A Map for Creating Conscious Relationships

IRAM

Inner Relationship Archetypal Model

Markus William Kasunich

IRAM: A Map for Creating Conscious Relationships
By Markus William Kasunich

Copyright © 2020 by Markus William Kasunich

I3Magi Light Press. All rights reserved.

www.info@markuskasunich.com

ISBN: 9781735738307
printed in the United States of America

This book is dedicated to Samjhi

To my beloved wife, partner, companion, muse, and cosmic playmate.
Words cannot express my eternal gratitude
for the depths of your radiant love.

Without you, this could never have come to fruition.

Table of Contents

PART IV: DYSFUNCTIONAL INFLUENCE

Dysfunctional Relationship Dynamics for Shadow Inner Adult and Wounded Inner Child

PART V: EXPANSIVE CONDITIONING

FOREWORD

By Stephen R. Burns

My parents have lived in the same house for nearly fifty years. Every time I visit them, it is a stroll through memory lane. The same creaks in the hardwood floor, the familiar smell of plants and dog, the same sense of quiet. Their house is an old brick bungalow, and the main hallway provides the richest amount of memories. Posted on the walls are pictures of my childhood. Graduation photos. Family gatherings at Christmas and weddings and other holidays. Even pictures of old girlfriends. All of them are neatly framed and hung with care. Like a carefully forged rainbow, they are snapshots of the life of my family.

Of my life.

Looking at them always takes me back to those moments. Those years. From my time in high school to my first days in university to the time when I was married. They remind me of who I was and what I was like. They also remind me of my good decisions and the more questionable ones, some of which still haunt me.

The pictures themselves hold no judgment. They are, instead, a mirror. Or at least, they can be. And if we're willing to look hard enough, if we're willing to dig, they provide answers for the way forward.

Aristotle once said that knowing ourselves was the beginning of all wisdom. For me, that understanding has come easily. Writers are reflective. Before you can create realistic characters in a novel, you have to mine your greatest resource: yourself. And the only way to do that is to become self-aware. However, there is a difference between knowing who you are and knowing what to do once you have that information.

When Markus asked me to edit his book, I had little experience in his world. I knew bits and pieces, the way most writers know bits of things. Despite that, I had no concerns when I agreed to edit it.

That changed almost overnight.

The challenges were not, however, the regular editorial challenges that exist in every book. It was the information itself. I would often find myself pausing in the middle of a section and unable to continue editing. I'd close my laptop, musing over what I'd just read, and drifting towards a place in my mind. A place very much like my parents' hallway.

The world of the unconscious can be a strange, and at times, forbidding place to explore. I felt, as I first started reading, very much an outsider. Much of the information seemed at odds with the organized religion that I'd not only grown up with, but taught as a minister for many years. And yet none of that prohibited me from dwelling on portions of the book, the ones that discussed archetypes and my past, and why certain behaviors in my life and relationships were locked in an endless cycle.

As an editor, there is no way to dance around the material. You have to absorb it in order to help bring the book to fruition. And that's what happened to me. Day after day, I absorbed the teaching in IRAM until a funny thing happened.

It started to change my life.

I would see something or hear something and say "well, that's expansive (positive)." Or, "I don't want to be contractive (negative)." Looking at the world energetically, and learning to forgive my past mistakes and honoring myself were game changers.

My old theology professors would have called a book like this "New Age" and dismissed it. And they would have been wrong. The unconscious is not a religious place. Spiritual, yes. Practical, yes. But not religious. What this book does is not so much change the picture as provide a different angle in how we see things. One that opens up a mirror.

As Markus says many times in his work, however, the mirror is not enough. We have to do the work. The inner work. But you can't do that unless you have the tools. I cannot hang a picture unless I have a hammer and some nails. This book provides those tools for any seeker, regardless of your religious experience. A hammer is not Catholic or Buddhist or an atheist. It's just a tool.

A few weeks ago, I visited my parents. As always, I took a stroll down the main hallway. The pictures hadn't changed. My crew cut high school grad photo. The family shot with my first girlfriend. My graduation from university. They brought back memories, as they often did, but it felt different this time.

Pictures capture memories, but they don't frame complexity. Like the times I was kicked out of the house as a teenager. Or how that first serious girlfriend cheated on me. Or the struggles with my sisters and extended family that caused me to walk away for long stretches. Those, too, are part of it.

They are not all sunshine and rainbows. And to ignore that is to miss the chance to move beyond that hurt and conditioning. A chance to move beyond that moment in time. A chance to move, most importantly, beyond the frame.

Those pictures will always look the same unless you address the dynamics that created those memories in the first place. The change in outward relationships evolves only when we change our inner relationships. It isn't easy. The sentiment we attach to those memories is real and powerful. And in some ways, when we explore those dynamics, it can feel like betrayal. This, I think, is the greatest struggle.

At least, it was for me.

We assume that by acknowledging our conditioning, we are blaming others. But what we learn in IRAM is the opposite. It isn't blame, it's acknowledgement.

And acceptance.

IRAM is not a prosecutor. It isn't a lawyer trying old cases. It isn't someone telling you that your parents were awful or that your husband destroyed everything. It is a map. A guide through the inner self to help us better understand our outer behaviors, and change them so that they are no longer self-destructive.

What this book does is allow you to embrace your past, and also to appreciate the missteps in your life. Not only by you, but those around you. Humility is a good thing, so long as it begins with an appreciation of self. But it's not true humility when we feel the need to be martyrs, when we think we must fall on the sword to help others. IRAM gives you the tools to understand that all of life has a place, even the parts that caused us pain.

For me, the changes in my life have been profound.

I no longer make fun of myself. I hold higher standards with how people speak of me and with me. I no longer allow myself to be a punching bag so others feel better. In some ways, this seems small, doesn't it? Like a simple pause in a comment where I normally would have taken a shot at myself to be funny. Or when I'd bring myself down so the other person wouldn't feel intimidated. Or the idea that I didn't deserve to live an abundant life.

A cheap story brings us nothing but conflict and shallow answers. But the stories that change us are the ones that linger on the essence of that conflict, the manner in which resolution is found, and how that affects the future.

I am not a cheap story. Neither are you.

You are valuable and important, and the world needs your voice. Not your conditioned voice, not the one weighed down by the baggage of others, but the one that yearns to be free. You. The real you.

We all have hallways that we walk down, be it in albums or on sites or on actual corridors. We remember how we were perceived and how we thought of ourselves. We remember the dynamics that surrounded it. And we don't need a guide to those places because it's ingrained within us.

What we need is a map to somewhere new. One that will light our journey towards better things, better relationships, including the most important one, our relationship with our inner self. The one that allows us to honor who we are in a new way and frees us to become the best version of who we want to be.

The ask is to listen and apply what you hear. The return is to witness new things in your life. New relationships. New confidence. New opportunities.

I can't promise you a perfect life after reading this book, but I can promise you the right road. I can tell you that if you trust what you learn, and if you are willing, you will find yourself in a new place. The same hallway perhaps, the same pictures, but with no rainbows and better lighting.

What a difference.

INTRODUCTION

What is Your "Relationship" with Your Relationships?

*"We meet ourselves time and time again
in a thousand disguises on the path of life."*
– Carl Jung

Our human relationships will always serve as a wondrous, multidimensional passion play of direct experience to explore the human condition. Relationships are a complex psychological forum where we consciously and unconsciously express our inner dynamics to rediscover our true nature. How we relate through the connection and association to others offers profound insight into the inner workings of our consciousness. It is through this powerful invitation that we are always being invited to explore in order to learn, evolve and mature.

What defines your experience of relationships? We would like to think that we have the freedom and the power to make intentional, conscious decisions that shape not only what kind of relationships we want and who we want to be with, but also how we engage in the dynamics of those relationships. There is, however, a deeper, unseen influence within us beyond the known and conscious choices that affect what relationships we create and gravitate toward, and how we navigate those experiences.

The concept of relationship can be defined as a state or a sense of relatedness, connection and association to people, groups of people, or conditions where one develops an alignment through a specific kinship or affinity. This connection with others is one of the most significant vehicles available to develop, explore and celebrate the depths of our human experience.

Though on the surface many may be aware what qualities, behaviors and types of people towards which they feel a conscious affinity, what remains unrecognized is the deep undercurrent of inner conditioning that is also unconsciously influencing that sense of affinity and idea of attraction.

Have you ever noticed that you continue to encounter remarkably similar dynamics in past and present relationships? You seem to encounter familiar types of people with the same patterns again and again, in spite of the fact that you are making great efforts to choose something different.

Even though you consciously want something else, it's as if there is a strange magnet and blind spot that does not allow you to fully grasp what you are creating. It is often difficult to fully understand to whom you are attracted or what is happening until the relationship is in ruins. Most people spend their lives unconsciously stumbling from relationship to relationship, from painful experience to painful experience, from pattern to recurring pattern, hopelessly repeating the same unwanted drama, while trying desperately to identify the underlying issues. But they still cannot unravel why the outcome remains unchanged.

Conscious intention, aspirational ideals or the unfaltering belief that you can have something better if you just keep trying is never enough. Relationships are created by conscious choices AND unconscious conditioning. It is the combined influence of both these powerful worlds within you that generates your experience and manifests the outcome. To change the recurring relationship dynamics, you must take the initiative to honestly examine not only your conscious motives, but also uncover, examine and transform the unconscious patterns unwittingly affecting that process.

Realize that every single relationship in your life (platonic, family of origin, extended family, co-workers, employers, teachers, friends, partners, romantic, lover and everything in between etc.) can powerfully highlight and reflect your overt and covert conditioning. Relationships are a mirror to the fragmented self as well as the divine qualities within. And each relationship, in its own unique way, is being manifested by this intricate dance of mixed awareness that includes conscious intention and unconscious conditioning. These human connections invite you to investigate your unseen inner dynamics, beliefs, hidden agendas and projections in every interaction with every person in your life.

Every relationship you will ever experience in your lifetime provides a powerful opportunity and invitation for self-reflection, healing, purification, transformation and celebration. This process is constantly unfolding regardless of your willingness to acknowledge it, your level of awareness, or your active participation.

You become more empowered when you actively engage in the opportunity that your relationships are providing you instead of ignoring or denying the gift that is being offered.

But how do you even begin? This task appears endless and overwhelming. It seems like it could take years of investigation, committed deep personal analysis, psychological training, study, countless hours of observed interactions with others, therapy or years of counseling and targeted introspection to wade through your inner jungle of the jumbled unconscious conditioning to finally get a grip on how all of these deep-seated patterns are playing out in your life. With the dauntless task that you are facing, at first, it seems utterly hopeless.

It may feel like you would be better off settling for what has been conditioned, manage it to the best of your ability, and reluctantly accept your lot in life because you do not have the understanding, the time, or the tools to deal with it.

The problem is that most people embark on this bold, inner journey into the uncharted territory of their unconscious without sufficient understanding, tools, or any sort of map or a guidebook. And they end up wasting a lot of time and energy in the process leaving them to feel very frustrated. As a result, they give up and concede to "living by default" because it is too much. This is exactly how I felt in the process. The deep frustration, unsettled feeling, along with a sincere knowing that I could create something more fulfilling prompted the inner and outer journey that inspired this material.

A Journey of Self-Discovery

I've had difficult experiences with interpersonal relationships as long as I could remember. By my early thirties, I had already had a string of failed, unfulfilling and deeply contractive romantic relationships that continued to haunt me. And it was not a lack of effort. I saw myself as a highly conscious, introspective, intelligent, kind, and loving person who had much to offer. So what was the problem? Why did I keep creating the same trauma and pain with different people?

Because of the inner work I had already begun to explore, I could also recognize the similar patterns from my romantic relationships playing out in my friendships, at work with my co-workers, my bosses and my neighbors. I knew these recurring patterns stemmed from the unconscious conditioning from my past, but I still could not get a handle on how to unravel or transcend them.

I had realized it was a waste of time to indulge in being a victim and spend my healing process blaming my family of origin, and my childhood for what had already happened. I had explored enough of that in my years of therapy to know that was not going to get me where I wanted to go. I knew these patterns were intimately connected to my childhood conditioning, and I could not undo the experiences or how they had affected me. But I also understood that this conditioning continued to shape my present experience at a deeper level, and I wanted a way to more effectively navigate them.

I had already devoted years to studying spirituality, creativity and psychology in and out of universities, alternative colleges, programs and groups, and I had done many years of ongoing therapy, seeing counselors, psychologists and psychotherapists.

I spent thirteen years in different immersive spiritual communities and ashrams in North America working intensely with people from all over the world, facilitating retreats and events as well as group and private counseling. I delved deeply into meditation and spiritual practices. I travelled the globe and sought out gurus, shamans, medicine men and women, alternative therapists, healers and spiritual teachers looking for the keys to break the code.

Disillusioned, I even gave away everything I owned except for the contents and gear of a 75 pound bag and spent almost a year as a wandering nomad, living off the land in the Rocky Mountains of British Columbia, Canada. Travelling alone, immersed in nature, hitchhiking from town to town. I went on an inner pilgrimage to uncover these illusive answers. During that solitary experience with minimal human contact, I continued my research and earnestly documented my personal observations and investigation of my conditioning and patterns that were alive in my inner world in order to more deeply understand them.

Through every step of self-discovery, I gained incredible insightful tools, techniques and wisdom from every experience in the process. After almost a lifetime of devoted research, investigation and inner work, years of traditional therapy, and now, after seeing my own clients for over fifteen years, I continued to see the same challenges and roadblocks with their growth. And I realized there had to be a more efficient and practical way to consciously navigate these patterns that would simplify the process for anyone.

I poured through those years of notes, personal journals, combined with my accumulated experience of healing and inner investigation. I closely examined nearly two decades of my study, observations, as well as the recurring patterns in myself, clients and everyone around me. Drawing on a combination of eastern and western principles, I set myself with the task to design a comprehensive "inner relationship guidebook."

In 2016, with the help of my wife Samjhi, I mapped out the initial structure of the material and worked with it for the first time at our annual immersive retreat. Though I was already quietly utilizing my informal system for many years in my private sessions with my clients, the first official comprehensive map was created and shared with the participants at that event. It had an unexpected and profound impact on all of those who attended.

Samjhi and I had also noticed more layers of our own subconscious patterns were emerging while we were teaching the material throughout the retreat. After all our years of individual inner work and self-investigation, the system continued to access even deeper aspects of the subconscious. We realized we were working with something that was inspiring radical and deep transformation.

I began to integrate the content into my holistic life and consciousness coaching practice, as I continued to utilize the model with my clients with incredible results. Many of the case studies in this book came from the insight and direct experience of those sessions. I spent the next four years assembling the content for this book and refining the map that we had originally designed. These questions were at the forefront of the process.

What if you had access to a comprehensive "inner relationship map" to make the whole process of inner investigation more efficient?

What if you could utilize a "relationship guidebook" to help you comprehend why you continually create the same recurring patterns and choose the same types of relationships with the same kind of people?

What if that map also provided not only the insight, but also the practical tools to navigate all your relationships with greater awareness?

What if this system could really assist you to make the sustaining changes that you are longing for?

What if you could have the power to make healthy and empowered choices that will ultimately help create the fulfilling experiences of relationships that you have always wanted?

The answers to these questions are found within the pages of the:

IRAM: A Map for Creating Conscious Relationships

This powerful inner map and relationship guidebook provides the necessary keys and resources to transforming and empowering all your inner and outer relationships.

> *"Yesterday I was clever, so I wanted to change the world.*
> *Today I am wise, so I am changing myself."*
>
> *– Rumi*

What does IRAM mean?

The term **IRAM** is an acronym that refers to the "Inner Relationship Archetypal Model," which describes a powerful map of the relative fragmented personality structure through archetypes, but it also suggests a deeper symbolic meaning.

In many spiritual traditions, the concept of the "I" refers to the personal identity structure that is wired into our relative conditioning. This is a platform where the inner conditioning plays itself out in our being.

The word RAM is a powerful Sanskrit chant that is comprised of two sounds RAA + OM. The first sound RAA refers to the place where karma is said to enter the body depicted at the navel area. Karma can be simply understood as the cause-and-effect result of all human behavior. Every experience of human conditioning can be either resolved or unresolved in the life of any individual. It is said that chanting the sound RAA stirs and awakens the latent unaccessed karma and subconscious conditioning.

The sound OM activates profound insight and intuition in the body in the third eye resting above the brow in the center of the head. This sound OM is said to vibrate to the full power of universal consciousness that can illuminate, resolve and eradicate karma and conditioning.

Mixing the two sounds RAA + OM together forms the full word RAM, which has the power to access the unconscious conditioning, awaken it and purge it from the being with potent universal awareness. Therefore, the term I-RAM describes the process of bringing the profound awareness of "RAM" into the "identity structure" of "I," where you explore the drama of human conditioning.

By bringing universal awareness of consciousness into our human conditioning, you begin to stir the pot and activate the karma which allows the latent conditioning to be purified and transmuted using this specific map of consciousness as a guide.

No map or system is entirely perfect. But using this powerful guide can be highly effective to more quickly assist you to get where you want to go. The IRAM is designed as a comprehensive guidebook, a tool and a map to understanding and utilizing the four different foundational quadrants of the being that are constantly engaging, communicating and relating together consciously and unconsciously.

It has been designed to assist you to develop a conscious understanding and deeper relationship to all the different fragmented aspects or archetypes of your being, and offer insight, tools and an approach for self-investigation. Once you understand and begin to consciously engage with your inner relationship in a new and empowered way, you are now able to shift and sustain more conscious relationships in the outer world.

Tips to Navigate Your Journey into the IRAM

Sincerely embarking on any inner pursuit has the potential to forever change your existing relationship to yourself. This seemingly innocent journey literally massages your inherent nature, loosens old conditioning, unravels the heart, and invites a deepening of insight into what has always been present within you.

Infinite aspects can emerge outward and tread wildly into a kaleidoscope of dynamics as they unfurl themselves. To those who are interested in honoring this dance, the source of these dynamics will eventually reveal its mysteries from within. This investigation opens the door to transformation and offers the potential of profound inner realization.

As you journey into the **IRAM,** realize that you are delving into the often-unexplored aspects of the subconscious world of patterns, conditioning and programming. Here are some suggestions to assist you in navigating this process.

The book is designed in a specific way to maximize your process: Years of research, case studies, retreats, workshops and personal experience have helped craft the format and order of the material in this book. There are many worksheets, exercises and invitations offered for self-reflection throughout the pages ahead of you. When you initially go through the process, read from the beginning; don't be tempted to jump around, and follow the steps as they are laid out. Allow the journey to unfold. Then you can continue to use the book as an ongoing reference and guidebook.

Take time to pause and reflect on the material that you are exploring: Take your time and allow the material to gestate within you. Move at your own natural speed. Give yourself permission to really be with what you are exploring. Sometimes you may need to stop and tune into what is being said and just take it in. I highly recommend that you pause at the end of each section or chapter and take time for self-reflection with what has been presented, especially if the ideas are new for you.

 One of the most powerful tools for self-reflection and personal observation is journaling: I cannot stress enough the profound transformational power of journaling your inner insights, observations and feelings throughout the course of this journey. Journaling develops observation skills and can reveal many hidden aspects of yourself. We usually document important things. When you record your journey, it is an act of self-validation as you become more available to your inner world.

Notice your mental, emotional and psychological reaction to what you are reading: Some of the material may "trigger you." Pay attention to any inner agitation you may have about a specific area of the book. Also notice areas that you may feel tempted to skip over or information you are having trouble absorbing. Those "triggers" may be powerful clues to help unlock your inner conditioning.

Pay attention to your outer world: It is impossible to remain unchanged as you embark on any journey of sincere inner reflection. As you continue to understand your inner conditioning and develop a conscious relationship to the dynamics in each of the 4 quadrants of the IRAM, you are transforming your inner world. As you transform this inner relationship, notice how this continues to affect the relationships in your outer world.

Use the book as an ongoing reference tool: The book is designed to help you not only construct a map of your inner dynamics, but also as an ongoing tool for your inner and outer relationships. Make notes, re-read sections and review the various worksheets. As you continue to evolve, you will discover the deeper nuances of your inner dynamics. This will continue to be a powerful resource for that journey as you express these dynamics in your outer world.

PART I
EXPANSION AND CONTRACTION

Inner Relationship Archetypal Model

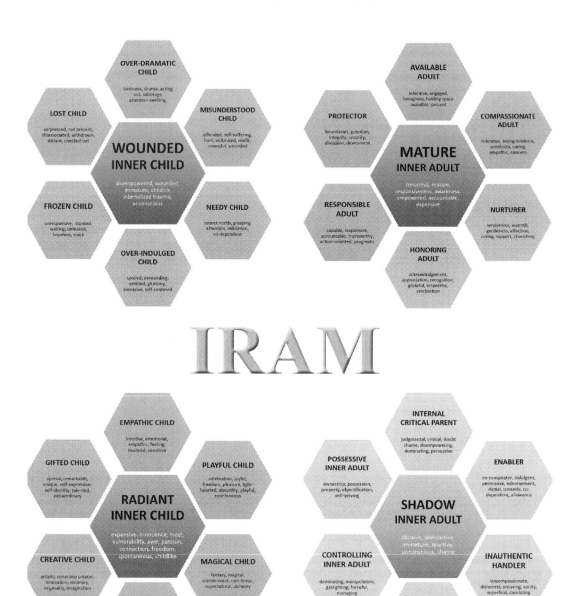

Exploring the IRAM (Inner Relationship Archetype Model)

The **IRAM** is divided into four foundational quadrants (Mature Inner Adult, Radiant Inner Child, Shadow Inner Adult and Wounded Inner Child) which are made up of 24 universal relationship "stories" also known as archetypes. There are six archetypes in each individual quadrant. Two quadrants "above the line" are different experiences of expansiveness while two quadrants "below the line" are steeped in different expressions of contractiveness. How these different fragmented aspects of your inner reality consciously and unconsciously communicate and relate to one another within you ultimately creates the basis of your outer world of relationships.

Expressions of Contractive Behavior in the IRAM

"The refused and unaccepted characteristics do not go away;
they only collect in the dark corners or our personality.
When they have been hidden long enough,
they take on a life of their own–the shadow life.
The shadow is that which has not entered adequately into consciousness.
It is the despised quarter of our being."
– *Robert A. Johson (Jungian Analyst)*

The SHADOW PARENT: The contractive expression of how your immediate family of origin, environment and culture "parented" you in an unconscious, reactive, immature, abusive or contractive perspective.

(Internal Critical Parent, Enabler, Inauthentic Handler, Unavailable Adult, Controlling Inner Adult and The Possessive Inner Parent)

The WOUNDED INNER CHILD: The expression of how your Inner Child internalized these immature or contractive behaviors into fragmented wounds, survival techniques, disempowered conditioning and childish behaviors to cope with the disharmonious projection of different expressions of "shadow parenting."

(Overdramatic Child, Misunderstood Child, Needy Child, Over-indulged Child, Frozen Child and the Lost Child)

The past unconscious examples of outer **Shadow Inner Adult** behavior created the now present wounds of the **Wounded Inner Child**.

Your unconscious present **Shadow Inner Adult** behavior continues to activate and engage your present **Wounded Inner Child** conditioning.

Expressions of Expansive Behavior in the IRAM

The unconscious or "lost gold" within you
contains the most direct access to your highest nature.
If this powerful untapped energy remains unexplored annd unowned,
there is no hope to express the fulfilled experience of your potential.

The MATURE ADULT: The representation of all the ideal, mature, expansive, conscious behaviors of maturity that were empowered through example. They were either modeled from our family of origin, environment or culture or later acquired, cultivated and empowered through the experience as expansive expressions of relationship behavior.

(Available Adult, The Nurturer, Compassionate Adult, Honoring Adult, Responsible Adult, and The Protector)

The RADIANT CHILD: The representation of all the radiant expressions of the Radiant Inner Child. These are empowered through examples of expansive parenting from your immediate family of origin, environment and culture. They are also the uncorrupted and inherent expression of your internal "divine" radiance.

(Empathic Child, Playful Child, Magical Child, Sacred Child, The Creative Child and the Gifted Child)

The past examples of **Mature Inner Adult** behavior created a foundation
for the expression of the owned and unowned aspects of **Radiant Inner Child.**

The present development of the **Mature Inner Adult** continues
to empower and support conscious **Radiant Inner Child** behavior.

Understanding the Relationship of Expansion and Contraction

You are only ever making a simple singular choice
which repeats itself in an infinite number of situations.

In order to relate to the different aspects of the IRAM, one must first learn to understand your direct and personal experience of expansive and contractive. The general idea of expansion and contraction seems simple enough, but it is not always easy to execute in your relative world. If you take time to carefully examine your decision-making process, you will discover that you are only ever making two choices in every facet of your life that comes in an infinite amount of inner and outer invitations.

Everyone can naturally access the "feeling" of expansion and contraction. It is an innate feeling at the heart of every inner and outer human experience: energy, emotions, thoughts, beliefs, conditioning, and behavior. It is also the foundational undercurrent of every circumstance, decision and action.

How you consciously and unconsciously relate to this fundamental principle influences everything, including all your relationships. What is the difference between these two states of being? To assist you to access, identify and understand the experience of each of these choices, consider how these two states can manifest in your experience.

EXPANSION	CONTRACTION
Openness	Closed
Connection	Disconnection
Empowered	Disempowered
The Feeling of "YES"	The Feeling of "NO"
Movement or flow	No movement or stuck
"On"	"Off"

Because you are comprised of a universe of interacting inner behavioral archetypes and different fragments, it is possible for your relationship to have some aspects to be expansive while others are contractive. For instance, you may have an empowered relationship with your creativity but have a disempowered relationship to drawing boundaries.

It is important to understand that you cannot have both an expansive and contractive relationship to a single aspect at the same time. For example, you cannot have an expansive and contractive relationship to creativity simultaneously. Mastering your ability to view your experience of every inner and outer relationship through expansion and contraction will radically transform your life.

In terms of the IRAM, the experience of **EXPANSION** is expressed as **Radiant** and **Mature** while **CONTRACTION** is expressed as **Wounded** and **Shadow.** The relationships to these four interacting quadrants make up the foundation of your inner world.

RADIANT + MATURE
EXPANSIVE

Expansive Qualities

healthy / aware / awake / conscious / harmonious
mature / whole / empowered / radiant / responsive

ABOVE THE LINE

BELOW THE LINE

dysfunctional / unaware / unawake / unconscious / discordant
immature / wounded / disempowered / shadow / reactive

Contractive Qualities

CONTRACTIVE
WOUNDED + SHADOW

# The Expansive Inner Relationship Feedback Loop
EXPANSION = Radiant + Mature

The empowered self-regulating relationship between **MATURITY** and **RADIANCE** activates the most powerful expansive feedback loop that is available in the experience of conscious expansiveness. Through this dynamic, each aspect of expansion inspires, deepens and enhances one another creating a powerful synergy. Without the empowered qualities of maturity, the **Radiant Inner Child** cannot ever be fully sustained to reach its full potential and without the infusion of the radiance, the **Mature Inner Adult** can never be fully realized.

In order to live "above the line" in the field of conscious expansion, this expansive feedback loop must be intentionally activated and sustained through the ever-evolving relationship between these two transformational elements of expansion. This process requires you to continue to explore, empower and refine your relationship to all the unique expressions of the expansive archetypes in your inner and outer relationships.

# The Contractive Inner Relationship Feedback Loop
CONTRACTION = Wounded + Shadow

On the other hand, the self-perpetuating relationship between **SHADOW** and **WOUNDEDNESS** activates the most destructive contractive feedback loop that is available in the experience of unconscious contraction. As the oppressive energy of the **Shadow Inner Adult** continues to exert and maintain its dominance over the **Wounded Inner Child,** it continues to fuel the childish expression of disempowerment. And as long as this unconscious relationship remains intact between these two different expressions of contraction, you will remain "below the line" in the field of contractive negativity.

Because these patterns have been conditioned and present for so long as default survival mechanisms, it can be extremely difficult to free yourself from the different expressions of immature reactivity. This process requires you to deeply explore the unconscious world of contraction, acknowledge its presence and be accountable for the patterns. Only then will you be able to bring awareness into the darkness and transform your relationship to these contractive elements. This will allow you to finally break the unconscious contractive feedback loop that has continued to bind you to the world of pain in all of your inner and outer relationships.

PART II
EXPLORING YOUR CONDITIONING

Exploring the Ego Structure through the IRAM

What is the ego? The ego is a psychological term commonly used to refer to a complex mechanism within your being that can also be described as a "human psychological interface." It is a necessary, evolutionary tool of survival that allows every person to uniquely engage with the human experience. Regardless of your level of personal or spiritual evolution, and as long as you are in a human experience, you will always have an ego structure.

This ego interface is made up of a system of conscious and unconscious energetic imprinting, emotional and mental behavior patterns constructed from an array of different experiences of conditioning. It is an interconnected web of learned behavior, habits, programmed and acquired conditioning, beliefs, memories, ideas, thoughts, and emotional experiences all woven together. It has evolved into a relative, superficial but complex matrix that experiences itself as a unique individual separate from your inherent nature. It has been referred to as your *identity, personality*, your *persona* or "*little self.*"

Many people have the misconception that that human ego structure is inherently contractive, negative, undesirable, or contains all the unrefined aspects of the human experience. We hear expressions like "He has a big or inflated ego" or "You are speaking from your ego." But it is important to understand that this fundamental ego structure is not inherently good or bad. In fact, your ever-evolving relationship to your ego is equally or even more important than the existence of the structure itself. Your unexamined ego structure is nothing more than the default, survival mechanisms that were unconsciously "programmed" by your life experience. It contains both expansive and contractive conditioning. And your personal relationship to your ego determines what relationship you will ultimately express in your inner and outer worlds.

If you choose, you do not have to be ruled by the pre-existing conditioning within you. You are completely capable of having an expansive or contractive relationship to the conditioning that makes up that ego structure, and can use your now evolved and more conscious relationship to that "interface" to more effectively navigate your inner and outer life. In other words, you can create a healthy, conscious and expansive relationship to your ego structure.

The IRAM is a powerful and comprehensive tool to explore that process to not only understand, but to more consciously navigate your relationship to that complex, multifaceted matrix of conditioning. Your relationship to the ego can be completely transformed through using the IRAM.

The question is: How well do you understand and know the already existing conscious and unconscious patterns within you? Because if you have not examined it, your present conditioning is already determining, influencing, dictating and ruling your internal and external behavior and choices on multiple levels of consciousness.

The Different Aspects of the Ego Structure

Pre-determined Traits: At birth, you begin with a certain amount of pre-determined data and programming. This is your foundational conditioning, which includes your tendencies and genetic predisposition from your parents. These attributes are hard-coded into your physical, energetic, mental bodies, and are psychologically wired as part of your experience.

Conditioning: This term refers to the programmed software that is now recognized as your "normal" operating behavior that exists within you. These conscious and unconscious behaviors, imprinting and conditioned programs have been acquired, perpetuated and fortified throughout the course of your life from repeated experiences in your nuclear family, culture, religious and social structures.

Beliefs and Values: Beliefs are deeply imprinted and cherished programming of the ego identity. They are comprised of mental ideas and thoughts combined with an emotional charge. The powerful bond of emotional and mental experiences is difficult to unravel without working in both the mental and emotional fields. The term "belief" can also refer to personal attitudes and assumptions associated with true or false ideas and concepts. Many people never examine if pre-conditioned unconscious beliefs are supporting the kind of relationships they desire.

Pain and Wounds: This refers to conscious and unconscious patterns of pain that have become imprinted memories within your ego structure. This programming of patterns that you learned through repeated exposure in your conditioning can deeply affect and dictate how you relate to and create pain in your inner and outer experience. When you trigger these wounds, you continue to accept them, endorse them, empower them and ultimately embrace them as your own because they have become familiarized.

Fragmented Aspects of Self: As the ego structure develops within an individual it splits into separate and interconnected fragments that take on individual personalities within the being. Within you, there are conscious and unconscious archetypes or stories: The Wounded and Radiant Inner Child and the Shadow and Mature Inner Adult. Each aspect plays a role in the support and functioning of the entire structure.

Your Adopted Outer Roles: These roles are the internal aspects, patterns, dynamics and/or worldly systems that you have unconsciously or consciously defined yourself by that are acted out in the drama of our society. The identification to these worldly stations, roles or archetypes are associated with your perception, occupation or vocation that ongoingly evolve throughout the course of your life: daughter, brother, friend, employee, boss, mother, caretaker, healer, warrior, grandmother… etc. We define our personality by aligning ourselves very strongly with these unconscious and conscious roles out of habitual patterns, conditioning and familiarity without considering if it actually serves our greater good.

Unraveling Your Inner Conditioning

The foundation for all patterns which influence your inner and outer relationships were formulated by recurring exposure to your family of origin, your culture and your environment. Without help, you will continue to internally mimic those relationships and vicariously live out both the expansive and the contractive patterns of that programming. The patterns are present and fully alive in you. So, it is your choice and responsibility to determine what your relationship will be to that conditioning, how deeply you want to explore it and how familiar and intimate you choose to be with your inner programming.

After the source of the initial conditioning is gone, it is now your responsibility what you are willing to do to unravel and transform that inner paradigm. Without conscious attention, it will never unravel by itself.

> *"Your task is not to seek for love,*
> *but merely to seek and find all the barriers within yourself*
> *that you have built against it."*
> *– Rumi*

It is important to leave helplessness behind, because you now have the power, experience and the tools to understand and "reprogram" that inner relationship through investigation, purification and integration. As an innocent and naïve child, you did not have the awareness, discernment or the psychological sophistication to adequately understand or integrate the conditioning you were receiving. So, you were forced to unconsciously learn to cope, compensate and survive. The fragmented ego structure served that purpose.

"Your father may have been the source of that critical dialogue and maybe he openly abused you for seventeen years. But still, you are continuing that inner dialogue and keeping it alive within you. As long as you continue to treat yourself the same way he did, and do not do anything to alter it, then you are not only agreeing that you deserve it, you have now become your own abuser. You will continue to play out the drama of the abuser and the victim in your inner and outer relationships until YOU decide to untangle the conditioning and choose something different."

Because so much of your conditioning lives deep in the unconscious realms and is playing itself out through your unexamined inner and outer relationships, it is important to examine the source of your conditioning. Investigating the dynamics of your family of origin, past environment and culture will help to develop more consciousness.

The circumstances that caused the original conditioning are an important aspect of the self-investigation process. The specific details will help you identify and explore the conditioned dynamics that continue to play out in your inner and outer world. But once you have examined that origin, it is not necessary to keep reliving the story.

Many people will continue to recycle their past story and keep it active in their present consciousness long after it has served its purpose. You can spend years perpetuating the wound under the guise of "working on it" but never really find resolution. Explore the past story with the intention of becoming deeply intimate with your dynamics. Cultivating awareness and shifting your relationship to those dynamics will be the necessary keys for transformation.

> *"It is easy to forget how mysterious and mighty stories are.*
> *They do their work in silence, invisibly.*
> *They work with all the internal materials of the mind and self.*
> *They become part of you while changing you.*
> *Beware of the stories you read and tell: subtly, at night,*
> *beneath the waters of consciousness, they are altering your world."*
> *– Ben Okri (Birds of Heaven)*

Exploring Your Primary Childhood Conditioning

This survey is designed to inspire a deeper awareness about your upbringing, your childhood patterns and your experience as a child. Some of these answers will help establish a deeper understanding of your foundational conscious and unconscious patterns.

Please use the questions as journaling prompts, beginning points of inquiry or as a path for further exploration. Be honest with yourself and answer the questions to the best of your ability. It may also be helpful to dialogue with family members as part of the process. Many of the patterns of conditioning are buried deep in the unconscious, and your memories hold incredible keys to help you understand yourself.

1. What was the cultural or ethnic background of your family members growing up?

FATHER _____ MOTHER _____ OTHER _____

2. Where did you grow up? (country, state, city, community). List the areas if you moved to different places as a child. _____

_____

_____

_____

3. What was the religious or spiritual background most practiced in your home growing up? _____

4. Did you have any siblings? If so, list them in order oldest to youngest, including yourself in the list. _____

_____

_____

5. How were you most likely to get attention as a child from your father, mother figure or your primary or influential caretaker? For many people, their siblings and other extended family members (grandmother, step-father, step-mother, aunt, cousins, etc.) played a prominent role in their upbringing.

If necessary, also explore the below process with those individuals as well. Please complete the two lists below by ranking the TOP 7 options in order (to only those that apply), on the line provided on a scale from 1-7 (with 1 being the most and 7 being the least likely).

Attention from your Mother figure:

_____ a) Temper tantrum

_____ b) People pleasing

_____ c) Injury or getting sick

_____ d) Withdrawing or hiding

_____ e) Being obedient or compliant

_____ f) Directly asking for attention

_____ g) Scholastic success (being smart)

_____ h) Athletic accomplishments

_____ i) Creativity

_____ j) Being funny or entertaining

_____ h) Making money

_____ k) Doing a good job or work ethic

_____ l) Being kind, compassionate, loving

_____ k) OTHER _____

Attention from your Father figure:

_____ a) Temper tantrum

_____ b) People pleasing

_____ c) Injury or getting sick

_____ d) Withdrawing or hiding

_____ e) Being obedient or compliant

_____ f) Directly asking for attention

_____ g) Scholastic success (being smart)

_____ h) Athletic accomplishments

_____ i) Creativity

_____ j) Being funny or entertaining

_____ h) Making money

_____ k) Doing a good job or work ethic

_____ l) Kindness, compassion, loving

_____ k) OTHER _____

6. Please rank in order (1-6) what manner, method or expression of love or caring that was most common in your home as a child by your mother and father figure (or other primary caregiver).

Your Mother Figure:

_____ a) Receiving of material gifts

_____ b) Quality time with parents

_____ c) Words of affirmation or devotion

_____ d) Acts of service

_____ e) Physical connection or attention

_____ f) OTHER _____

Your Father Figure:

_____ a) Receiving of material gifts

_____ b) Quality time with parents

_____ c) Words of affirmation or devotion

_____ d) Acts of service

_____ e) Physical connection or attention

_____ f) OTHER _____

7. To the best of your ability, rank the TOP 7 options in order (to only those that apply) that best describes the experience of what you most felt growing up as a child in your family household (also explore other extended family members, if necessary):

Your Mother Figure:	**Your Father Figure:**
_____ b) Heard	_____ b) Heard
_____ c) Understood	_____ c) Understood
_____ d) Cherished	_____ d) Cherished
_____ e) Wanted	_____ e) Wanted
_____ f) Adored	_____ f) Adored
_____ g) Possessed or owned	_____ g) Possessed or owned
_____ h) Guilted	_____ h) Guilted
_____ i) Dominated	_____ i) Dominated
_____ j) Celebrated	_____ j) Celebrated
_____ k) Attacked	_____ k) Attacked
_____ l) Manipulated	_____ l) Manipulated
_____ m) Ignored	_____ m) Ignored
_____ n) Acknowledged	_____ n) Acknowledged
_____ o) Espoused	_____ o) Espoused
_____ p) Sexualized	_____ p) Sexualized
_____ q) Shamed	_____ q) Shamed
_____ r) OTHER _____	_____ r) OTHER_____

8. Rank the TOP 7 options in order (to only those that apply): Who did you feel closest to as a child?

_____ a) Mother_____

_____ b) Father_____

_____ c) Step-Father _____

_____ c) Step-Mother_____

_____ c) Grandparent (Name) _____

_____ d) The natural world (explain)_____

_____ e) Sibling(s) (Name)_____

_____ f) Friend(s) (Name)_____

_____ g) Extended Family Member (e.g. cousin, aunt, uncle) _____

_____ h) God/ Consciousness / Spirit Guide (Describe)_____

_____ i) Family pet (Describe)_____

_____ j) Imaginary Friend (Describe)_____

_____ k) OTHER (explain)_____

Journaling Your Observations:

1. Describe yourself as a child. What kind of child were you? (obedient, rebellious, quiet, outgoing?)

2. What were your hobbies and interests growing up?

3. Did your childhood behavior dramatically change or shift dramatically at any point while you were growing up? Did a specific circumstance occur to inspire that change (change of school, loss of family member, abusive circumstance, etc.)?

4. What were some of the predominant belief systems and values that you remember in your home growing up that left a lasting impression on you? Please explain.

5. What was the emotional atmosphere in your home growing up? (For example: A lot of anger, repressed emotions, over-dramatic, explosions, encouraged to express only happy feelings, etc.) Explain your observations.

6. Were there any noteworthy, monumental events or circumstances that impacted you as a child that you can remember? (moving home, changing schools, a wonderful family trip, etc.) Please describe.

7. Were there any tragic, abusive, destructive or psychological events or circumstances that impacted you as a child that you can remember?

8. Are you still in contact with your parents or any family members today? Explain the nature of your present-day relationship with the various members of your family of origin.

PART III
CONTRACTIVE CONDITIONING

OVER-DRAMATIC CHILD

tantrums, drama, acting out, sabotage attention-seeking,

MISUNDERSTOOD CHILD

offended, self-suffering, hurt, vicitmized, misfit, resentful, wounded

LOST CHILD

surpressed, not present, disassociated, withdrawn, distant, checked out

WOUNDED INNER CHILD

disempowered, wounded, immature, childish, internalized trauma, unconscious

FROZEN CHILD

unresponsive, stunted, waiting, defeated, hopeless, stuck

NEEDY CHILD

unmet needs, grasping attention, validation, co-dependent

OVER-INDULGED CHILD

spoiled, demanding, entitled, gluttony, excessive, self-centered

The Wounded Inner Child

The Wounded Inner Child is the primary gateway to healing and integration.
When you invite your woundedness out of subversiveness
and into your awareness you finally begin to honor the past pain.
You also minimize its contractive influence on your life.
And you begin to offer yourself the potential of something more.

Among the many fragmented aspects of your relative identity or persona, the **Wounded Inner Child** remains one the most important and influential within your consciousness because it offers so much potential for powerful healing, transformation and integration.

The **Wounded Inner Child,** the disempowered side of the healthy Inner Child, represents all the conscious and unconscious, unresolved, unexpressed and internalized, undesired childhood experiences, behaviors, emotions and relationships that were conditioned by your outer environment. This includes any disempowered experience that created some form of internal conflict or any contraction within the personality structure of the child.

Much of this primary conditioning was compartmentalized and held within this fragmented aspect of self as a survival mechanism. Too much of what was being experienced in the outer world was overwhelming, unharmonious, confusing, painful and misunderstood by the less complicated and innocent psychology of the child. The open, naïve and receptive child originally engaged with its experience with complete trust, so these traumatic wounds had to be repressed into this unwanted subversive fragment that now functions in the disempowered aspect of the wounded consciousness.

All these outer contractive influences inadvertently help form the principal programming and examples of known, appropriate and accepted behavior that would then be explored in the world as the child continued to grow and mature. The problem arises when even as the individual matured and no longer needed these survival patterns, the unconscious programming not only remained intact but also continued to have a subversive influence on behavior.

These behavioral patterns were internalized by the immediate environment: parents, siblings, extended family systems and the external culture. The child was programmed with its wounded core issues by the:

1. **Conscious and unconscious relationships to every aspect of the outer experience,**
2. **External interactions and behavior within the family tribe, culture and society,**
3. **The child's unique interpretation, reaction and identification to these examples.**

Eventually examples of this conditioned behavior would become the habitual patterns that you would continue to unconsciously attract, explore and express through all of your inner and outer relationships throughout the course of your life.

This fragmented **Wounded Inner Child** aspect of your identity structure will continue to perform its duty as the unconscious "safe keeper" of these issues, play its role in maintaining the survival systems, and therefore unconsciously continue to project these patterns of behavior in the inner and outer world until some form of "resolution" of these undesired, rogue patterns is somehow realized.

The Archetypal Conditioning of the Wounded Inner Child

The **Wounded Inner Child** has many different traits depending on the circumstances of its conditioning. Each person will develop a combination of different behaviors based on what works to get the attention and validation that it needs. Consider all the unhealthy survival techniques that you've acquired.

Many of those practices still function unconsciously within the wounded world of the Inner Child. If left unexamined, they will continue to express themselves in all of your inner and outer relationships. Identifying your Wounded Inner Child's story will allow you to understand how you can respond to this aspect of yourself, and what internal medicine or remedy you need to apply. Though every wounded archetype exists, everyone has a unique personalized expression of those wounds. And there are usually two or three primary reoccurring archetypal "stories" most actively expressed in your relationships. Here is a brief overview of the six Wounded Inner Child archetypes:

The Over-Dramatic Child: This aspect is the excessive exhibitionist that embodies the collective voice of drama for Wounded Inner Child. It will utilize all expressions of drama as a desperate "cry of alarm" to get attention. This saboteur agitates all conscious and unconscious drama: temper tantrums, illness, and accidents. This is an immature cry to be rescued from pain, and a survival tactic for ongoing acknowledgement and validation. In creating this excessive drama, the Overdramatic Child fortifies its identification to an internal sense of being wrong and continues to feed its deep sense of scarcity.

The Misunderstood Child: This wounded aspect feels like it experiences life more intensely than others. It takes things personally by internalizing situations and relationships. It desires a deep need to feel understood yet believes that no one will ever understand, which creates isolation. Therefore, this aspect of the Wounded Inner Child is drawn to understand and identify with others' pain. Sometimes this need to be understood is so strong that it will resort to self-inflicted wounds and self-perpetuating struggle to release the intense emotions and frustrations.

This tangible proof of their suffering is an attempt to create (inner and outer) validation, evoke sympathy and create support, even as they believe they are undeserving of that attention.

The Needy Child: This aspect feels a desperate need to have pain validated which quickly turns into a behavior of "neediness" and attention seeking. There is a constant desire to have their suffering acknowledged by others. They feel born broken, unloved and lacking wholeness. They consistently seek to fulfill their deep unmet needs from an outside source usually becoming co-dependent and disempowered. They are driven by an internal scarcity that they hope can be fulfilled by another.

The Over-Indulged Child: This aspect of the Wounded Inner Child feels entitled, ungrateful, demanding and demands that every desire be indulged. They feel resentful if it is not delivered. This experience of being "spoiled" grows from a lack of true boundaries, structure and support in their upbringing. This over-indulgence creates a desperate and compulsive need to have attention, support and boundaries expressed through feeding and manipulating outer desires and acknowledgement. But underneath this excessiveness, pampering and over-indulgence, there is a deeper feeling of insecurity, lack of nurturing, emptiness and a sense of emotional impoverishment.

The Frozen Child: This aspect of the Wounded Inner Child feels crippled, paralyzed, immobilized and thrives in the story of their own hopelessness of not knowing "how to" function or what to do to move forward. This keeps the Frozen Child enslaved in the story that "something is wrong with me" and "I can't do it." There can be an indefinable fear of "getting it wrong" and feeling of being profoundly stuck. There is also an inability to commit, desperately hoping that someone else will rescue, nurture and support them because on some level they believe they are ultimately damaged and powerless. This frozen experience of paralysis supports an inner insecurity, fear, need for dependency and unconsciously absolves them from any personal responsibility for their inaction.

The Lost Child: This aspect of the Wounded Inner Child is the embodiment of unconscious dissociation. It has developed the ability to "check out" and withdraw and become lost to itself as a survival mechanism. As a result, it feels profoundly alone, unseen, and possibly unworthy to openly ask or receive love. It has retreated from life due to the burden of an intense unexpressed or unprocessed trauma.

This withdrawn state creates a safe distance which can still garner a tempered experience of attention while remaining somewhat out of reach of any potential danger. This cultivated distance unconsciously avoids intimacy out of a sense of survival. Therefore, the Lost Child consciously or unconsciously craves an acknowledgment of value, sensitivity and nurturing beyond the aloof outer layer of protection. When there is an invitation of connection, the Lost Child has an inability to accept the offer because of its detached state that maintains the feeling of being lost, alone and forsaken.

OVER-DRAMATIC CHILD

tantrums, drama, acting out, sabotage attention-seeking,

LOST CHILD

surpressed, not present, disassociated, withdrawn, distant, checked out

MISUNDERSTOOD CHILD

offended, self-suffering, hurt, vicitmized, misfit, resentful, wounded

WOUNDED INNER CHILD

disempowered, wounded, immature, childish, internalized trauma, unconscious

FROZEN CHILD

unresponsive, stunted, waiting, defeated, hopeless, stuck

NEEDY CHILD

unmet needs, grasping attention, validation, co-dependent

OVER-INDULGED CHILD

spoiled, demanding, entitled, gluttony, excessive, self-centered

THE WOUNDED INNER CHILD
Over-Dramatic Child

"A man who has not passed through the inferno
of his own passions has never overcome them."
– Carl Jung

We live in the age of heightened drama because we have neglected our inner
relationships. We demand to be enthralled by an outer culture to combat that growing
desensitization and the profound feeling of inner loss. Disempowered attention-
seeking temporarily soothes the pain but never creates true connection and always
leaves the attention seeker grasping for more.

Understanding the Dynamics of The Over-Dramatic Child:

The Over-Dramatic Child is easily recognizable. This reactive archetype embodies drama and "acts out" on behalf of every aspect of the Wounded Inner Child. It is desperately seeking attention, affirmation and reassurance. The Over-Dramatic Child is created because of a conditioning of outer neglect, rejection and abandonment that leads to internalized reactivity, stress and anxiety because it believes it will never be given the nourishing attention that it needs.

Drama has many expressions from the subtle and unconscious to the overt and more conscious. It is more complex than your typical stereotype of "drama king or queen." Most people have some form of conditioned over-dramatic reactions. Every individual will express their personal flavor of acting out based on their unique conditioning.

Not all overdramatic behavior appears "overtly contractive" on the surface. But even in the example of "attractive" and so-called "positive drama," as enjoyable or entertaining as they may be, they are still disempowering and co-dependent. The craving for attention is always fueled by a deep sense of insecurity and scarcity. Even then, the drama is never fulfilling, and the Over-Dramatic Child is always left craving more.

Types of Attention seeking: Over-dramatic behavior has two primary categories of expression. They can either appear delightful, entertaining and enjoyable (superficially positive) or shocking, revolting and inappropriate (superficially negative). Either way, each of these forms of expression are designed to consciously or unconsciously garner attention to soothe the Over-Dramatic Child.

Externalized forms of attention seeking are expressed directly and outwardly. These more obvious expressions of drama tend to focus on attention seeking through outer behavior that directly involves another. This can include positive and entertaining forms of attention seeking or disturbing forms of drama. They can be subtle or obvious.

Some examples of obvious externalized drama are:

Being the life of the party ● the rebel or rule breaker ● insults, profanity or vulgarity towards another ● socially inappropriate behavior ● the class clown ● excessive talking ● humor ● complaining ● teacher's pet ● over-assistance ● lying ● melodramatic or over-emotional behavior

Some examples of more subtle externalized drama are:

Over-sexualized attire to garner attention ● wearing expensive designer clothes to broadcast wealth ● intentionally dressing to be noticed ● dominating, interrupting or hijacking the conversation ● name dropping ● inappropriate sharing ● self-bashing ● self-deprecating dialogue

Internalized forms of attention seeking are focused inward and tend to be more passive. It is self-centered, inwardly narcissistic, and self-sabotaging. It appears on the outside to be aloof or withdrawn, but the attempt is to garner attention by being vague and intentionally inaccessible.

Some examples of obvious externalized drama are:

accident-prone behavior ● self-injury ● different forms of self-sabotage ● clumsiness ● being generally awkward ● focus of self-indulged vanity ● perpetually losing track of the time ● over self-rumination ● self-absorption with your own process ● excessive pampering

Some examples of more subtle externalized drama are:

feelings of ineptitude ● unconscious low self-esteem ● vanity ● being inaccessible or unreachable ● aloofness ● withdrawn ● disengaged ● self-judgment ● excessive self-doubt ● avoiding intimacy ● false modesty ● withholding talent, wisdom or insight ● over self-identification ● moody

Examples of the behavior of the Over-Dramatic Child

- **Exhibitionist, provocative or seductive behavior**
- **Constant seeking of reassurance or approval**
- **Excessive sensitivity and emotionally sensitive to criticism or disapproval**
- **Pride and attachment and strong identification to their own personality**
- **Outer dress and style are designed to draw attention, debate and controversy**
- **Creates somatic symptoms (of physical illness) to get attention "accident prone"**
- **Has a pattern of unconscious dramatic self-sabotaging**
- **A desperate need to always be the center of attention**
- **Impatient frustration with delayed gratification**
- **Inappropriate interruption of the flow of conversation**
- **Rapidly changing and seemingly exaggerated emotional states (moody)**
- **Fabricates an inappropriate, contrived and deeper intimacy than is present**
- **Making rash decisions**
- **A tendency to be easily influenced by others**
- **Openly expresses strong, dramatic opinions and perspectives**
- **Blames personal failures or disappointments on others**
- **Easily influenced by others, especially those who treat them approvingly**
- **Being melodramatic, over-emotional and reactive**
- **Ingrained patterns of exaggeration, embellishment and hyperbole**
- **Denial of their level of over-dramatic patterns**

The condemnation, judgment and shame projected on the Over-Dramatic Child: The Over-Dramatic Child is one of the most recognizable yet misunderstood aspects of the Wounded Inner Child. The common insult, "drama queen," refers to the obvious attention-seeking aspect of the Over-Dramatic Child, but there are many layers of subtle expression to over-dramatic behavior.

Because this expression of the Over-dramatic Child is so expressive, it becomes an easy target to judge the collective expression of immaturity in the being. As a result, the Over-Dramatic Child is condemned for acting out and shoulders a disproportionate amount of shame in relation to the other archetypes of the Wounded Inner Child. As a result, this obvious reactive behavior is managed or subdued at the expense of deeper investigation of the source of the drama.

The desire to be acknowledged, validated, and praised are natural psychological needs that are vital for healthy mental and emotional development. Getting attention is a fundamental behavior necessary for survival. For instance, a newborn baby is dependent on care and attention and instinctively reacts by acting out through crying to obtain a mother's attention.

This is a form of natural and functional attention- seeking. But the Over-Dramatic Child's contractive relationship to drama is amplified because it is motivated by a deep woundedness of deprivation and desperation.

An individual's childish relationship to drama and attention-seeking is a conditioned behavior based on how caretakers, adults or parents responded to this instinctual need. Any excessive need for unhealthy attention always begins with a contractive past, spawned from some form of neglect. The more that these fundamental needs were ignored during early development, the more the Over-Dramatic Child must depend on excessive attention seeking as a necessary tactic to ensure survival.

The ongoing projection of inner or outer judgment and shaming of this now conditioned "crying out for attention" never helps to resolve the conditioning. Labeling this behavior "wrong" only fortifies the existing scarcity and accentuates the already reactive attachment to drama. This creates another layer of "negative attention seeking" which continues to fuel the hunger for attention in an endless loop. For the deprived Wounded Inner Child, any form of negative attention, though painful, is still preferable to no attention at all.

Over-Dramatic behavior is always reactive, immature and disempowered: The Over-Dramatic Child is always reacting to its inner sense of unconscious scarcity. It does not believe or realize that it can self-generate enough self-love and adoration to fulfill its needs. It has been conditioned to not trust its own inner abundance. As a result, this Wounded Inner Child manipulates its inner and outer behavior to gain this desperately lost attention. The Wounded Inner Child does not have an example of how to cultivate attention in a healthy way, so the behavior it exhibits is instinctual. Like a fearful infant that cannot take care of itself, it is acting out as a survival mechanism because it knows no other methods to ask for its needs. This behavior is deeply disempowered because it is always co-dependent on an outside source to provide its attention and acknowledgement.

The internal saboteur: The internal saboteur is the "undercover agent" of the Over-Dramatic Child, and it is one of the most disruptive but unseen elements of the Over-Dramatic Child. It can wreak havoc on your balance, expansive choices, goals and dreams. This undermining agent of the Over-Dramatic Child is responsible for all examples of sabotage on every level.

If the Over-Dramatic Child is an active component of your Wounded Inner Child dynamics, then the internal saboteur is quietly influencing some aspect of your behavior whether you are aware of it not. Every individual has their own personalized expression of the internal saboteur unique to their conditioning. The key to responding to the inner saboteur is to take the time learn the movements of this contractive undercover agent of destruction. You must identify the quality, flavor, and expression of the sabotage.

The greatest tactics of the internal saboteur utilities are stealth, complacency and unawareness. This aspect of the Over-Dramatic Child dwells in quiet shadows of the unconscious. If you are unaware of its presence, you will not be able to effectively respond to the wounded subversive disruptions.

The internal saboteur longs to be discovered: The saboteur ensures that all expansive behavior is foiled until adequate attention is given to highlight its woundedness. It longs to be discovered and is quietly disrupting the consciousness until the pain is acknowledged and appropriately addressed.

In the physical body, if a serious injury remains unattended, it becomes infected, potentially inflicting further damage to the physical body. This can create a host of ongoing issues until the original wound is addressed. In some cases, the infection can have lasting effects that could now be worse than the original injury. The same is the case with the Over-Dramatic Child. The ongoing subversive damage of the internal saboteur can, in the long run, create more destruction if left unattended.

In the beginning the saboteur was an immature, subversive tactic of the Wounded Inner Child to desperately draw the attention inward because it had no other choice. But if this destructive agent is left unattended, it will function in a reactive manner, undermining expansive opportunities because it has been left unchecked for so long.

Examples of self-sabotage: Self-sabotage can take on so many different expressions in the being that are not easily recognizable without self-investigation. There is a lot of shame and guilt around these covert manifestations of the Over-Dramatic Child because it is very difficult to ascertain the origin of the seemingly unconnected behavior traits. This makes it even more difficult to examine. Here are some examples of self-sabotaging behavior. Remember that your personal expression of the self-sabotage is completely unique to your past experiences and conditioning.

- **Ongoing Issues related with time management:** Ongoingly being late, not finishing tasks on time or repeated experiences of procrastination. Impatience or frustration with delayed gratification.

- **General difficulty with resolution:** Issues with completing tasks, overloading oneself with too many events and assignments (even if these are "fun experiences"), difficulty maintaining structure and schedules, ongoing difficulty with being able to shift from one experience to another (multitasking)

- **Psychological manifestations in inner and outer relationships:** Emotionally sabotaging relationships if they are too expansive (or too good to be true), ongoing issues with getting too close or intimate, unconsciously choosing deeply contractive partners, friends and companions who align with your past traumatic patterns of pain or mistaking the familiarity of past pain as true connection.

The physiological effects of trauma can form an unconscious addiction to drama:
A psychology which has become habitually programmed to equate lack of attention as dangerous will react seeing lack of attention as a fundamental threat. Constantly acting out of a perceived sense of survival from past trauma can become highly addictive to the Over-Dramatic Child.

The attention temporarily soothes the fear, scarcity and emptiness and induces the pleasure-inducing mechanisms and eases the anxiety. People can easily become addicted to the rush that the drama provides because even though it is only temporarily rewarding, it feels good and seems to fill the gap.

The reward for ongoing drama is dopamine (the brain's happy drug) and at some point, the immature aspect of the being becomes addicted to the drama for the sake of the drama. The Over-Dramatic Child may continue to artificially induce drama out of habit, even when it is unnecessary to get the temporary fix or the quick high because it has now become addicted to the temporary pleasure.

This behavior can be seen with actors, entertainers, public figures and performers who use the outer admiration and attention to soothe their unresolved inner wounds. They perform for the "high" of public adoration and become codependent to the outer validation. This drives their need to remain relevant and stay in the public eye in order to continue to get fed with attention.

Unfortunately, the drama no longer has to be "positive" or entertaining to obtain this high. In many cases, they will do whatever it takes to continue to get attention. In some cases, "negative" drama actually induces more intense experiences of survival and feelings of conflict and can arouse a stronger opiate experience of dopamine.

Like any drug, the drama must become more potent and extreme as one builds up a tolerance to the attention. It is never enough. And that means the Over-Dramatic Child continuously requires more intense versions of threatening, darker, and more destructive drama to induce the same high, like a drug addict that requires a higher dose of the drug to get the fix that they are craving.

This attention-seeking behavior is a psychological coping mechanism that has become an ongoing addiction from the prolonged effects of the trauma and unaddressed pain in the Wounded Inner Child. And though you cannot completely erase the residual effects of early trauma in the Wounded Inner Child, you can find more expansive ways of navigating the conditioned reaction to rewire the programmed addiction to drama with something more sustainable.

"Every one of us is touched by the addict archetype. The only question is how much of our lives is consumed by it. Besides the usual suspects–drugs, alcohol, food, and sex–one can be addicted to work, sports, television, exercise, computer games, spiritual practice, negative attitudes, and the kinds of thrills that bring on adrenaline rushes. In its positive aspect, this archetype helps you recognize when an outside substance, habit, relationship, or any expression of life has more authority over your will power than does your inner spirit. Confronting addiction and breaking the hold that a pattern or substance has on you can impart great strength to your psyche."
– Carolyn Myss

Manipulation of attention never creates fulfillment: Any attention that the Over-dramatic Child creates from the outside world through its immature drama is ultimately unfulfilling and not sustainable. Drama does not create an empowered inner state even if the Wounded Inner Child ultimately gets the attention that it desires. The high of the outward attention will always fade. And if the Over-Dramatic Child continues to desperately grasp for this attention, it can never attain the fullness of inner validation. It is cursed to live a contractive feedback loop that is fueled by co-dependency, addiction and fosters nothing but ongoing disempowerment and dissatisfaction. Whatever attention is consciously or unconsciously manipulated from a state of contraction, it cannot and will not create an expansive state. Fulfillment is only sustained when one learns to "fill" the deep inner scarcity and desperation with a mature inner attention until the woundedness is "fully" acknowledged, lovingly validated and resolved.

Prone to exaggeration by inflating reality to create attention and build self-esteem: Exaggeration is a common personality trait of the Over-Dramatic Child that either consciously or unconsciously gains validation through this expression of attention-seeking. By definition, exaggeration is literally a form of lying through misrepresentation. But through the eyes of the Over-Dramatic Child, it is simply considered hyperbole, inflated for dramatic effect.

Exaggeration is a form of overcompensation for an inner insecurity. This lack of self-esteem is the cause for the attention-seeking behavior of the Over-Dramatic Child, who is attempting to restore inner balance and reclaim the lost validation from their past. The unconscious coping behavior of exaggeration does little to directly address the foundational wounds. And though the perpetual inflation may generate a significant amount of superficial activity and outer attention, this drama is a reactive mechanism attempting to immaturely manage the existing woundedness and feeling of disempowerment. Here are some common examples:

- **Over-emphasis on accomplishments**
- **Excessive talking and mindless commentary**
- **Over-activity and being busy = self-importance**
- **Always having to be the "go to" person**
- **Pretentiousness**

The entertainer, class clown or the center of attention: This expression of the Over-Dramatic Child can effectively exploit positive drama "by showing off." It is captivating and the "audience" is more than willing to be entertained. On the surface this seems innocent and fun and the Over-Dramatic Child may display a sense of bold confidence and self-assurance in this display. The problem arises when the Over-Dramatic Child begins to over-identify with this role and the attention that comes with it. A co-dependency forms when it is unconsciously fueled by insecurity, the deep need for approval and outer acknowledgment. This dramatic expression can take many forms:

- **Exploiting talent, skills or gifts in order to dominate being the center of attention**
- **Immature and childish humor, impressions and comedy to be the "class clown"**
- **Needs to be the boisterous, lively, entertaining, and fun, "life of the party"**
- **In a social event they are always switched "on" and working the crowd**
- **Can create attention through captivating storytelling**
- **Dominating, interrupting or hijacking the conversation**
- **Can be overly charming, eccentric and captivating**
- **Showing off their physical abilities or prowess**

Melodramatic or reactive attention seeker: This form of attention-seeking usually expresses itself through the manipulation of psychological or emotional behaviors and character traits to attract attention. In this situation, the Over-Dramatic Child uses a heightened sense of melodrama to accentuate the situation in order to gain attention. Because this form of drama can be emotionally draining and eventually becomes exceedingly difficult to take seriously, the melodrama must continue to get more outrageous in order maintain the attention. Since the Over-dramatic Child is willing to do whatever it takes to garner any form of attention, these over-dramatic behaviors will be increasingly unfiltered, indiscriminate, and unsuitably intimate. This expression of drama can take on many forms:

- **A heightened theatrical drama expressed as a "drama queen" or "diva"**
- **Can act as a puffed-up, "bigger than life" version of themselves**
- **Inappropriate or unfiltered sharing without care for consequences**
- **Self-bashing and victimized commentary to get recognition**
- **Disempowered acts of "playing the victim" or "damsel in distress" for pity**
- **Shifting, exaggerated emotional states combined with erratic reactivity**
- **Excessive sensitivity and over-emotional to criticism**
- **Childish temper tantrums, fits, dramatic emotional outbursts and histrionics**

Self-injury and chronic illnesses or acute somatic manifestations: Deep patterns of psychological trauma can create ongoing unconscious manifestations. This type of pattern from the Over-Dramatic Child are self-inflicted and internalized as different forms of inner subterfuge that disrupt healthy functioning. Many internalized expressions of drama take on unconscious somatic (body oriented) manifestations. Not all physical manifestations, illnesses or sabotage are necessarily psychosomatic, so it is important to eliminate any direct causes to understand possible unconscious traumatic influences.

Without inner observation and self-inquiry, it can be difficult to identify these subtle patterns since they do not seem connected to any obvious triggers. As a result, this form of internalized over-dramatic behavior may continue for years without being recognized. If left unchecked, these patterns will become normalized and be even more difficult to detect. That is why it is important to not assume "that is just the way you are" without adequate self-investigation. Here are some examples:

- **Ongoing clumsiness and "accident prone" behavior**
- **Allergies, spontaneous aliments, chronic illnesses, headaches**
- **General awkwardness, being jumpy**
- **Over-sensitivity to physical touch, tactile self-soothing habits**

Patterns of self-absorption, ineptitude and low self-esteem: These internalized expressions of the Over-Dramatic Child usually revolve around various forms of contractive self-absorption. Superficially, these behaviors do not fit the classic "melodramatic" expressions. But with closer study, one will notice that these subversive behaviors are designed to "draw an individual in" to obtain attention through more passive tactics. Here are some examples:

- **General expressions of insecurity, awkwardness, or unconscious low self-esteem**
- **Conscious or unconscious feelings, attitudes or behaviors of ineptitude**
- **Subtle disparaging, belittling or self-doubting dialogue**
- **General expressions of pessimism, cynicism or self-doubt**
- **Over self-identification and inner judgment**
- **Strange, odd or macabre (subtly dark, disturbing or uncomfortable) behavior**

Outer withholding, aloofness or disengagement: These subtle patterns of internalized drama can take the form of withholding or passive disengagement. This covert behavior is mercurial and exceedingly difficult to identify in the outer world. Because of its fluid and aloof nature, it is even more difficult to authentically acknowledge these patterns in oneself. It requires a high level of honesty and ongoing self-investigation to be willing to observe and explore the nuances of this form of subversive drama. When confronted with being accountable to the behavior, many will become even more inaccessible and unreachable. General patterns of aloofness which draw attention are:

- **Withholding talent, wisdom or insight but alluding to having it**
- **Vague communication style that avoids details and offers minimal information**
- **Being an inaccessible "wallflower" who is seductively coy and seemingly shy**
- **Obvious disengagement, disdain for connection and withholding**

Histrionic Personality Disorder (HPD): Have you ever heard the expression "throwing a hissy fit"? This expression refers to an excessive dramatic pattern characterized by the psychological behavior known as Histrionic Personality Disorder. This disorder is usually identified by a "dramatic cluster" of dysfunctional attention-seeking patterns that acutely manifest to obsessively seek approval.

The combination of these different patterns can be covert, overt, internalized or externalized drama, sabotage or expressions of grandiosity, exaggeration, aggressiveness, self-indulgence and seduction. This cluster of patterns function together as a fluid array of interdependent tactics working together focused on gaining as much attention as possible.

The individual is usually quite skilled at quickly shifting their behavioral approach to adapt to the situation to consciously and unconsciously attract the maximum amount of attention. People who exhibit this reactive pattern of attention-seeking can be highly functioning and exhibit a keenly developed sense of social skills. They are effective communicators, charming, resourceful and highly narcissistic. They are commonly described as being over-dramatic, seductive, sexually provocative, and manipulative using their talent, intelligence and physical appearance to draw any attention they can in order make themselves the center of attention.

They have great difficulty with connection and intimacy in interpersonal relationships. They have issues with accepting failures, become easily bored, and crave constant stimulation. They are competitive and ruthless if threatened. They are invigorated by risky and dangerous people and situations. They prefer to withdraw from difficult situations instead of engaging with it responsively, because there is less possibility to leverage attention.

Along with other immature behaviors of attention grabbing, here are some common patterns that are usually wired into the drama matrix:

- **Denial about how much they seek attention:** An individual with heightened HPD is unwilling to honestly admit or address their attention- inducing behaviors. The idea of deconstructing the Over-Dramatic Child's matrix of the acquired survival mechanisms threaten their very sense of survival. In the mind of the Wounded Inner Child, this system of behavior, however immature and taxing, is usually "working" for them. They are skilled at getting what they need, even if it requires constant effort and is not sustainable in the long run. They are unrealistic about the contractive effects of the prolonged behavior and therefore they are unwilling to recognize its existence.

- **Emotional shallowness or superficiality:** Because of the need to quickly shift between different attention seeking tactics, it is impossible for those with HPD to sustain emotional depth, even if they allow themselves to briefly access it. For one thing, emotional intimacy is an offering not a taking, so it is difficult to superficially leverage enough attention through that form of vulnerability. Also, if the Over-Dramatic Child connects more deeply to their emotional experience, they would begin to feel the emotional impoverishment, desolation and scarcity that is at the core of the condition. Superficiality, though not satisfying, is a survival tactic that keeps things on the surface in to ignore the pain.

- **Fabricates inappropriate and contrived intimacy to create recognition and attention:** In extreme manifestations of HPD, the Over-Dramatic Child will consciously or unconsciously invent varying degrees of inauthentic intimacy. This is a method to induce attention and contrived connection for the agenda of maintaining their control over the flow of attention. As a skilled manipulator, this feigned display of intimacy will align their naïve subject and assure constant attention through empathy, guilt and loyalty. This fabricated sense of intimacy is combined with the tantalizing promise of something more even if they are unable to authentically offer a true expression of intimacy.

- **Provocative, engaging and seductive:** Like a psychological vampire, they have cultivated highly provocative and seductive skills which have become refined in their outer nature. This tactic is vital to manipulate a constant stream of attention. They know how to flaunt what they've got, and they love the rush of the provocative attention-seeking game. Seduction is key to success.

- **A tendency to be influenced and align with those who give them attention:** Any individual with HPD is functioning from varying degrees of disempowered reaction and immaturity. At the core, they desperately crave to be recognized, adored and cherished. Therefore, they are impressionable, especially by those who seem to fill that superficial need for attention. The disempowered state of inner scarcity is so prevalent they do not believe that they can ever fulfill their own needs. As a result, they are willing to cede their integrity and can be easily convinced to "sell their soul" for the promise of continued attention.

- **Jealous of others' attention:** Because of the acute level of woundedness, they feel threatened if attention is focused on another. That is viewed as competition, an assault on their territory or their audience that may upset the carefully created status quo that they worked so hard to achieve. The jealousy can become delusional and turn vindictive if they deem it is necessary.

Histrionic Personality Disorder is the example of a contractive feedback loop of the immature behavior of the Wounded Inner Child that is fueled and manipulated by the Shadow Inner Adult. This contractive relationship continues to influence the immature Over-Dramatic Child through the contractive association of the Shadow Inner Adult aspects of the Controlling Adult, Possessive Adult and Inauthentic Adult.

OVER-DRAMATIC CHILD

tantrums, drama, acting out, sabotage attention-seeking,

LOST CHILD

surpressed, not present, disassociated, withdrawn, distant, checked out

MISUNDERSTOOD CHILD

offended, self-suffering, hurt, vicitmized, misfit, resentful, wounded

WOUNDED INNER CHILD

disempowered, wounded, immature, childish, internalized trauma, unconscious

FROZEN CHILD

unresponsive, stunted, waiting, defeated, hopeless, stuck

NEEDY CHILD

unmet needs, grasping attention, validation, co-dependent

OVER-INDULGED CHILD

spoiled, demanding, entitled, gluttony, excessive, self-centered

THE WOUNDED INNER CHILD:
The Misunderstood Child

"The victim mindset dilutes the human potential.
By not accepting personal responsibility for our circumstances,
we greatly reduce our power to change them."
– Steve Maraboli

Understanding the Dynamics of The Misunderstood Child:

More than other aspects of the Wounded Inner child, the Misunderstood Child embodies the idea of the consummate (poor me) victim mentality and self-imposed suffering. This victim mentality has many different manifestations, but at the core it is connected to a profound sense of inner deficiency and an obsession with that woundedness. Even though the Misunderstood Child may speak about making efforts to remedy their pain, they are too psychologically impaired to take the necessary steps. Instead, this ego fragment chooses to be consumed in their perceived or actual woundedness.

"Self-pity is one of the most destructive non-pharmaceutical narcotics.
It is addictive and gives momentary pleasure
and separates the victim from reality."
– John W. Carpender

The Misunderstood Child also has a complex internal conflict with their prolonged sense of suffering. In some ways, they loathe it. It keeps their life in a state of contraction, making them feel like they cannot experience the same contentment that others enjoy. However, the unresolved pain offers them a sense of "broken uniqueness." They feel it sets them apart from others as they connect to the pain around them, and becomes the very thing that they use to get the attention that continues the cycle of self-pity. They can be highly sensitive and protective of their pain because their personal sense of woundedness is so deeply woven into their personal identity.

Feeling understood is a foundation for acceptance and love: Every child longs to be understood and appreciated. This validation helps the child form healthy feelings of self-worth and self-understanding. But for the Misunderstood Child, this feeling of being misunderstood is at the root of their self-perpetuated suffering.

Feeling undervalued or misinterpreted can create a host of unconscious conditioning that will eventually be internalized as self-rejection, create a continued pattern of self-inflicted pain, and promotes the isolation of being a misunderstood outcast. Without self-love, the ability to feel a sense of understanding or experience internal hope and optimism is profoundly crippled.

The Unsolvable Problem

 The Misunderstood Child has a deep need to be understood but believes no one will ever understand them. One of the most common tactics of this contractive aspect of the Wounded Child can be referred to as the "unsolvable problem." This term refers to the pattern where an individual continues to create a "behavioral contractive feedback loop" exhibiting an almost defiant unwillingness to entertain any possibility of a solution. It allows them to wallow in the insolvability of the problem. This is the example of the consummate pessimist or that individual you may know who always sees the glass as "half empty."

Simply put, the Misunderstood Child is uninterested in looking for any expansive solution to the problem. They unconsciously need the problem to continue to either manipulate attention or justify their pain. This way they can remain the victim and utilize the attention they get from others. Without the problem, they cannot remain in their cycle of struggle.

Examples of behavior of the Misunderstood Child:

- **Embodies the misunderstood outlier, misfit or outcast**
- **Exhibits a general lack of responsibility for their life.**
- **Does not take actions to improve life circumstances**
- **Has a tendency to get caught up in challenging circumstances**
- **Feels a general sense of helplessness**
- **Blames others for problems. May try to elicit guilt.**
- **More invested in complaining and getting sympathy rather than real change**
- **Sometimes feels special and important because of their unique circumstances**
- **Holds grudges against those who have wronged them and does not forgive easily**
- **There is a tendency to exaggerate pain to elicit sympathy**
- **Strong dependency on the "Martyr" complex**
- **There is an indulging by "living in the wound" of past or present situations**
- **Sometimes attracted to vocations that identify with human pain and suffering**
- **Can take things over-personally and project unnecessary misunderstanding**
- **They are intensely sensitive and experience life "more deeply" than others**
- **Exhibits passive-aggressive behavior patterns**
- **Deep inner dissatisfaction is projected as "someone or something else's" fault**
- **Can feel entitled and project that they "should" be treated in a specific manner**
- **Over-investment of pain or perceived pain at the expense of responsibility**
- **Attempts to coerce caretaking by demanding attention because of their pain**
- **May look for special treatment but feel like they don't deserve it**
- **Does not feel the right to ask for their own needs**
- **Perpetuates a state of pessimism, jadedness, doubt and complacency**

Feeling wronged, persecuted or victimized by anything or anyone
is not a long-term adaptive behavior.
It does not empower you to be resourceful, grow or be successful.
It is immediately contractive, stagnant and hinders the environment for change.

Attracted to challenging and negative circumstances: This aspect of the Wounded Inner Child focuses on the pain and suffering in the world even if presented with a different option. Their internal filter is tuned to get caught up in the most challenging situations in order to keep their pain active and justify their woundedness. They believe there is no other option for them. They cannot understand that they are actively invested in continuing to ignite their own wound.

General sense of powerlessness, helplessness and hopelessness: There is a strong conditioned belief of powerlessness and helplessness with no possibility to change the situation. At some point, the wound of being repeatedly misunderstood and unacknowledged generated an overwhelming loss of hope. The Misunderstood Child gave up on being lovingly seen and appreciated from the outer world. Instead, they began to internalize the pain of that profound sense of hopelessness that defined their self-perpetuating patterns of suffering. This continued to foster the general feeling of loss of power and being helpless to do anything to escape the contractive state of being.

Does not take actions to improve life circumstances: Though the Misunderstood Child may profess its desire to change, it is too crippled to take the necessary actions to improve the present contractive circumstances. The identification to suffering is deeply ingrained, as is a strong belief that the pain is deserved. The overwhelming sense of helplessness combined with previous failed attempts to transform this pattern have taught the Misunderstood Child that an expansive life is out of reach. Feeding the wound has become the only thing they understand.

To continue an ongoing story of suffering is the Misunderstood Child's
method of control and punishment disguised as healing.
- Samjhi

Feeling special and unique because of their pain: Some people are only "happy" and feel alive when they are suffering because it defines their existence. When examining the Misunderstood Child, one can see examples in the common persona of the tragic romantic. This profound pain defines their experience of love. It makes them feel special because of their "impossible" circumstances.

To project this misunderstood love, they will fall for an inaccessible or unavailable subject. They cannot bring themselves to confess their feelings, so they continue to secretly worship the fantasy from afar. They feel alive in the longing and suffering for their unaware beloved because it supports the belief in struggle.

Indulges in "living in the wound" of past or present situations: The Misunderstood Child indulges in the practice of "living in the wound" because on some level they do not really want to change the relationship to pain and suffering.

This plays out in many ways. The Misunderstood Child:

- becomes unconsciously enamored by the struggle of the "healing process" and remains stuck in perpetual healing without ever getting through the process. If there is no change in the inner and outer experience, then it is likely that the Misunderstood Child is keeping the wound alive.

- will continually revisit and become obsessed with contractive circumstances from the past. These past issues can be powerful opportunities to recreate something new moving forward. But the obsession with the past pain without solution continues to give the woundedness attention and energy and keeps it active in the present.

- will indulge in excessive bouts of self-pity. Feeling sorry for yourself does not allow the opportunity to change because the focus is constantly on what is wrong with the present situation and feeling "bad."

- refers to the wound as "my pain" or "my issues" with a sense of strange affectionate personification and emotional charge which suggests deep attachment.

- will continue engaging in an active inner and outer dialogue of self-condemnation which actively cripples the ability to choose an expansive alternative. This condemns self for the existence of pain and judges how you are dealing with it. Making yourself wrong for any aspect of the wound never helps release yourself from the wound.

- is also known for indulging in the "if only things were different story." Focusing on what "could have been" is a way of negating what has happened and keeps the Misunderstood Child disempowered in a fantasy that can never be, because you cannot change the past events, the "what if" reality does not help to empower a new path moving forward. It keeps you stuck in "could have, should have, or would have" but can never be.

Embodies the misunderstood outlier, misfit or outcast: The Misunderstood Child is the epitome of the "eternal outcast" who romantically survives on the fringes of society just waiting to be discovered. This role legitimizes its sense of misunderstood suffering. The deep woundedness perpetuates the "lone wolf" mentality.

Even when they are sincerely embraced for who they are, the Misunderstood Child does not believe that it truly deserves the acceptance, even though it craves that acceptance. If this pattern of woundedness is not resolved, the Misunderstood Child will return to the outlier position which, though painful, is more manageable and familiar.

Drawn to vocations that identify with human pain and suffering: Since the Misunderstood Child identifies so profoundly with the idea of woundedness, they may unconsciously be attracted to vocations that also identify with human pain and suffering. It allows them to project their own sense of woundedness in an external arena. The intensity of the outer "pain drama" and ongoing suffering can be legitimately and excusably felt, explored without personal ownership.

Taking things over-personally, being offended and over-sensitivity: This contractive aspect of the Wounded Inner Child feels like it experiences life "more deeply" than others. But that is nothing more than an "over-dramatic sensitivity" that can be used for attention. Deeply empathic feelers do not need to project misunderstanding. But for the over-sensitive Misunderstood Child, there is an unconscious dysfunctional pattern that longs to be misunderstood and justifies this position of woundedness. Taking things "personally" ensures that the individual will always be a victim.

The Misunderstood Child over-explains their situation: They offer unnecessary levels of details and explanation because they believe they will always be misunderstood. This tactic backfires because they confuse the listener with the chaos of those details, lose track of their own point and create the very feeling they were hoping to avoid. The fear of being misunderstood creates the outer experience of being misunderstood.

The Martyrdom Complex

Any Individual who has developed a martyr (victim) complex, focuses on the needs of others while neglecting their own. They refuse to admit that this is done for selfish reasons, either to fill a psychological need or as a tactic to avoid personal responsibility or accountability.

This self-sacrifice is the ultimate self-inflicted pain. The seeming ingratitude from the world fuels internal resentment. This martyr can take many forms:

- They may portray themselves as the misunderstood or "unsung hero" saint or caretaker who has abandoned their personal dreams or needs in "service" to another or a greater cause.

- Using this positioning of martyrdom, they may emotionally manipulate others into doing their bidding by presenting themselves as the noble sufferer.

- They blame the selfishness of others for their real or perceived personal repression and oppression.

- The positioning of martyr justifies their excuse for unfulfilled greatness, as well as reassuring their inherent innocence. "If only the world could see my talent, my genius, my greatness…"

- This pattern allows the individual to maintain a cynical perception of people's intentions, perpetuating the feeling of being misunderstood, unknown and unseen.

- The deeply misunderstood martyr never has to accept personal responsibility for their own decisions, choices that have continued their personal suffering.

- The martyr expects and assumes that everyone should understand their perspective, their pain or their story. Because they have spent so much time focusing and caretaking others, they are secretly waiting for the day when it is their turn to be acknowledged or have their needs met without having to ask. Ironically, if they did have the opportunity to have this need fulfilled, they more than likely would deny the offering because they identify so deeply with their suffering.

Common Misunderstood Child phrases to watch for:

- **My situation is impossible.**
- **It's your fault that I am unhappy.**
- **They should be treating me differently.**
- **After all I have done for them, the least they could do is…**
- **You will never understand.**
- **You do not know what it is like to be me.**
- **It never works out for me.**
- **Suffering is where I draw my strength from.**
- **"No pain, no gain."**
- **I have always been a misunderstood misfit.**
- **Suffering helps me realize that I am alive.**

Does not recognize or ask for needs: As a part of the martyred self-imposed conditioning of suffering, the Misunderstood Child rarely, if ever, asks for what they need. In many cases, this pattern of the Misunderstood Child is perpetuated simply because there is little or no recognition of their own needs, which makes it virtually impossible to be able to request assistance when it is needed.

If they do recognize it, they believe that any request is likely to be rejected or ignored. And because of the conditioning, they are unconsciously drawn to ask for help from those who will not or cannot show up for them. This only fortifies the belief that they will never get the help that they need.

Exhibits passive-aggressive behavior patterns: The Misunderstood Child can project anger and envy at those who are accomplished or those they perceive are moving forward when they cannot and will not. "Why is someone who is less talented, intelligent or capable than me more successful?" They resent the success of others because they feel that others did not "struggle" enough to deserve their achievements. For them, anything that is without pain is also without value.

Another example of passive aggressive behavior can occur when someone offers the Misunderstood Child a way out of their perpetual contractive feedback loop. They will say things like "You do know how hard it has been for me" or "it is not as simple as it looks," and refuse the offer of assistance. The Misunderstood Child is ultimately angry at themselves for their inability to break through, but they cannot admit that they are, in fact, their biggest obstacle to transcending their own struggle.

The Misunderstood Child makes everything complex and complicated: The more complicated the situation, the easier it is for this aspect of the Wounded Inner Child to remain trapped and engaged in their own conflict. This messy chaos creates a familiar state of accepted confusion. As a result, they tend to "muddy the waters" with complexity as an ongoing distraction, so they do not have to examine the true nature of their circumstances.

They may proclaim "You do not understand how complex it is for me," or " it is just so complicated, I am not sure you will ever understand," or "you are oversimplifying a much more complex situation." In a sense, they unconsciously maintain the energy of self-misunderstanding by refusing to comprehend their own condition. The continual chaos fuels that disempowered state.

OVER-DRAMATIC CHILD

tantrums, drama, acting out, sabotage attention-seeking,

MISUNDERSTOOD CHILD

offended, self-suffering, hurt, vicitmized, misfit, resentful, wounded

LOST CHILD

surpressed, not present, disassociated, withdrawn, distant, checked out

WOUNDED INNER CHILD

disempowered, wounded, immature, childish, internalized trauma, unconscious

FROZEN CHILD

unresponsive, stunted, waiting, defeated, hopeless, stuck

NEEDY CHILD

unmet needs, grasping attention, validation, co-dependent

OVER-INDULGED CHILD

spoiled, demanding, entitled, gluttony, excessive, self-centered

THE WOUNDED INNER CHILD
The Needy Child

"We're only as needy as our unmet needs."
– John Bowlby (Founder of Attachment Theory)

Understanding the Dynamics of The Needy Child:

The dynamic of neediness begins within an expression of "inner neediness," where one has unconsciously learned to starve themselves with a lack of self-nurturing and sincere self-attention. This conditioned internalizing of inadequacy originated from the behavior of their specific family, parents or role models.

Experiences of neglect, abandonment and rejection have created a dysfunctional pattern of self-abandonment that drives an outward seeking to have those unmet needs satisfied by others. This contractive expression of the Wounded Inner Child perpetuates the dynamic by continually neglecting themselves to stay in a state of emotional emptiness.

The undernourished Needy Child begins to seek, demand or elicit attention and validation through its interactions with the outside world. Having abandoned itself, it is willing to pursue co-dependent behaviors to soothe the longing, and do whatever it takes, however inappropriate, to feel nourished. The depths of the wound will determine the extent to which one is willing to go to feel "loved."

The Different Expressions of Neediness

There are two common manifestations of the Needy Child that are expressed through either or a combination of approval-seeking and/or attention-seeking. Both forms of "seeking" begin from the unconscious belief of deep insufficiency.

1. **Neediness as a form of approval-seeking:** Neediness is really an unconscious belief and confession that others are and have "more" of everything than you. The behavior unconsciously disempowers an individual as it looks outward. Neediness demands reassurance and approval that you are enough.

2. **Neediness as a form of attention-seeking:** Human beings exist with a certain level of healthy self-attentiveness that benefits from positive attention from others. It becomes pathological when your desire to be reinforced becomes compulsive, seeking excessive attention and becoming attached to the source of that attention.

Meeting Healthy Emotional Needs vs Unhealthy Emotional Neediness

A **healthy emotional need** is a basic human requirement for healthy development. This centers on "basic" feelings like love, fear, anger, sorrow, gratitude and peace, all of which is derived from the understanding and support of one person for another.

The need and expression of this human emotional connection is present in everyone, but it will usually increase during periods of excessive stress or physical and mental illness and during various stages of life, such as infancy, early childhood, and old age when a higher level of support is necessary. This expression of healthy support is called "interdependence."

On the other hand, **unhealthy emotional neediness**, as expressed through the Needy Child, has a dysfunctional relationship to obtaining those outside needs. This compulsion can be expressed through an inappropriate desperation to meet these needs by latching or clinging onto an outside source. If the dysfunction is strong enough, it can override the "healthy" expression of human connectedness. Instead, it will feed emotional co-dependence driven by insecurity, fear and lack of confidence.

Emotionally "needy" projections from the voice of the Needy Child:
Any internal or external dialogue that places responsibility for getting needs met on an outside source, on another person or somewhere else besides themselves without any personal responsibility is the victimized and manipulative voice of the Wounded Inner Child:

- **"I have needs!"**
- **"I need your approval."**
- **"I need you to tell me how good I look."**
- **"I need for you to be available for sex whenever I want it."**
- **"I need you to make me feel lovable and worthy."**
- **"I need (all of) your attention."**
- **"I am nothing without your love."**
- **"I need you to make me feel secure."**
- **"I need you to make me feel important."**
- **"The best part of me is you."**
- **"I need you to fill my emptiness.**
- **"Without you, I cannot fill my emptiness."**
- **"I need you to make me feel special."**
- **"It is your job to make me happy."**
- **"Without you, I do not know who I am."**
- **"You complete me."**

Interdependence vs Co-dependence

Emotional interdependence is the healthy emotional and/or psychological reliance between two or more people. There can be various degrees of interdependence depending on the nature of the relationship. The key that makes the relationship "interdependent" is that the individuals within the relationship do not abandon themselves for the other as they remain autonomous.

Your sense of self and your conscious connection to your inherent nature is maintained and continues to thrive within the connection. This consensual relationship is also mutually valuable for all in involved. Independence and connection maintain a conscious healthy inner relationship while there can still be deep devotion to a partner, friend, loved one, family member, community, or society.

Emotional co-dependency is an unhealthy emotional or psychological reliance between two or more people. There can be various degrees of co-dependence depending on the nature of the relationship.

In this situation, a person's unhealthy patterns or behavior (consciously or unconsciously) are enabled. Examples can include addictive patterns, immaturity, irresponsibility, or under-achievement which can result in varying contractive behaviors. Among the core characteristics of co-dependency, the most common theme is an excessive need for approval from an outside source.

Someone who is part of a co-dependent relationship is someone whose thinking, emotions and behavior is organized around another person, process, or substance. Emotional co-dependence is driven by a contractive, unconscious and "selfish" urge that demands without consent and is not equally expansive for all parties involved. There is little or no connection to their sense of themselves, as they have deserted their own needs in favor of the outside party.

Denied self-care fuels dishonest selfishness: The "neediness" of this aspect is inauthentic. The denied form of self-caring has descended into selfishness to obtain unfulfilled needs. The individual does not want to admit that their behavior is driven by a compulsive desire to have their needs met. The attention the Needy Child is seeking is not willingly offered and therefore there is little concern for the one giving it. The validation is "hijacked" without permission.

Even though the "Needy Child" has managed to coerce the needed attention, they remain unfulfilled because on some level they realize that the attention was not freely given. This bitter dissatisfaction drives the ongoing cycle, which fuels their internal sense of scarcity and anger.

The self-denial of outer care and assistance: Another unconscious manifestation of the Needy Child can be seen in the unwillingness to accept assistance when it is legitimately needed. This pattern may be driven by several unconscious wounds. On some deep level the individual has internalized or has been conditioned to believe that the assistance is not truly deserved. They may even sabotage the experience of feeling cared for when it is given, not fully believing or allowing the experience. That lack of self-worth stems from past experiences of profound disappointment when their needs were unfulfilled.

Instead of feeling this deep pain, the unconscious Needy Child may reject assistance and suffer the consequences to unconsciously protect themselves from feeling the wound of being let down yet again by another. Even though this pattern protects the individual from feeling the wound of abandonment or rejection, it creates a sense of isolation and withdrawal from true connection.

Also, they may not even believe or trust that people will be there for them, and therefore they will reject any opportunities, essentially rejecting or abandoning themselves before someone else can. It requires immense vulnerability and trust to allow themselves to be loved, especially if they unconsciously feel like they do not deserve it. This ongoing cycle of denial creates internal tension, obsessive worry about their needs, control, ongoing anxiety and a general feeling of fear of trusting anything, especially the unknown.

Examples of the behavior of the Needy Child:

- **Inability to make decisions for themselves**
- **Intense fear of abandonment, anxiety and nervousness**
- **Oversensitive and emotionally overwhelmed by criticism or disapproval**
- **A pattern of victimized worry, pessimism and cynicism**
- **Great difficulty being alone for long periods of time**
- **May tolerate and/or justify abuse or mistreatment from others to be liked**
- **Minimizes or denies their own needs placing others' needs above their own**
- **Tendency to act naïve, innocent or be in denial**
- **Demonstrates an ongoing pattern of helplessness**
- **Difficulty starting or completing tasks without assistance**
- **Displays an aversion to mature adult decision-making without assistance**
- **Becomes easily emotionally overwhelmed**
- **General pattern of "people pleasing"**
- **A pattern of lack of self-confidence, insecurity and lack of self-worth**
- **Can be disingenuous or inauthentic to justify being accepted or liked**
- **Consistently attempts to elicit praise, validation or "fishes for compliments"**
- **Can become passive-aggressive, manipulative and resentful**
- **They feel like their needs can only be met by another**
- **Obsessively avoid potential or perceived conflict or confrontation at all cost**
- **Emotionally imitating, mimicking or adopting traits of another**
- **Demonstrating clinginess or smothering in relationships with others**
- **Attention-seeking through indulging in unnecessary debate**
- **Tendencies to get jealous of others' independence**
- **Looks to another to fulfill their unmet emotional gaps, needs and internal emptiness**
- **An obsessive need to know how the "other" person is feeling in order to feel secure**

Demonstrating "clinginess" in relationships with others: "Clinginess" stems from an inner scarcity that is rooted in damaged self-worth. It can also be expressed as a passive aggressive power play to control a relationship or situation out of fear of being alone or being abandoned. Unhealthy desperation fueled by inner insecurity in any behavior feels smothering, contractive and unattractive to others. Clinginess is the expression of the out-of-control addictive quality of dependency.

The need to elicit praise, validation or attention: The feeling of receiving praise, validation and attention is the lifeblood that sustains and continues to feed the contractive patterns of the Needy Child. Without the continued draw of attention from the outer world, the pattern and the subsequent relationships that feed that conditioning will collapse. Therefore, the desperate need to manipulate the situation to get this validation is paramount. Cutting off the flow of this attention may deeply disturb the Wounded Inner Child, potentially creating an emotional breakdown. In the eyes of the Needy Child, obtaining this validation is a survival issue.

The tendency to be inauthentic: The intense need to be liked means the Needy Child can change depending on who they are talking to or where they are attempting to get attention. This behavior can take many forms. It can be loud and overbearing, overly positive, or abrasive, or it can be carefully scripted, rehearsed, polished and well thought out. The Needy Child can be very skilled in knowing how to draw people in. They may use mirroring language, be able to intuitively read the situation, stimulate the necessary subjects or perspective and know how to engage others. They seem to know exactly what to say, relate and sound inviting. They may even play roles and behave as the person who they think you want them to be in order to be liked to get validation.

The inability to make decisions for themselves: It is difficult for the Needy Child to make decisions because their process is usually based on others. Therefore, they may find themselves seeking approval during the decision-making process, asking for other opinions or waiting until someone else makes the decision on their behalf. Their behavior is so focused on the attention of others, they are unwilling to decide out of fear that they will not be liked or that it will be wrong. They may even use the inability to make a decision as a reasonable opportunity to justify getting help and seeking attention.

Oversensitive and emotionally overwhelmed by criticism or disapproval: Even moderate disagreement or perceived disapproval may overwhelm the Needy Child, activating unconscious survival patterns. The individual may emotionally overreact as a defense mechanism to protect themselves. If you perceive this inflated reaction, know that the Needy Child is activated.
This subversive tactic may be used to deflect the potential disapproval while simultaneously creating the desired attention.

Avoiding possible conflict and confrontation at all costs: Avoiding potential conflict can be another manifestation of the same deep-rooted fear of disapproval. Avoiding confrontation means internal and/or external self-sacrifice at their own expense for another in order to deflect engagement that could possibly lead to rejection. Disapproval is a bigger enemy than being inauthentic. Keeping the peace means you are more likely to get your needs met by a "happy" other person. The Needy Child will go to great lengths to soothe the potential conflict to maintain the fragile state of appeasement.

Tendency to get jealous of others' independence: The Needy Child is co-dependent and unwilling to cultivate self-sufficiency. As a result, they can become envious with someone who shows empowered independence. They feel their own shortcomings and envy the sense of freedom in the other. This may also intensify their fear that they will be rejected as the other begins to soar past any co-dependency with them.

An obsessive need to know how the "other" person is feeling in order to feel secure: In order to maintain that delicate constructed balance of "approval" from another, the Needy Child will obsessively be focused on how the other is feeling. They need this information to keep everyone happy in an attempt to feel secure and to control things for favorable outcomes. An extreme example of this co-dependent state is a victim ensuring that their abuser is happy to preserve peace (out of fear of abuse).

May tolerate and/or justify abuse or mistreatment from others to be liked: The Needy Child will tolerate mistreatment in order to maintain a co-dependent relationship. The mistreatment is a reasonable trade-off for what the relationship provides. To avoid conflict or disapproval, they will justify an abusive relationship. On an unconscious level they do not feel they are worthy of more. The outer mistreatment is reflective of their existing inner treatment and belief system.

Tendency to act naïve, innocent or be in denial: The Needy Child will be more interested in creating a palatable story than admit the reality of the situation. This may be because they do not feel worthy, are unwilling to feel deserted or experience the wound of disapproval. That creates a tendency to feign innocence or choose naïveté as a coping mechanism. These are all just softer forms of denial.

Emotionally imitating, mimicking or adopting traits of another: Individuals who have no idea who they are, who they want to be, or who they should be will adopt traits of people who offer them approval. The personal inner identity of the Needy Child is unstable, so they will revert to mimicking as a form of flattery. The Needy Child is so "outer focused" on their identity they spend all of their time seeking approval instead of cultivating an empowered inner relationship. This is not to say that emulating admirable traits from another is always co-dependent, but ultimately one must eventually cultivate these traits as an authentic expression. Imitation to seek approval is unsustainable and fuels disappointment.

Can become passive-aggressive, manipulative and resentful: When the attention tactics fall short, the Needy Child can become passive-aggressive and handle the situation through varying methods of manipulation. This breeds resentment. The Needy Child has made self-sacrifices for attention, and upon failure, become angry and disappointed with themselves, though they are unwilling to admit their culpability.

Attention-seeking through indulging in unnecessary debate: The key words here are "indulging" and "unnecessary." While there may be novelty and play in most forms of banter and debate with others, there is a point which the engagement becomes a ploy to subversively "hijack" attention. But because this tactic is unowned, it becomes passive-aggressive under the guise of something else. Neediness drains energy out of healthy relationships. And if someone is needlessly creating "a passive-aggressive forum for attention" through debate, they are essentially treating the other person as nothing more than an audience for garnering attention and self-validation.

OVER-DRAMATIC CHILD

tantrums, drama, acting out, sabotage attention-seeking,

LOST CHILD

surpressed, not present, disassociated, withdrawn, distant, checked out

MISUNDERSTOOD CHILD

offended, self-suffering, hurt, vicitmized, misfit, resentful, wounded

WOUNDED INNER CHILD

disempowered, wounded, immature, childish, internalized trauma, unconscious

FROZEN CHILD

unresponsive, stunted, waiting, defeated, hopeless, stuck

NEEDY CHILD

unmet needs, grasping attention, validation, co-dependent

OVER-INDULGED CHILD

spoiled, demanding, entitled, gluttony, excessive, self-centered

THE WOUNDED INNER CHILD
The Over-Indulged Child

"Man is not, by nature, deserving of everything that he wants.
When we think we are automatically entitled to something,
that is when we start walking over others to get it."
– Criss Jami

Understanding the Dynamics of The Over-Indulged Child:

The image of the spoiled child is a highly recognizable archetype. It is often characterized in cultural narrative through music, books, TV, film, celebrities, leaders and public figures. This conditioning is expressed through self-centered behavior, recurring and uncontrollable outbursts of temper tantrums, and the insatiable need for instant gratification.

It can manifest itself as disrespect toward authority figures or perceived threats to its status quo. The Over-Indulged Child needs to be the center of attention. This unbridled narcissism can also be expressed through a dramatic self-deification of megalomania.

This self-centeredness is usually programmed during the developmental stages of maturation. Typically, the behavior is a result of a child always getting what they want by manipulating its environment through destructive behavior. Because this aspect of the Wounded Inner Child has come to so deeply identify with the superficiality of materialism, it can be cruel, aggressive and even vengeful if it is denied. *"I want what I want, and I don't care what I have to do to get it."*

"A sense of entitlement is a cancerous thought process
that is void of gratitude and can be deadly to our relationships."
– Dr. Steve Maraboli

The developmental importance of feeling disappointment: Disappointment can be defined as the psychological reaction to an outcome that does not match up with the initial expectations. It is a natural part of healthy human development. The Over-Indulged Child has been continually sheltered from any feelings of loss and disappointment. The inner facility to engage with that experience was never fully developed. Healthy experiences of disappointment shape self-reliance, conviction and introspection.

Disappointment offers an opportunity to examine the way you see yourself, others and the world around you. It can help you determine what is important and adjust unreasonable expectations. It breeds deeper commitment, effort, and most of all it inspires adaptation as you gain insight. Without these developmental experiences the Over-Indulged Child is constantly disempowered and inept in the face of disappointment, which only continues its desire for indulgence.

"If we are ready and quiet enough,
we shall find compensation in every disappointment."
– Henry David Thoreau

The Over-Indulged Child confuses "wants" as "needs": In the dysfunctional conditioning of the Over-Indulged Child, there is a profound misunderstanding between wants and needs. They have difficulty making this distinction and therefore react when a want is not granted as if a need has been denied.

Objective needs are those that are met through tangible things, or material items tthat could be physically measured. These include shelter, food, water and oxygen.

Subjective needs are those conditions necessary to ensure our healthy psychological existence. Some examples of these subjective psychological needs are self-esteem, a sense of security and approval and adoration. There are distinct (objective and subjective) needs that must be met by each and every human being in order to function well in society, and to survive. The inability of meeting these needs can lead to a person suffering from physical or psychological illness or dysfunction that can deeply affect quality of life.

Wants are something craved or desired. To feel a strong wish for some preferred or favored object, circumstance, condition, experience or event. A want is not necessary or essential. They are optional. Unlike needs, wants will differ because they are relative from one person to another.

Wants are powerful incentives to consciousness because they can inspire and motivate us to achieve, grow, and expand in our thinking and perception of self-worth and personal value. But issues will always arise when anyone conveniently deceives oneself into believing that a want is actually a need. This distorted perception creates intensified emotional reaction, addiction or compulsion as an individual may become obsessed with obtaining a particular desire as if it is necessary for survival.

Types of over-indulgence: Not all types of over-indulgences are the same. The dysfunctional behavior can be created as a result of one or a combination of several different types of over-indulgence. Here are three examples:

1. **Overabundance or excessive giving**
2. **Over-nurturing, smothering and emotional coddling**
3. **Loose structures or wavering boundaries**

Over-nurturing, smothering and emotional coddling: When nurturing is indulged to the point where the behavior feeds the wants of the child rather than its needs, then it has crossed the line into indulgence. This occurs when the child is consistently conditioned to have their caregivers do something for them that they should be doing for themselves.

The child learns to expect the indulged behavior and never claims its own independence or the confidence that comes from that empowered experience. When children are emotionally coddled, they become too insecure to fend for themselves and continue to crave and demand this over-indulged attention.

Loose structures or wavering boundaries: Having too few boundaries create and enable the over-indulged child. Healthy relationships are based in trusting and honoring our personal agreements with one another. This builds a sense of character and inner conviction with accountability. When a child constantly witnesses that the rules are not enforced, they will indulge their desires regardless of what has been said. They have been conditioned to understand that rules do not apply to them.

Consistent boundaries create security. Maintaining limits demonstrates discipline, nurturing and caring. Without them, a child will feel unconsciously wounded that there was not enough authentic caring and react accordingly.

> *"It's a very child-centered universe right now, and in some ways,*
> *we want to see our kids empowered and being able to advocate for themselves.*
> *But there's a fine line between that and going over the boundary*
> *of the too-empowered child who thinks*
> *they have the right to every toy they point to."*
> *– Elaine Levy Cooper, Ph.D.*

Examples of the behavior of the Over-Indulged Child:

- **It's never good enough – constant seeking for fulfillment in the outer world**
- **A heightened sense of self-importance, grandiose and potential megalomania**
- **Satisfying and indulging in selfish wants is more important than empathy**
- **Can exhibit sociopathic tendencies**
- **Total wanton and disregard for rules, systems and authority**
- **Self-centered, selfish and self-absorbed**
- **Exhibits varying degrees of narcissism**
- **Lack of gratitude or appreciation**
- **Can become demanding, cruel and aggressive if denied**
- **Deeply insecure without outer validation**
- **Very materialist, status driven and image oriented**
- **Exhibits excessive vanity**
- **Has perpetual tantrums and emotional unstable if feels dissatisfied**
- **Needs to be the center of attention**
- **Focused on instant gratification**
- **Has difficulty with owning the consequences of their actions**
- **Denial of personal responsibility and blames others**
- **Emotional scarcity or impoverishment**
- **Avoids introspection**

Deficiency, insecurity and unfulfilled attention: It may not be apparent, but the root of the Over-Indulged Child's issues stem from insecurity and unfulfilled attention. The behavior develops as an unconscious survival pattern. It arises when there has been a dysfunction in meeting the deeper and emotional and psychological needs of the child during the early stages of development.

Unknowingly, the child does not want material gifts. Rather, it is an attempt to experience love by demanding more of anything. In particular, attention, gifts and experiences overcompensate for the scarcity it is unable to articulate. The child measures these outer experiences as a form of validation. They do not fill the necessary gaps but provide immediate ego gratification. Either way, one or more of these elements of deficiency are almost always present in the unconscious seeking that are present in this aspect of the Wounded Inner Child.

There is a constant seeking for fulfillment in the outer world: As a result of this deficiency, the Over-Indulged Child will never feel truly satisfied with anything it acquires through its demands from the outer world. As this immature aspect of the Wounded Inner Child is getting those desires met through manipulation, it will never truly feel fulfilled. In fact, acquiring attention through manipulation will eventually reveal a deep sense of inner resentment because the Over-Indulged Child is reminded again and again of the unconscious inner deficiency that drives its compulsion.

Unfortunately, the more the Over-Indulged Child becomes pampered on the outside, the more it ceases to look inward, to be self-reliant. That sense of inner knowing is built from a process of learning through mistakes, refinement and self-exploration. Self-development creates self-respect. The very behavior that showers the revered over-affection on the Over-Indulged Child will ultimately create dependency and disempowerment.

A pattern of sociopathic "lack of empathy": The term sociopath refers to someone who has antisocial personality disorder (ASPD). People with ASPD cannot understand others' feelings. They will break rules, ignore social morality and make self-absorbed decisions without feeling remorse for the harm they cause. The Over-Indulged child can become so dysfunctional that it can develop strong patterns of sociopathic behavior. When the pain and compulsion of satisfying their own cravings become all-pervasive, they lose touch with their connection to humanity.

Individuals with this personality disorder will have no problem in exploiting others in harmful ways for their own gain or pleasure, and frequently manipulate and deceive other people. They can do this through charm or intimidation. Irresponsibility is a core characteristic of this disorder.

Those with antisocial personality disorder are impulsive and reckless. They may repeatedly disregard and jeopardize their own safety and the safety of others. They display a brazen temper and can lash out violently without provocation. These individuals are prone to substance abuse and addiction, and the abuse of various psychoactive substances is also common.

Outer focused, materialistic, status driven: As part of the preoccupation with vanity, the Over-Indulged Child is commonly materialistic and obsessed with outer image at the expense of sincere introspection. This conditioning understands how to manage and manipulate that relationship with the material world. The Over-Indulged Child has become profoundly co-dependent on the constant stream of attention. To maintain its fragile egoic state of power, the Over-Indulged Child focuses all of its energy on maintaining that source.

Heightened sense of self-importance, grandiosity and megalomania: On the furthest end of the narcissism spectrum, we may find the pathological egotist known as a Megalomaniac. This is a psychological disorder that manifests through delusions of grandeur and an insatiable obsession with obtaining and maintaining ultimate power. An Over-Indulged Child lives on the lesser end of this spectrum. But left unchecked and indulged long enough, it can easily lead to this condition since this is the epitome of inner ego indulgence personified.

Desperately needs to be the center of attention: The Over-Indulged Child maintains its sense of control and manipulation through this strategic positioning, which ensures that everyone and everything in its world orbits around them.

Focuses on instant gratification: The Over-Indulged Child does not believe that the abundant flow of support, attention and love will always be available. Because of this, the Over-Indulged Child makes impulsive and even reckless decisions based on short-term satisfaction without concern for the possible implications of those immature and careless actions.

No ownership, accountability or responsibility for its actions: This aspect of the Wounded Inner Child typically denies any sense of self-responsibility for its actions, has little or no accountability, and refuses to own its part in the unfolding circumstances. The Over-Dramatic Child will blame others with no remorse. Since the Over-Indulged Child sees itself as beyond reproach, it is virtually impossible for it to take any form of authentic accountability for its actions.

Disrespect for rules, systems and authority: Because they have never been taught proper boundaries, the Over-Indulged Child has contempt for rules and regulations. In many cases, they may break the rules for no other reason except to exert their sense of self-importance.

When combined with sociopathic tendencies, self-importance and a conditioned ego that knows nothing else except being indulged, this aspect is willing to be dangerous and destructive to satisfy their personal desires regardless of the "rules."

The Over-Indulged Child also shows disdain for authority figures. The child's ego has been groomed to be the center of attention, and in some ways is also comfortable in the position of making demands and running the show. Healthy, well-adjusted authority figures that create appropriate boundaries and deliver consequences for misaligned acts threaten the power position that this contractive aspect cherishes.

In the original conditioning of the dysfunctional behavior, the caregivers that were supposed to support and nurture did not meet the needs of the child. As a result, there is a traumatic and unconscious wound of betrayal that remains unresolved that will play out through the heightened rebelliousness towards authority.

The Over-Indulged Child is secretly seeking loving boundaries: A child who perpetually pesters their caregivers may be searching for the healthy limits they need for their development. The destructive behavior they exhibit is used to discover what outrageous behavior will finally get that parent to care and respond. An Over-Indulged Child's spoiled behavior can spill over into every aspect of their present experience as they mature into young adults.

But secretly, they long for something more fulfilling. They may not admit it, but they know that their selfishness is getting in the way of something more expansive that they may not know how to fully articulate. They are seeking the "tough love" and genuine concern that it takes to put their developmental "needs" above superficial "desires."

> *"Humility is not thinking less of yourself,*
> *it is thinking of yourself less."*
> *– C.S. Lewis*

Lack of gratitude or appreciation: Common in the patterning of the Over-Indulged Child is the obvious lack of gratitude. Why does this aspect of the Wounded Child avoid it?

Sincere gratitude opens an individual to a deeper humility. It is psychologically impossible for an individual to be in the contractive state of entitlement and the expansive state of thankfulness simultaneously. The power of gratitude erodes the egoic power position that maintains the over-indulgent structure. Therefore, this aspect of the Wounded Inner Child will avoid the experience at any level.

> *"What separates privilege from entitlement is gratitude."*
> *– Brené Brown*

Over-indulgence is a survival method designed to avoid the trauma of deep hurt. If the façade and structure is dropped, then the child will feel the profound betrayal, isolation and hurt that lies beneath the surface. Avoiding gratitude prevents the humility of the unravelling.

OVER-DRAMATIC CHILD

tantrums, drama, acting out, sabotage attention-seeking,

MISUNDERSTOOD CHILD

offended, self-suffering, hurt, vicitmized, misfit, resentful, wounded

LOST CHILD

surpressed, not present, disassociated, withdrawn, distant, checked out

WOUNDED INNER CHILD

disempowered, wounded, immature, childish, internalized trauma, unconscious

NEEDY CHILD

unmet needs, grasping attention, validation, co-dependent

FROZEN CHILD

unresponsive, stunted, waiting, defeated, hopeless, stuck

OVER-INDULGED CHILD

spoiled, demanding, entitled, gluttony, excessive, self-centered

THE WOUNDED INNER CHILD
The Frozen Child

"It is by going down into the abyss
that we recover the treasures of life.
Where you stumble, there lies your treasure.
– Joseph Campbell

Understanding the Dynamics of The Frozen Child:

What dynamics create this debilitating sense of immovable, unresponsive handicap in this contractive aspect of the Wounded Inner Child? This feeling has commonly been described as being completely "stuck," the inability to shift into action out of the frozen state. The contractive dynamics of the Frozen Child can be best described as a crippling behavior or perpetual state of powerless and terrifying "stuckness."

Traumatizing experiences create these deeply frozen psychological tendencies in an individual. The tragic pain for the individual is compounded by the fact that they know that they are "stuck" but are somehow psychologically inhibited from moving forward and changing their situation. There is a feeling of profound hopelessness and guilt that dominates their self-assessment.

This state is created by abuse. An individual has become too fearful to move forward because they have been so battered physically, emotionally or psychologically. Resignation becomes a dysfunctional form of survival and/or protection. They do not feel safe enough to take the initiative to transform their own circumstance. They believe that they no longer have the ability, they are not worthy, or the effort is not worth the struggle. There is a feeling that they are too broken and therefore incapable of the transformation that they desire. They invest completely in this victim mentality.

The Debilitating Effects of Trauma

When examining the effects of trauma, one must always consider the context of every individual's perception and their unique makeup. Everyone internalizes events differently through the filter of their own experience. Whatever may be traumatic for one individual may not be for another.

"Trauma that is not genuinely felt will be reenacted
in either symptom or behavior and ultimately
be recreated in intimate relationships."
– Robert Naborsky, MD

The all-pervasive dynamics of debilitating "stuckness," also known as the Frozen Child, are a manifestation of past abuse. This unprocessed experience of pain will be consciously suppressed as a coping mechanism, creating a diminished level of functioning. The degree of the debilitating state is linked to the depth of the trauma.

Unlike the Lost Child, who does not easily recognize the plight of its own dysfunction (because of the severe levels of detachment and fragmentation), the Frozen Child can usually recognize varying degrees of its own nature. This generates shame and guilt for the inability to move forward. And while they have a sense something is amiss, they are unsure how to resolve it.

The Different Forms of Trauma

Acute or intense trauma: This can be defined as a catastrophic (sometimes single) event that creates deep distress to the psyche. These are life-changing events and potentially life threatening: Rape, violence, profound (psychological, mental, emotional and physical) abuse, natural disasters, loss of a loved one, war, financial collapse, death, divorce, or a severe car accident are just some examples.

Moderate trauma: Though no trauma should be minimized, there is a category of lesser incidental experiences that also create a level of distress but are less severe. Some examples are: verbal abuse, leaving home, separation, emotionally painful experiences, medical procedures, neglect, bullying, teasing, failing at school or at a job, break-ups, minor accidents or intermittent emotional distress

Chronic trauma: Multiple occurrences or extended periods of either acute or moderate trauma can create lasting dysfunction to an individual's psyche. Some of these seemingly moderate experiences of trauma repeated ongoingly can create lingering patterns, habitual reactions, management tactics, repression, dissociation, and a host of other manifestations that become problematic to treat and un-learn. A cluster of trauma experiences form the conditioning of the Frozen Child.

Examples of the behavior of the Frozen Child:

- There is a profound feeling of being stuck, paralyzed or frozen
- They do not work for their own best interests (procrastination)
- Invest more energy in the problems than potential solutions
- They focus on the fear of failure more than they value learning from mistakes
- They are afraid they "will not get it right."
- Express a debilitating state of being overwhelmed
- They feel like they are incapable and do not know "how to do it."
- View themselves as being insignificant, a failure and unlovable
- Experience a lack of confidence in their abilities
- Self-critical, ashamed and frustrated by their own desperate state of inaction
- Live in the contractive experience of "waiting" or "trying" to change
- Rationalize their own excuses and justifications for not moving forward
- Mistrust almost any change and believe the world is inherently unsafe
- They exhibit a behavior of hypervigilance and being "on edge"
- Experience reoccurring bouts of anxiety, disorientation and panic attacks
- They appear to be overly sensitive with mood fluctuations
- Have a tendency for procrastination, stalling and avoidance behaviors
- They feel judged, pressured, controlled and criticized
- Hold grudges, do not trust, and are highly suspicious of others
- Exhibit varying degrees of obsessive-compulsive behaviors
- Can easily fall into relationship patterns of co-dependency and enabling
- They may spend a lot of time holding on to the past and projecting it into the future

Rationalization, excuses and justifications: The Frozen Child has become adept at rationalizing its victim behavior in order to avoid addressing the deeper issues. There is always inner conflict, because the coping mechanism is not dissociated from consciousness and there is an awareness that these justifications are hiding something deeper. Even as the Frozen Child invests in excuses, it craves resolution for the unprocessed issues. That conflict creates the feeling of unworthiness and other psychological patterns. In other words, the individual is aware of the "façade."

"The illusive road of someday
often leads to the inevitable town of nowhere."
– Anonymous

The Great wait: The pattern of waiting is a common behavior exhibited by the Frozen Child. This static state is always dependent on some outside event to occur for the next move to take place. You can always offer a thousand justifiable reasons why it is necessary to wait, but at the root of the inaction there is an underlying fear that feeds the excuse for a lack of forward movement. Because waiting is a façade for something much deeper, it is also accompanied by guilt and shame.

Procrastination: The Frozen Child's behavior invests in a perpetual life of non-advancement. Procrastination is defined as the act of "putting off" an (often urgent, necessary, uncomfortable or important) impending action until a later time by focusing on a (less urgent, unnecessary, comfortable or less important) immediate task in the moment. This is a form of misdirection, distraction or avoidance. An individual will keep themselves distracted by the seductive, short-term procrastination in exchange for meaningful empowered action that is focused on long-term visions, goals and dreams that create real transformation.

Trying: The word trying is often defined as *making an attempt to do something.* The phrase making an "attempt to do" inplies a perpetual state of striving towards something but never achieving it. Even though trying creates the illusion of expansion action, it is almost always contractive when it is used as an alternative to sincere action.

Perfectionism: "Not wanting to get it wrong" or "not wanting to make a mistake" is an excuse to avoid action, take a risk or move forward. This is a symptom of fear that is often related to past trauma or distress. This tactic is used to protect from potential criticism. The individual believes that by acting "incorrectly" or "out of line," there could be a real or perceived threat, danger or pain. This approach focuses on the fear of failure rather than refining potential mistakes in order to move forward. Though the excuse of not wanting to get it wrong is conscious, the deeper reasons for the pattern remain unaddressed in the unconscious.

Experience reoccurring bouts of anxiety, disorientation and panic attacks: This pattern can be manifested in varying degrees depending on the nature of the internal distress. The reoccurring behavior is a sign of the unprocessed pain. It is activated by outer circumstances and acts as a painful reminder of the trauma that created the pain in the first place.

"All growth is a leap in the dark,
a spontaneous unpremeditated act
without benefit of experience."
– Henry Miller

Feeling judged, pressured, and criticized: The Frozen Child believes that the world is pressuring them to do something they are incapable of doing, or they feel a general experience of judgment and criticism. Because their level of internal judgment and self-disapproval is so high, but unowned and unacknowledged, they not only fear experiencing this, but they also tend to manifest this behavior everywhere as a self-fulfilling prophecy.

This cycle of self-judgment and failed attempts to change creates hopelessness, a sense of unworthiness and secures the frozen state of victimhood that becomes increasingly more difficult to break the longer the pattern repeats. Eventually as this continues, the Frozen Child may fall into believing the "I don't know how to do it." story.

Hypervigilance and being "on edge": Based on the pain of past traumatic events and the belief that consciously or unconsciously the world is inherently a dangerous and threatening place, the Frozen Child remains poised in a state of hypervigilance, waiting for the next threat to reveal itself. They exhibit suspicion with everything and everyone. They have conditioned themselves to be in a constant state of defensiveness. This includes impending circumstances or people that could cause discomfort, stress or potential harm.

They stay "on edge" because they inherently do not feel safe. This reactionary pattern is directly related to the memory of the unprocessed (mental, psychological, physical or emotional) trauma. This behavior can often be seen in war vets, abuse survivors and rape victims. As a result, it is difficult for these individuals to develop enough trust and vulnerability in order to feel safe and are intensely protective and quick to overact.

Avoiding personal responsibility and staying the disempowered victim: As long as the Frozen Child continues to avoid personal responsibility for their own immobilized state, they will continue investing in the stories that perpetuate it. The key to getting unstuck is first realizing you are stuck. As long as there is no accountability for the deeper "why" of the frozen state, nothing will change.

Perpetuating a frozen state expends a significant amount of internal energy: The Frozen Child often exhibits ongoing bouts of fatigue and often complains about being too tired to move forward. Since the Frozen Child is aware of its own state of "stuckness," it is consciously or unconsciously exerting tremendous amounts of internal energy to "hold back." The amount of energy it requires to sustain its frozen state drains the Frozen Child and creates the very fatigue it uses to excuse its lack of action.

OVER-DRAMATIC CHILD

tantrums, drama, acting out, sabotage attention-seeking,

MISUNDERSTOOD CHILD

offended, self-suffering, hurt, vicitmized, misfit, resentful, wounded

LOST CHILD

surpressed, not present, disassociated, withdrawn, distant, checked out

WOUNDED INNER CHILD

disempowered, wounded, immature, childish, internalized trauma, unconscious

FROZEN CHILD

unresponsive, stunted, waiting, defeated, hopeless, stuck

NEEDY CHILD

unmet needs, grasping attention, validation, co-dependent

OVER-INDULGED CHILD

spoiled, demanding, entitled, gluttony, excessive, self-centered

THE WOUNDED INNER CHILD
The Lost Child

"The psychological distress symptoms of traumatized people
simultaneously call attention to the existence
of an unspeakable secret and deflect attention from it.
This is most apparent in the way traumatized people
alternate between feeling numb and reliving the event…"
– Judith Lewis Herman

Understanding the Dynamics of The Lost Child

This aspect of the Wounded Child is sometimes difficult to identify. The dynamics of the Lost Child differ from person to person depending on the circumstances. But there are some general clues that can help one identify the behavior. The Lost Child expresses itself through a deep sense of withdrawal, isolation, and varying degrees of dissociation that create an overwhelming experience of feeling lost, hopeless and destitute.

This state originates from a profound trauma so repressed in the unconscious that it does not have any self-understanding of the level of its own detachment. Everything has gone into "lockdown" to survive.

Because of this disjointed state, it is incredibly challenging to access, reclaim and integrate these lost aspects of the Wounded Inner Child. It has a profound mistrust of vulnerability due to the fear of being victimized again. The trade-off for the act of safe-guarding is the inability to feel connected. To feel safe and protected, it must stay "under the radar," sacrificing its accessibility to the world and accessibility to aspects of itself.

The experience of the Lost Child can be likened to hiding your own set of keys somewhere for safe-keeping. But you have hidden them so well, that even you forget their location. You may remember that the keys are safe, but you cannot remember where and sometimes why they were even hidden in the first place. You may even forget that you hid them at all. This creates confusion, frustration and fear as you wander around with limited or no access to large portions of your own home. As time passes, you may even forget that you ever had access in the first place.

Examples of the behavior of the Lost Child:

- **Exhibit a strong tendency towards depression and loneliness**
- **Project a strong feeling of aloofness**
- **They have blackouts, cannot account for or lose big gaps of time**
- **Seem to easily "check out" and go into trance states**
- **They have difficulty sleeping**
- **May have difficulty remembering big portions of their childhood**
- **There is a strong tendency towards anxiety or compulsive behaviors**
- **Exhibit polarized mood swings they do not seem to understand**
- **Have difficulty connecting to or understanding their emotional experience**
- **Experience being "out of place"**
- **Low sense of self-worth, self-esteem, and confidence**
- **Keep to themselves and spend a lot of time alone**
- **Difficulty in expressing playfulness, spontaneity and sense of joy about life**
- **Project a strong sense of control over themselves and their environment**
- **Find it difficult to make decisions**
- **Experience low energy, heaviness or a lack of motivation**
- **Display escapism, dissociative behavior and compartmentation tendencies**
- **Feel numb and disconnected from themselves and the world**
- **Hiding a big, shameful secret from themselves**

The Destructive Effects of Trauma, Abuse and Distress

The human consciousness has an extraordinary capacity to survive under terrible circumstances. Anything that an individual will not or cannot assimilate goes into the great holding area of the unconscious, like a deep vault or vast reservoir. Everything is recorded just below the surface of the conscious mind. Hypnosis has proven that, under the right conditions, the conscious human mind can recall even the tiniest details of an event.

Disassociation is the ultimate survival mechanism that allows the consciousness to "break down" tragic experiences into manageable pieces (fragmentation) until it is safe to integrate the once overwhelming information from the holding tank of the unconscious back into conscious awareness. During normal development, children have been known to practice a form of "healthy" disassociation with new, foreign or complex experiences. They put this information into the deep storage area until they have the psychological maturity and faculties to integrate the new information into their belief system.

The unconscious also acts as a place where they can use their imagination to mature emotionally, mentally and psychologically. This is part of the natural learning process of expanding beyond the comfort zone. Healthy children dissociate less and less as they develop a wider bandwidth of experience to process the information.
But when the trauma is ongoing and toxic beyond the healthy bounds of being manageable, the unconscious keeps the fragmented information in storage and out of touch as a means of survival. This is the repressed underworld which creates the core wound of the Lost Child.

Eventually these unresolved issues will surface, piece by piece, into subtle areas of our personalities and behaviors. At first, they may not make sense or even be detectable, but these fragments are looking to be integrated into consciousness, if the person is ready on some level to resolve them, like bubbles rising to the surface.

Extreme abuse and trauma create profound levels of disassociation. It can take years to surface, depending on the circumstances of the incident(s) and the stability and makeup of an individual. It is not an exact science, and the process or re-integration is unique to each person. Through self-analysis, assisted counseling, guidance, therapy and personal introspection, there is always hope that the conscious mind may, at the right time, begin to see the clues and hints provided to aid the process.

Dissociation or dissociative behavior: This can be defined as a psychological experience in which individuals feel disconnected or "lose touch" in some way from the world around them. However, everyone has a different "breaking point" when this will occur. This coping mechanism is activated to manage this distress. The Lost Child compartmentalizes traumatic experiences to keep us from feeling too much pain, (physical, psychological, emotional, mental and spiritual). When dissociation occurs, you experience detachment from reality, and there is an aspect of you that becomes inaccessible.

The internal stress of dissociation: If the level of dissociation is deeply buried, it is not uncommon for these fragmented aspects of information to re-surface at odd times from the underworld of the unconscious. The Lost Child may therefore exhibit a strong tendency towards anxiety or compulsive behaviors and have polarized mood swings they do not seem to understand. They may also have difficulty sleeping, low energy, a lack of motivation, and find it difficult to make decisions. These are all symptoms of internal stress and possible unraveling.

Have difficulty connecting to or understanding their emotional experience: One of the major defense mechanisms employed to keep the dissociation intact is the ability to minimize emotional connections. If the emotional experiences remain non-existent, the pain remains untouchable and inaccessible.

The Lost Child has difficulty connecting emotions in the body with the physical understanding of those emotions. This makes it exceedingly difficult to articulate any emotional state. Even though this detachment from the emotional body "protects the Lost Child" from feeling the past pain, it comes at the cost of emotional numbness.

83

Difficulty in expressing playfulness, spontaneity and sense of joy about life:
The inability to experience joyfulness and the accompanied expansive elements
of the Radiant Inner Child is a notable clue in recognizing the unconscious wound
of the Lost Child. To contain the pain, the Lost Child has difficulty in expressing
playfulness, spontaneity and joy but may not be able to understand exactly why. This
sense of frustration and confusion is common.

The sacrifice of intimacy: Unfortunately, most intimate connections are sacrificed in
exchange for protecting the unknown secrets that belong to the fragmented pieces of
the Lost Child. Even though there is a deep longing to be known, unconsciously there
is a pact to protect these fragments of memories at all costs, even if it is at the expense
of human connection.

As a result, the Lost Child tends to distance itself from deeper intimacy and projects
an air of aloofness as a means of protection. Since this behavior is a result of
unconscious conditioning, it is difficult for the individual to understand why they feel
so isolated, depressed and alone. They will spend a lot of time feeling out of place,
wondering "What is wrong with me?"

Project an aloof character and tend to spend a lot of time alone: The Lost Child
is easily threatened and overwhelmed by the unpredictable emotional energy of group
dynamics because it can potentially stir up the dissociated trauma from the past. The
Lost Child projects an unconscious energy of anger and defensiveness that results
in an unspoken message to leave them alone. They may not even be aware of it or
understand why they are ignored. This also leads the Lost Child to enjoy spending a
lot of time alone so the currents of the past trauma can remain subdued. If they do go
out in groups, they tend to stay in the periphery of the engagement.

Control: Controlling things, people, and situations are a necessary coping mechanism
for the Lost Child. The level of control reflects the depth and intensity of the level of
unconscious fear of its unravelling. It is a deflection tactic to keep the conscious mind
busy focusing on something other than what is hidden. This also creates a false sense
of security. People tend to control out of a fear of being controlled. Self-imposed
behaviors of control are the unconscious psychological reactions to these unthinkable
acts of violation and pain they have experienced.

Difficulty making decisions: Decision-making may be difficult. The Lost Child
stays unknown and out of touch to itself in an apathetic state of inaction as a means
of safety. But unlike the dynamics of the Frozen Child who sees the path and knows
what it should do but feels stuck, this lost aspect cannot recognize its own contractive
situation. For them it is better to not know. This creates a sense of disconnection and a
lack of desire to act or make decisions that could rock the boat or upset the system.

Gaps of memory, time, checking out, and escapism behavior: All of these behaviors are examples of the dysfunction survival mechanism to keep information disassociated, untraceable, and fragmented. Denying access to large portions of childhood memory and personal history is necessary to cut the connection.

In the case of the Lost Child, the ability to access compromising personal history is manipulated and erased, creating a thick fog of confusion and distraction. Any seeming movement on the pathway to this hidden information is quickly diverted to daydreaming and escapism behavior. The escapism becomes habitual.

Events can be rewritten to omit the trauma. There can also be moments of "checking out" where the individual loses gaps of time, especially if the outer circumstances have some sort of association with the repressed trauma. Either way, the individual's own understanding of their personal history, memories and the ability to access this information is always compromised.

Hiding a big, shameful secret from themselves: It is important to realize that there is a "big secret" at the heart of the dissociation. That secret is shrouded with a fog of confusion and misunderstanding that can be clouded by false memories. Keeping the secret from yourself is the key to this reactive survival mechanism. Getting to the heart of that traumatic secret is a delicate process that requires safety, honesty and courage. Even though the Lost Child feels it is the keeper of that secret, on some level it knows something is hidden beneath the surface even if they cannot understand or explain it.

Misdiagnosis of the pattern of the Lost Child: The Lost child is one of the most elusive, mercurial and intangible aspects of the Wounded Inner Child. It survives through feigned unconsciousness and repression.

The reactive manifestations of these dynamics are designed to subversively mislead introspection, throw you off the path, and keep you in a constant state of ignorance. Therefore, the patterns of the Lost Child are easily confused with other aspects of the Wounded Inner Child dynamics, and the physical manifestations that result from the strain of the repression are misdiagnosed.

This is the ultimate "shell game" of the unconsciousness. It maintains a perpetual state of disempowered, apathetic unawareness. Even the mere attempt at investigation can be met with a series of physiologically and physically exhausting deceptive roadblocks. Because most survivors of abuse or violence are not even aware of their traumatic past, they rarely seek help or even identify the subtle clues and seemingly unrelated manifestations in their psyche. To those who are lost in the fog of this unconscious self-deception, these "unconnected" issues are not even recognized as issues. The power of this Wounded Inner Child aspect lives in its effectiveness to maintain a sense of apathetic compliance, internal confusion and complacency maintaining its subversive mission "that it is safer not to know that you know."

Your Personal Wounded Inner Child Dynamics

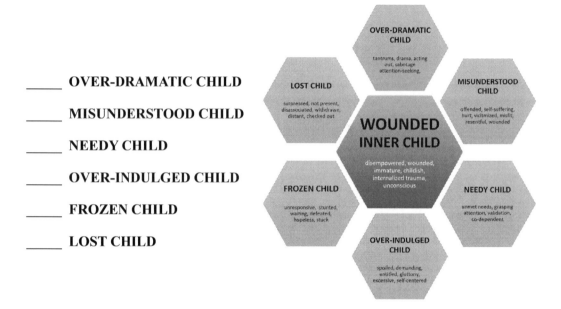

_____ **OVER-DRAMATIC CHILD**

_____ **MISUNDERSTOOD CHILD**

_____ **NEEDY CHILD**

_____ **OVER-INDULGED CHILD**

_____ **FROZEN CHILD**

_____ **LOST CHILD**

After reading the chapter about **The Wounded Inner Child,** take some time to consider which of the six archetypes best describe your personal conditioning. Rank the above list on a scale of 1-6 (1 being the most influential and active and 6 being the least).

Remember that all the Wounded Inner Child archetypes exist within every individual's conditioning, but everyone usually expresses these dynamics in a personal way that is totally unique to them based on their specific life circumstances.

Usually, several of the dynamics are more prevalent than others in your inner and outer experience. The intent of this process is to isolate the most active patterns so you can create more awareness. This allows you to consciously work with those archetypes, so it is important to recognize which patterns are the most influential.

Consider the dynamics in your past and present (inner and outer) relationships. If you observe those relationships, you will begin to see the recurring patterns playing out. Be honest with yourself. Since in most cases you will be delving into the unconscious world, it may require some introspection and self-analysis. It helps to explore specific examples in your life through journaling. Use the information in the past chapters regarding the six Wounded Inner Child Archetypes as a guide to help you in your process.

INTERNAL
CRITICAL PARENT

judgmental, critical, doubt
shame, disempowering,
dominating, persuasive

ENABLER

co-conspirator, indulgent,
permissive, ednorsement,
denial, concede, co-
dependent, allowance

POSSESSIVE
INNER ADULT

ownership, possession,
property, objectification,
self-serving

SHADOW
INNER ADULT

abusive, contractive,
immature, reactive,
unconscious, shame

CONTROLLING
INNER ADULT

dominating, manipulation,
gaslighting, forceful,
managing

INAUTHENTIC
HANDLER

uncompassionate,
dishonest, uncaring, vanity,
superfical, caculating

UNAVAILABLE
ADULT

unaccountable, checked
out, disengaged,
irresponsible

The Shadow Inner Adult

The **Shadow Inner Adult** is the destructive, shadow side of the Mature Inner Adult that has been unconsciously conditioned within you. You have been exposed and conditioned with the contractive "Shadow Parenting" from the behavior, patterns and beliefs of the adults, role models, caretakers that were part of your circle of influence during your childhood. You now continue to play out those same unconscious behaviors in your relationship with your Wounded Inner Child. That inner relationship influences your external relationships.

An unresolved **Shadow Inner Adult** unconsciously determines the relationship with your Wounded Inner Child and how you relate to the world around you. When left unexplored and unexamined, you will default to that conditioning and parent yourself in similar manner.

Most do not acknowledge or even realize the abusive power of this contractive side of the Shadow Inner Adult because the behavior is so familiar. You become desensitized because of the years of deep and continued conditioning, and therefore it just seems like a reasonable part of your identity. But if you more deeply examine the nature of these behaviors, you will realize that just because they feel "normal" because they have been passed down the family line) does not mean they are expansive.

In fact, these are the surprising and difficult "patterns" of behavior that eventually show themselves in all of your relationships. Why do I always create someone who is controlling? Why is every partner always emotionally unavailable? These immature behaviors are usually unexamined, unconscious and will remain unknown. But they will continually be projected in your inner and outer relationships until they are finally examined, accepted and eventually resolved within you.

> *"It is clear that we must make a shadow, or there would be no culture;*
> *then we must restore the wholeness of personality that was lost*
> *in the cultural ideals, or we will live in a state of dividedness*
> *that grows more and more painful throughout our evolution."*
> – Robert A. Johnson (Jungian Analyst)

The **Shadow Inner Adult** is one of the most powerful, subversive and influential aspects of your inner structure, which is why these patterns are kept hidden and unexplored in the unconscious. Initially, it can be very difficult to confront these abusive patterns because their very existence breeds a lot of shame, guilt and judgment. It is challenging to admit that they are still actively playing out in your consciousness. It is vital to learn how they function and manifest in your inner and outer world. There is so much potential for profound growth and awareness in the exploration, acceptance and integration working with these behaviors.

The Shadow Inner Adult is usually seen as the "bad or wrong" parts of you, but in reality, they are deeply reactive, unexplored and unconscious aspects of your consciousness that were conditioned as survival mechanisms that will eventually consciously or unconsciously reveal themselves in all of your relationships.

The Archetypal Conditioning of the Shadow Inner Adult

The Shadow Inner Adult has many overt and covert methods to express its contractive conditioning. These tactics range from abuse, control, disempowerment, to domination, manipulation and persuasion. The reactive and immature behavior maintains the Contractive Feedback Loop with the Wounded Inner Child. Each person will employ a different combination and expression of these shadow archetypes depending on their foundational conditioning.

Many attempt to approach the Shadow Inner Adult with the "make it go away because it is bad" philosophy, which will never be sustainable or truly effective. In the short term, it is nothing more than a form of suppression. And the desire to "kill the contractive ego" does nothing more than quietly fuel the very contraction that it is proclaiming to "heal." Everyone has some level of a corrupted psychology that has been uniquely programmed due to their individual circumstances. It is important to realize that your personal set of patterns is no better or worse than anyone else.

The most important action that you can take in relating to your Shadow Inner Adult is the recognition of its presence in your behavior. You do this by bringing awareness into the different Shadow dynamics and archetypes. Cultivate an intimate understanding of how it functions within your conditioning.

Eventually you will come to accept that it is and always will be part of your conditioning. In a strange way, you will have to learn to appreciate and befriend the Shadow side of yourself. This does not mean enabling or glorifying it. But when you begin to embrace its presence and respond to the different dynamics, you offer yourself the opportunity to consciously recreate your behavior and choose something more conscious and expansive.

"The most dangerous psychological mistake
is the projection of the shadow onto others.
This is the root of almost all conflicts."
– Carl Jung

The Internal Critical Parent: This aspect of the Internal Shadow Adult is the most recognizable form of abuse that one can identify because it is expressed as an "inner voice" of intense criticism, and judgment toward the Inner Child. Unfortunately, people have become so accustomed to the insidious nature of this inner dialogue that they rarely recognize its powerful contractive effect.

Essentially, it is a shaming of you (the Inner Child) for perceived imperfections. This form of abusive dialogue fortifies the cycle of negativity. It never allows the experience of being "good enough" by sabotaging and diminishing any expansive aspect of the Inner Child. There are many degrees of this internalized self-criticism depending on the nature of the initial programming. The Internal Critical Parent ultimately projects blame by magnifying any of your perceived internal flaws or even creating these "flaws" where they do not exist.

The Enabler: This form of abuse occurs when the Shadow Inner Adult takes on the role as a co-conspirator, ally and supporter to the undisciplined behavior of the Wounded Inner Child without consequences. This alliance is created with the immature child at the expense of healthy parenting or a mature role model.

There is a lack of accountability or an illusion about the reality of the circumstances that enables the Wounded Inner Child to run amok without appropriate consequences. This behavior not only allows, but fuels this lack of accountability. Eventually, it creates, through the conscious or unconscious collusion, an unhealthy co-dependency and absolution.

The Inauthentic Handler: This dispassionate and uninterested Shadow Inner Adult "handles" the inner child without connection to its emotional needs. The Shadow Parent misrepresents itself as available and caring, but it is not authentically engaged with the deeper needs of Inner Child. This contractive form of behavior seeks to justify its actions by creating a superficial persona of noble behavior while inauthentically handling the inner child, with no depth or true caring. The behaviors of the Inauthentic Handler are always rooted in superficiality, deceit and selfishness.

The Unavailable Adult: In this form of delinquent behavior, the Shadow Inner Parent is completely irresponsible, disengaged and unaccountable to the inner or outer child. This "checked out" space allows for the Shadow Adult to remain unavailable, clueless and absent to the Inner child's behavior. The Unavailable Adult therefore stays comfortably detached to any consequences of its neglect. This is complete abandonment of any sense of personal responsibility. The prolonged effects of the passive form of abuse are deeply impactful.

Controlling Inner Adult: This aspect of the Shadow Inner Adult manipulates all facets of expression. It maintains control by suppressing, over-powering and bullying the Wounded Inner Child so it can be easily managed. This control is driven by an unconscious fear of the potential inability to handle any given circumstance. Therefore, all aspects of the Inner Child need to be subdued and maneuvered into a comfortable position that is overseen by the Controlling Inner Adult. At the root of the abuse is a sense of powerlessness. This translates into a need to create and maintain a desired set of existing belief systems and a sense of regulated order.

The Possessive Parent: In this form of contractive behavior, the Shadow Inner Parent claims ownership over the Inner Child through objectification and possession. Through domination, all the expansive and contractive features of the Inner Child can be leveraged for its own selfish desires. The Possessive Adult does not acknowledge individual autonomy. And tt views the "child" simply as a possession of the Shadow Inner Parent with little concerns for the abusive consequences. This is deeply destructive to the child's sense of individuality and personal freedom because all expression, behavior and personal accomplishments will be claimed, dominated and owned by the Possessive Inner Adult.

INTERNAL CRITICAL PARENT

judgmental, critical, doubt
shame, disempowering,
dominating, persuasive

POSSESSIVE INNER ADULT

ownership, possession,
property, objectification,
self-serving

ENABLER

co-conspirator, indulgent,
permissive, ednorsement,
denial, concede, co-
dependent, allowance

SHADOW INNER ADULT

abusive, contractive,
immature, reactive,
unconscious, shame

CONTROLLING INNER ADULT

dominating, manipulation,
gaslighting, forceful,
managing

INAUTHENTIC HANDLER

Uncompassionate,
dishonest, uncaring, vanity,
superfical, caculating

UNAVAILABLE ADULT

unaccountable, checked
out, disengaged,
irresponsible

THE SHADOW INNER ADULT
The Internal Critical Parent

The most powerful, dangerous and damaging skill of the Internal Critical Parent is its tactical ability to disguise itself as the voice of expansion.

Understanding the Dynamics of The Internal Critical Parent

This powerful voice was programmed and reinforced into being during your earliest childhood years. During its foundational development, a child will always seek to be nurtured through acceptance by parents, role models, guardians and immediate authority figures. The internalized feelings of not being acceptable originated from the conscious and unconscious contractive dialogue, behavior and example of parents. This internal voice undermines your sense of self-worth.

This programmed inner voice will mimic the language, behavior and toxicity of your role models. Your inner critic will be a familiar voice, constantly undermining you in the same way. If this messaging was accompanied by physical, verbal, emotional or psychological abuse, then the voice will be more deeply conditioned within an individual. Either way, the more toxic the initial messaging from your family of origin and environment, the more intense and toxic the power of your inner voice will be.

The Internal Critical Parent is created in one or more of these ways:

- Direct experience
- Indirect experience or observation
- Internalization and interpretation

Direct or personal experience:

You do it to yourself because it was done to you.

These words and phrases were spoken **directly** to you as a child. Your inner voice has developed from the actual physical contractive voice of criticism that you heard from your parents, role models or authority figures.

As you pay attention to the language of the internal critic, you will notice that the phrases, tone and intensity mimic the behavior of the contractive parenting you received. If the origin of your inner expression is relatively easy to identify, it is usually because it was so ever-present in your development. There may be a level of overt self-hatred that fuels the intensity of that voice.

Indirect experience or observation:

You do it to yourself because you saw it done to others.

You may have also witnessed this behavior indirectly as it played out in your immediate sphere to others in your family structure, to one or more of your siblings or to others in your environment. You may not have experienced the behavior directly, but it is still deeply wounding. In many of this these cases, the quality of your inner critic may be less overt, more subversive and harder to detect. There may also be a level of guilt and shame associated to the experience.

Internalization and interpretation:

You do it to yourself because you created an internal interpretation.

You can also internalize and interpret what your parents did not directly say, or their seeming lack of interest and withdrawal of love and affection. Unclear, unspoken or passive-aggressive contractive behaviors of the Shadow Inner Adult can be deeply traumatizing. This particular expression of the Internal Critical Parent is dangerous because it does not always seem to have a recognizable source, and the internal voice is more subversive in nature.

There is an internal questioning that arises because nothing was ever spoken or witnessed directly. It is important to realize that almost everyone has a certain degree of internal doubt, judgment and self-criticism within them. This expresses itself as an internal critic, but the intensity of its expression and the depth of the contraction is conditioned by what was "normal" for you. This voice is not the same as self-analysis. It is possible to explore internal inquiry and investigation without being toxic, destructive or hurtful.

The powerful influence of doubt: Every interaction with the Internal Critical Parent is designed to fuel inner uncertainty and mistrust in oneself. Doubt attempts to dismantle your empowered state of maturity and radiance. Doubt breeds an environment of inner chaos and confusion where the Internal Critical Parent thrives.

The three tactics of the Internal Critical Parent (oppression, disempowerment and persuasion): All expressions of your contractive dialogue will fall into one of these three major categories. If you closely examine your inner voice and conditioning, you will notice it usually favors one approach. Understanding the quality of your inner voice of criticism is necessary to assist you in applying the appropriate expansive remedy to work this aspect of the Shadow Inner Adult.

- **Oppression** is the most overt and direct expression of criticism. This form of inner maltreatment is identified through its brutal persecution. It is laced with violence and cruelty. It is designed to dominate the Wounded Inner Child by "beating" it into submission.

  "You will always be stupid and absolutely useless!"

- **Disempowerment** is a less overt form of persecution, though it still may contain a certain level of cruelty. It undermines confidence through demoralizing the Wounded Inner Child. It can be identified as a disheartening state of hopelessness and self-doubt.

  "You will never accomplish anything more than this."

- **Persuasion** is a covert form of manipulation and criticism that challenges your inner knowing. Through the power of suggestion this expression creates an inner subterfuge of uncertainty that makes you constantly question yourself. The persuasion begins with the seeming "voice of reason or inner debate."

  "Don't you think you should reconsider? The last time you tried this you didn't get very far. You don't want to make a fool of yourself again, do you?"

The Insidious Voice of the Internal Critical Parent

Without deep personal inquiry and examination, the voice of the Internal Critical Parent is left unchecked. It becomes intimately woven into the fabric of your internal dialogue because of your blind spot of its contractive nature and the familiarity of its expression. You hardly notice the debilitating implications of its presence. It can even seem somewhat "friendly" in its desire to aid the situation and offer its perspective. Therefore, you not only accept the dialogue but come to trust the advice and quietly adhere to its influence.

This destructive voice not only expresses itself through the bombardment of negative inner dialogue but also through powerful visualizations using your imagination, memory and past traumatic experiences against you. Its tactic is to fortify its position so it will dredge up deeply shameful incidents, rejections and mistakes from your past. It is important to realize that the intensity of the internal critic will be loudest when you are "triggered" by an event that has similar dynamics to your past. In other words, the experience of the event is familiar especially when you are upset by someone, make a mistake, feel confused, embarrassed or afraid.

Examples of Behavior of the Internal Critical Parent

- **Always contractive or negative in its expression**
- **Promotes inner and outer doubt**
- **Attack, criticism, blame, self-abuse and judgment**
- **Focuses on comparison**
- **Exudes a false sense of power and importance**
- **Fuels shame (making yourself wrong)**
- **Promotes guilt (seeing your actions as wrong)**
- **The Inner Critic can be disguised as a familiar voice of reason**
- **Expresses justification and defensiveness**
- **It twists truth as a tool to diminish or reduce worth**
- **It is devious but highly predictable**
- **It requires the "fuel" of attention to survive**
- **It keeps alive the past faults, flaws and failures**
- **It uses excuses to justify its position**
- **Convinces you that the external world agrees with its contractive assessment**

The inner critic creates a false sense of importance: The Internal Critical Parent has an inflated sense of power. It propagates its own importance in your internal process. In the beginning, it may feel like you have no control over the powerful will of this voice. But the seeming power of this voice is its biggest protective ploy and it is truly nothing but a hollow illusion. This behavior, like any conditioning, is only an ongoing narrative that you have the power to change in any given moment.

Devious but also predictable: This aspect of the Shadow Parent is sly but predictable. The more you know its movements and patterns, the more you can recognize the behavior of the conditioning. Once its predictable nature is unmasked and you are aware of the quality of expression and its preferred tactics, you can shift the relationship.

Don't "Should" on yourself: The word "should" is one of the most influential tools exploited by the Internal Critical Parent. The expression "should" is infused with guilt and condemnation. You "should" have known better. You "should" be doing something different. When you hear a string of "shoulds" in your inner dialogue, examine the subtle contractiveness of the voice that is speaking.

Your inner critic feeds the "dead" memory of past experiences: The voice of your Internal Critical Parent is nothing more than echo of past pain and a "dead" memory that is continually resuscitated by you out of habit.

The Internal Critical Parent will draw on past experiences to promote its current agenda, *"See, this is just like the last time you did this and you failed"* or *"Every time you do this, it turns out the same way."* It is an ongoing and reoccurring program that continues to replay itself because you allow it. Change happens when you finally make the decision to shift your inner relationship to the experience.

Some Common Internal Critical Expressions and Phrases:

- **Who do I think I am?**
- **I will never amount to anything**
- **I do not deserve…**
- **I am pathetic and hopeless**
- **I am never good enough**
- **I will never be as good as…**
- **Nobody loves me or everybody hates me**
- **I am stupid or dumb**
- **I should give up before I really make a fool of myself**
- **It's just not worth it or don't bother**
- **I really have nothing to contribute…**
- **Do I really want to go through this again?**

The difference between observation and inner judgment: If you want to transcend the subversive nature of the voice of the Internal Critic, you need to recognize the recurring patterns. Without focused introspection, this voice will continue to influence you. That observation needs to be as objective as possible. If you notice judgment inject itself into your internal thought process, then you can be certain that the voice of the Internal Critical Parent is present. The more you practice this skill, the easier it becomes to identify the quality of that contractive voice and distinguish it from true expansive or neutral observation.

Observing your own judgment: An effective technique to transcend self-contractive dialogue is to observe your inner criticism with compassion until you are no longer affected by it. Observe your judgment but be understanding with yourself and your process.

In the beginning, this may seem difficult. One of the protective mechanisms of the critical parent is to fool you into continuing to punish yourself when you initially observe a moment of internal judgment. In other words, you continue judging yourself for your behavior of judging. This maintains the negative feedback loop. It gives the illusion that actual observation is occurring. In reality, you are being drawn back into the familiar clutches of the abusive self-punishing inner critic.

Understanding the power of emotional awareness: The Internal Critical Parent is also activated by unacknowledged contractive emotions that linger in the recesses of your unconscious. The inner dialogue of the internal critic can be associated to a series of matching contractive emotions. When those powerful corresponding emotions remain unacknowledged, they have the power to further fuel the voice of the Internal Critical Parent and give it the momentum it needs to stay active.

Therefore, honest self-reflection and emotional awareness are crucial skills required in transcending the grasp of the inner critic. You reclaim your power by choosing your thoughts and your mindset. Once there is awareness, and you find ways to accept and release those emotions, clarity can arise without distortion. And without access to the lingering contractive energy, you can deflate the power of the Internal Critical Parent.

Tips for Healthy and Effective Self-Observation and Self-Analysis

If you know your enemy and you know yourself,
you need not fear the result of a hundred battles.
If you know yourself but not the enemy,
for every victory gained you will also suffer a defeat.
If you know neither the enemy nor yourself,
you will succumb in every battle.
– Sun Tzu (The Art of War)

Create a foundation of expansion when you begin reviewing your inner world:
Do not approach your Inner Critic with disdain, resentment or anger. Contraction
only generates more contraction. As you discover the different facets of your being,
see the entire experience as a treasure hunt. Be intrigued, fascinated and exhilarated
by every new finding. Know that for every new observation gleaned, your realization
deepens. Beginning with an expansive perception creates new opportunities and new
relationships.

Observation is an ongoing process of refinement: As with any aspect of self-
mastery, you must continually refine your observational skill. The voice of the
Internal Critical Parent never completely disappears. It just finds more subtle methods
to express itself. As you grow in awareness, you become more adept at observing the
more subtle expressions of this sly contractive behavior.

**Examine yourself as a witness without creating a subjective opinion about your
observations:** Survey your inner dialogue and internal patterns of contraction as if
they do not belong to you. Watch them. Be objective. Interact with the inner world
like a scientist executing a thought experiment for the purpose of building self-
awareness.

**Pay close attention to the "train of contractive thoughts" and observe where it
leads:** You always have a choice to follow a train of thoughts to their conclusion.
The question is, do you like where this path is leading? Once these "thought trains"
become more familiar – where they begin, what triggers them, what conclusion they
tend to lead to– you can more easily choose to refrain from going in a direction that
does not serve you.

Ask yourself: Are these critical thoughts and self-perceptions true? Just because
the Internal Critical Parent weaves a convincing story does not mean that any of it
is true. Never trust any aspect of a story from the contractive aspect of the Shadow
Parent no matter how reasonable it may seem. It is up to you to distinguish fact from
fiction, and truth from illusion. Just ask yourself, "Is any of this true?" This will give
you better discernment to cut through the spell of self-doubt.

INTERNAL CRITICAL PARENT

judgmental, critical, doubt shame, disempowering, dominating, persuasive

POSSESSIVE INNER ADULT

ownership, possession, property, objectification, self-serving

ENABLER

co-conspirator, indulgent, permissive, ednorsement, denial, concede, co-dependent, allowance

SHADOW INNER ADULT

abusive, contractive, immature, reactive, unconscious, shame

CONTROLLING INNER ADULT

dominating, manipulation, gaslighting, forceful, managing

INAUTHENTIC HANDLER

Uncompassionate, dishonest, uncaring, vanity, superfical, caculating

UNAVAILABLE ADULT

unaccountable, checked out, disengaged, irresponsible

THE SHADOW INNER ADULT
The Enabler

Indulging unhealthy behavior at the expense of yourself is misguided and dysfunctional. To help, allow or condone this contraction without discernment requires denying a truth about the inner and outer reality of your circumstances. In this way, everyone involved (the abettor and the receiver) are always disempowered and damaged by enabling.

This form of abuse takes place when the Shadow Inner Adult takes on the role as a co-conspirator to the undisciplined behavior of the Wounded Inner Child. This alliance is created with the immature child at the expense of healthy parenting or a mature role model.

There is a lack of accountability, weak boundaries, or an illusion about the reality of the circumstances that enables the Wounded Inner Child to run amok without appropriate consequences. This behavior not only allows, but also fuels this lack of accountability. It eventually creates an unhealthy co-dependency.

Understanding the Dynamics of The Enabler

The dynamics of the Enabler can take on many manifestations. This aspect of the Shadow Inner Adult emboldens dysfunctional relationships, behavior and conditioning. It is based on a co-dependent dynamic between a rescuer and the perceived victim. It is a conditioned strategy to fix a situation but never addresses the underlying issues.

It's human nature to protect the ones we love and prevent them from experiencing unnecessary hardship. But this form of behavior is fear-based and the obsessive need to "help" does not allow for growth. You may even defend an individual and promote a specific type of behavior to continue, even if it is unhealthy to themselves and the people around them.

Though intentions may be good, The Enabler "softens the blow" to such a degree that you create a false reality that can prevent an individual from experiencing the natural consequences of their choices. This allows you to continue your unhealthy behavior. All forms of enabling have a contractive effect on both the enabler and on the individual, who is being enabled, regardless of the intentions.

Examples of the behavior of the Enabler

- **Co-dependency, "the need to be needed"**
- **Excessive reliance on other people for approval and a sense of identity**
- **Over-responsibility or compulsive need to protect, fix or help**
- **Self-sacrifice - Forgoing one's own needs for those of another**
- **Lack of boundaries**
- **Lack of discernment and healthy judgment**
- **Ignoring, masking, or endorsing unhealthy behavior**
- **Martyrdom motivated by guilt**
- **Collusion with an abuser**
- **The desperate need to be the rescuer to satisfy internal inadequacy**
- **Always playing the role of the perpetual confidant**
- **Tendency to over-control circumstances that feel unmanageable**
- **Denial, lack of honesty and inauthenticity about the severity of a situation**
- **Underlying resentment for responsibility**
- **Promotes addictive or unhealthy behaviors in others**
- **"Good intentions" become justification for excessive pampering or enabling**
- **Dysfunctional and inauthentic emotional communication**
- **Low self-worth**
- **High level of self-pride**
- **Exhibits reactive polarized patterns of extremes**
- **Acting on the ideal rather than the reality of a situation**
- **Enabling is an expression of martyrdom and self-sacrifice**
- **Display dysfunctional state of "lost sense of self," emptiness and lack of self-identity**

The distinction between empowering and enabling: It is important to understand the difference between empowering and enabling behavior. Healthy caregiving is always motivated by an expansive choice for both parties. On the contrary, enabling behavior is driven from a contractive position. It is compulsive and fear-based with no regard for consequences.

It is not uncommon for behavior that begins from an empowered space and fueled by good intentions to slip into dysfunction. The original purpose gets lost as the behavior shifts. Enabling should be viewed as an expansive choice gone awry.

Ask yourself these questions to determine if you have Enabler tendencies in your relationships:

- **When helping another, do you put your own needs aside?**
- **Do you ignore or minimize unacceptable behavior?**
- **Do you find yourself resentful for the responsibilities that you take on?**
- **Do you have difficulty expressing your own emotions or opinions?**
- **Do you ever mislead, lie or omit information to cover for another's actions?**
- **Do you deflect or assign blame onto other people to protect the real perpetrator?**
- **Do you take responsibility for the consequences of someone else's behavior?**
- **Do you avoid or censor behaving in a particular manner because you are fearful of a potential confrontation or a blow-up?**
- **Do you continue to offer help even when it is not acknowledged, appreciated or valued?**

Co-dependency, "The Need to be Needed"

Being dependent on a personal support structure is a healthy expression of interdependency. But those who become excessive in this "dependency" and seek to satisfy their own internal inadequacies are co-dependent. It is one of the trademark dynamics of the Enabler.

Co-dependency is a relationship in which a person is manipulated by another who is affected with a pathological condition. It refers to the dependence on the control of another. It also involves placing a lower priority on one's own needs, while being excessively preoccupied with the needs of others. Co-dependency can occur in any type of relationship, not just romantic partnerships.

Codependency may also be characterized by denial, low self-esteem, or control patterns. An Enabler's self-esteem is dependent on their willingness to "help" in inappropriate ways. This offered "help" allows the Enabler to feel in control of an unmanageable situation. By attempting to "solve" an individual's problems on their behalf, the Enabler minimizes any motivation for that individual to take responsibility. Without that motivation, there is little reason for that individual to consider change.

We see the dynamics of co-dependency play out in relationships where one of the partners or family members suffers from addiction. In extreme cases, it strengthens the co-dependency of the relationship. It is an attempt of the Enabler to manage a horrible and deeply traumatic or abusive situation out of fear. You fear for your safety or the ramifications that may result from exposure. One can be co-dependent to a substance, behavior, belief or an individual. The dynamics of this vicious cycle allows an individual to maintain the destructive behavior through co-dependent enabling.

Acting on the ideal rather than the reality of a situation: One of the most difficult tasks for the Enabler personality is dealing with reality. The Enabler not only denies what's actually happening, but also projects the ideal scenario and chooses behavior based on that projection. The ideal may or may not have any basis in truth. This aspect of the Shadow Inner Adult will trade the reality of the situation for a constructed fantasy. This is far more than "positive or aspirational thinking." The ideal is something that the Enabler desperately needs.

The Enabler will:

- attempt to focus and highlight the infrequent (inner or outer) "good moments, choices or behavior" while consistently ignoring an ongoing sea of tragedy, contraction and abuse around them.

- project an idealized version of an individual saying "I can see their latent potential" while denying glaring behavior that does not support their narrative.

- identify to what they want or wish circumstances to be, ignoring the truth about what is really going on and develop an unhealthy loyalty to that illusion.

- will base their complacency, consent and collusion on the constructed ideal and is unwilling to examine the consequences of the behavior.

For the Enabler, sustainable growth and the lasting fulfillment that comes from that is never possible for anyone who is invested in illusion. Just because one can recognize someone's inherent potential does not mean that potential is realized. An individual may not be willing, interested or capable of being a living example of that ideal. Current behavior always demonstrates the actual level of realized potential. But the Enabler rarely bases its choices on that living example and chooses to remain in a state of denial by investing in a future ideal.

> *"Our greatest glory is not in never failing,*
> *but in rising every time we fail."*
> – *Confucius*

The necessity of failure and feeling pain: So much of the fear that fuels this aspect of the Shadow Inner Adult stems from the direct avoidance of pain. It may be a justifiable reaction to past events, but to grow, the Enabler must accept potential failure and feel the associated pain. The experience of pain and failure is unavoidable for real growth. Ironically, an attempt to avoid pain creates more pain that you are attempting to prevent. Only failure allows you to refine behavior and receive the gift of self-analysis.

If the Enabler never embraces this aspect of life, they will continue to live ruled by the perpetual fear of the unknown. Enabling another is a projection of the Enabler's attempt to manage their pain without honestly facing it. By minimizing someone else's painful situation, you are unconsciously attempting to mitigate their own experience or perceived failure. When you start to engage in deeper self-examination, the need to project on others vanishes. And it allows for an expansive opportunity of self-empowerment.

Enabling can fuel a false perception of power: There is nothing more seductive than the Enabler's inner dialogue of justification in the belief that they have the power to change another person through their actions. The Enabler builds this false perception of the situation through their dysfunctional illusion of supporting or helping fix someone's life. They often justify their illusion by deluding themselves with their own importance. *"They would be nothing without me."* Or *"They do not know how much I do to help them."*

Anytime the sincerity of the authentic assistance shifts to self-importance, the Enabler has been enticed by an egoic ideal of their own power. Indulging in this fantasy of influence is a coping mechanism. It soothes feelings of inadequacy and attempts to reclaim a lost sense of inner personal power. This temporary construct, however, is unsustainable because the Enabler is dependent on something outside their control.

Enabling is a short-term but temporary solution: While enabling suppresses short-term conflicts, it carries the penalty of prolonging a dysfunctional (inner or outer) relationship. In so doing, Enablers become unwitting accomplices in their own entrapment. This makes it all the more difficult to break the cycle of inner or outer abuse. If the Enabler does not acknowledge the avoidance of pain as the short-term fix, they will inevitably repeat the current circumstances again and again at the expense of true freedom.

Enabling usually fuels patterns of unconscious resentment: The Enabler will always be unfulfilled by their seemingly helpful behavior. They will feel that they are always on the "giving end" of the relationship. A common manifestation of the Enabler behavior is a deep, unconscious resentment that is projected on the person that they are "helping." The resentment exemplifies the unbalanced nature of the relationship. The unconscious resentment is a manifestation of unowned issues with self-care and self-attention.

Misplaced loyalty can create enabling and collusion: Collusion is an agreement between individuals to actively shield the unhealthy conduct from themselves and the outside world. The Enabler denies the unhealthy behavior at the expense of their own integrity. This dysfunctional collusion is justified by misplaced loyalty, with the hope that the abuser will change if they have enough support and time. It is an active conspiracy of denying the truth to themselves and others.

INTERNAL
CRITICAL PARENT

judgmental, critical, doubt
shame, disempowering,
dominating, persuasive

POSSESSIVE
INNER ADULT

ownership, possession,
property, objectification,
self-serving

ENABLER

co-conspirator, indulgent,
permissive, ednorsement,
denial, concede, co-
dependent, allowance

SHADOW
INNER ADULT

abusive, contractive,
immature, reactive,
unconscious, shame

CONTROLLING
INNER ADULT

dominating, manipulation,
gaslighting, forceful,
managing

INAUTHENTIC
HANDLER

Uncompassionate,
dishonest, uncaring, vanity,
superfical, caculating

UNAVAILABLE
ADULT

unaccountable, checked
out, disengaged,
irresponsible

THE SHADOW INNER ADULT
The Inauthentic Handler

"Allow yourself to think only those thoughts that match your principles and can bear the bright light of day. Day by day, your choices, your thoughts, your actions fashion the person you become. Your integrity determines your destiny."
– Heraclitus

Understanding the Dynamics of The Inauthentic Handler

Authentic examples of caring by a parent, role model or authority figure are vital to healthy development. When these virtues of behavior become tainted with inauthenticity, when the parent merely creates a persona of caring, it creates deep turmoil in the developing psyche of the child. This, in turn, is the beginning or the development of the Shadow Inner Adult aspect of the Inauthentic Handler.

The underhanded nature of this superficial behavior can be difficult to identify by the victim and the outside world. The parental figure may verbalize the "appropriate" example behavior, but the experience of the child is incongruent with said behavior. This contrived simulation, fueled by deceit, creates inner conflict within the child. Do they trust their perceptions or trust their parent's "good intentions"? Because of their developmental need for validation, the innocent child will desperately hold onto their loyalty even in the midst of the hollow façade. Ultimately, the child feels betrayed, but is unable to express this conflict.

The self-serving nature of the Inauthentic Handler: This contractive Shadow Inner Adult behavior is as self-engrossed as it is devious. When confronted, the Inauthentic Handler will defend its position by presenting decorated accomplishments (albeit superficial in nature) that they provide for the child, but will conveniently avoid the necessary self-inquiry or objective observation to acknowledge if the child is actually getting everything they need. Therefore, it is never really about truly "being there." It is about their vanity.

It is difficult for the Inauthentic Handler to acknowledge their uncaring state. They use external justification to support their position through comments like, "I am doing all the right things. I provide all the necessities." "What more do you want from me?" "My kid doesn't want for anything – he has the best clothes, goes to the best schools and has a great life. He has nothing to complain about."

This self-denial will block any attempt to self-explore their deeper intentions beyond a superficial level. The Inauthentic Handler's self-deceit can be so absolute that it can manifest as righteous conviction and absolute confidence of their generated delusion. Any challenging of their persona may be met with opposition through behavior-controlling tactics like shifting the blame, shaming and guilting because of the unconscious fear of the being exposed.

The Inauthentic Handler lives in a superficial world as a protective mechanism to avoid feelings of inadequacy and repressed wounds. The Inauthentic Handler is narcissistic. They have shallow relationships and see people, including their children, as interchangeable. People exist to support their fragile self-image and ego structure at the expense of a more authentic connection. Their children are therefore "handled," and serve only to support their vanity.

Examples of the behavior of the Inauthentic Handler:

- **Questionable personal integrity**
- **Deceit, dishonesty and fabrication (teaching a child to lie by example)**
- **Misleading public façade or image**
- **Varying levels of sociopathic behavior**
- **Perception is far more important than authenticity**
- **Half-hearted or ingenuine parenting**
- **Ongoing non-committal behavior**
- **Insincere, superficial and shallow**
- **Patronizing behavior**
- **Superficial situation handled or managed with a lack of emotional connection**
- **Double standards, hypocrisy or incongruent behavior ("Do what I say, not what I do.")**

Questionable personal Integrity: The inner corruption and inauthenticity is programmed in early development to play a role in order to be accepted and loved. Along with the constant example of inauthentic role models, openly corrupt morals and contradictory behavior, children are taught to compromise their principles and integrity as a necessary survival tactic.

They consistently forfeit their own internal authentic experience in exchange for an artificial outer identity. The result can be a lack of trust in honoring and openly expressing their intimate feelings, as well as an underlying suspicion in the authenticity of others. Personal character is sacrificed. This creates a dysfunctional inner culture.

To fill this internal void, most default to a composite of their parents, friends, and idols. They unconsciously accept the imposed roles and superficial behaviors rather than question their validity within their own authentic personal journey.

Hypocrisy and double standards: In relation to the Inauthentic Handler, hypocritical or two-faced behavior is demonstrated through the comment, "Do what I say and not what I do." In this example, parental figures do not heed their own advice, but still expect their children to heed the rules and philosophies that they are not willing to embody. This pretense creates a deep mistrust in authority.

Excessive vanity: This affliction takes the form in one's compulsive obsession with their outer image as well as their social status. Vanity seeks approval to fuel their identity. Where pride is an inner experience of self-belief, vanity requires endorsement. In the case of the Inauthentic Handler, vanity profoundly influences self-identification, where outer status is more important than sincerity.

Ongoing non-committal and erratic behavior: The Inauthentic Adult is not inspired by an inner conviction that is derived from an act of self-referencing. Any loyalty is aligned with the portrayal of their superficial outer image. As a result, their behavior is erratic and inconsistent. They typically do not expose much devotion to a belief that is not in alignment with the social norm and best serves their present needs.

Insincere, superficial and shallow: The Inauthentic Handler does not engage in self-analysis or deep inner work. This can also be observed in conversations and engagements with the outer world. They are heavily invested in banter and gossip. When a situation or individual challenges them to go deeper, the Inauthentic Handler lashes out to maintain the illusion. They will shift the conversation from potentially exposing their superficial image. Much better to "save face" than consider self-reflection.

Deceit and denial: Parents that model inauthentic behavior as an acceptable method of handling things are teaching their children to lie. There are always some forms of lying (like "little white lies") that people will tell in the context of certain social circumstances or interpersonal relationship, but for the Inauthentic Handler, habitual lying has become normalized. It uses a variety of subtle forms of deception to "handle a situation" in interactions to sustain their persona. This allows the Inauthentic Handler to get comfortable with the habit of lying, while denying their true uncaring intentions. Pathological lying as a model of parenting and handling life situations can create the foundation for ongoing and future destructive sociopathic behavior.

Sociopathic behavior is selfish and objectifies others to achieve their personal fulfillment. They have a disregard for rules and commonly utilize deceptive tactics with a disturbing level of ease. Sociopaths find it difficult to make plans and prefer to believe they can nimbly navigate problems as they appear. They are risk takers, easily bored, ignore personal boundaries and justify outrageous actions and behaviors.

The "handling of children": In the description of this aspect of the Shadow Inner Adult, the term "handler" is deliberately used to illustrate the superficial lack of sincere parenting. There is also the inherent objectification of the child (or the inner child) as a self-serving means to an end.

The fabricated image of being a "good parent" becomes a façade to the outside world in order to fulfill the excessive vanity of a persona, but there is little willingness for the perpetrator to be honest about their lack of attention and genuine effort. Parenting is "phoned in" or completed with "half-hearted effort or concern" which is more associated with the term "handler" rather than "parent."

The Inauthentic Handler usually grants heavy praise, attention and rewards to the child for anything that sustains the superficial image and creates the desired perception from the outside world. Children are trained to enforce the inauthenticity even when they have an inner moral conflict with the behavior or the image that they are being demanded to support. This creates a psychological schism in the child.

The victim of this deceptive behavior has no choice but to turn this unconscious and unacknowledged pain inward on themselves creating the shame that something about them must be inherently wrong or unlovable or surely their "loving" and "caring" parent would surely show up for them in an authentic way.

INTERNAL CRITICAL PARENT

judgmental, critical, doubt shame, disempowering, dominating, persuasive

POSSESSIVE INNER ADULT

ownership, possession, property, objectification, self-serving

ENABLER

co-conspirator, indulgent, permissive, ednorsement, denial, concede, co-dependent, allowance

SHADOW INNER ADULT

abusive, contractive, immature, reactive, unconscious, shame

CONTROLLING INNER ADULT

dominating, manipulation, gaslighting, forceful, managing

INAUTHENTIC HANDLER

Uncompassionate, dishonest, uncaring, vanity, superfical, caculating

UNAVAILABLE ADULT

unaccountable, checked out, disengaged, irresponsible

THE SHADOW INNER ADULT
The Unavailable Adult

*If you choose not to decide, you still have made a choice
and that unowned, disempowered decision
is nothing more than a cowardly "no".*

In this form of delinquent behavior, the Shadow Inner Parent is completely vacant in any role with any aspect of the Inner or Outer child. This "checked out" space allows for the Shadow Adult to remain absent to the Inner Child's actions and unaccountable for any consequences because of the neglect. This is complete abandonment of any sense of personal responsibility.

Understanding the Dynamics of The Unavailable Adult

The term "unavailable" can be illustrated in many ways when it comes to the behavior of the Shadow Inner Adult. Role models, parental figures or guardians who are emotionally, psychologically immature, irresponsible, or physically not present, are all variations of the neglectful behavior of the Unavailable Adult.

Most adults who display this behavior are immature and psychologically ill-equipped with unexamined personal issues from their past. It creates a deficit in their ability to meet the necessary emotional, psychological and physical needs of a child.

Research has identified the profound importance of all infants and developing children having an appropriate, warm and loving connection to a parental figure during the fundamental years (ages 0-5). And regardless of the reason, the unavailable behavior of a distant and unconnected role model can create trauma and lasting effects on the psyche and inner and outer conditioning of the child.

Some Examples of the Unavailable Parenting Style:

- The parents' selfish emotional or physical needs, desires and/or wants are always the first priority.

- Most unavailable parents are unable to encourage, teach or empower their children. They are indifferent in their behavior toward their children and lack the knowledge to meet their children's even basic needs.

- Parents who are distracted by ongoing or prolonged circumstance of stress such as financial, emotional and social difficulties, distance themselves from the emotional connections with their children, leaving them deeply traumatized by abandonment.

- Social isolation and lack of friendship and support from relatives leaves the children suffering from loneliness, fear and anxiety.

- A parent who is unwilling or unable to demonstrates through act, word or deed the experience that the child is loved and adored. The unavailable parent may never verbally acknowledge or say "*I love you.*"

- A parent who is physically present but is emotionally unreachable and therefore unapproachable creating an overwhelming sense of isolation in the child.

Examples of the behavior of the Unavailable Adult:

- **Overwhelming lack of inner and outer responsibility**
- **An attitude of delinquent detachment**
- **The refusal to "show up" for themselves or others**
- **Denial and abandonment of necessary "adult" responsibilities**
- **Physically, emotionally and psychologically absent**
- **Demonstrates lethargy, laziness and slothful behavior**
- **Presents themselves as aloof or distant to deflect responsibility**
- **Does not listen well**
- **Not "present" or "checked out" in the moment**
- **Living in the illusion or the fantasy of the future or the past**
- **Exhibits a crippling sense of apathy**
- **Recurring excuses, justification, apologies and unfulfilling promises**
- **Words do not match actions or behavior**
- **Living in a state of the non-committal maybe or "soft no"**
- **Propagates a victimized mentality**
- **Demonstrates selfish and self-serving behavior**
- **The inability to express authentic acknowledgement, attention or adoration**

The refusal to "show up" for themselves or others: In many cases the Unavailable Adult refuses to show up for others, because they are unwilling to show up for themselves and will not admit either. This unwillingness to respond is typically seen instead by the Unavailable Adult as their inability to do what it takes.

They cannot be honest about their choice. So they will say things like, *"I am not sure what you want me to do"* or *"I don't know what I am doing"* or *"I am doing the best that I can do here."* To hide their unwillingness to make a sincere attempt, they will feign complete ignorance, minimize or deny the entire circumstance and the people involved, along with their need to participate in an engaged way.

Reoccurring excuses, apologies or unfulfilling promises: One of the greatest side-stepping tactics, beyond denial and avoidance, is the Unavailable Adult's masterful practice of excuses. They can offer a well-rehearsed justification to lessen the reality of their choice of disengagement. These attempts are nothing more than an attempt to conceal the true reason for the unavailability.

The truth about the "fear of failure": One of the biggest ploys utilized by the Unavailable Adult is professing the inability to act or show up because of a crippling fear of potential failure. They are unwilling or unable to make the effort or show up to avoid failure. But this is nothing more than a glorified excuse.

The Unavailable Adult is already functioning in a constant, ongoing state that can be defined as "failure" because they are unwilling to engage and failing to act. Even though they proclaim they are not showing up because they are afraid of potential failure, what they are really unwilling to face is their existing state of inadequacy. It is nothing more than an egoic ruse to justify their perpetual victimhood and unavailability.

Exhibits ongoing indecision, non-commitment and a "soft no": You can identify the Unavailable Adult through the choice of words that create the illusion of active engagement even though they are not engaged. "Maybe," "trying" or "waiting" are a few of these expressions. These words are used to justify this illusionary active state. But when you unravel the expressions and the underlying energy, you will see they are nothing more than the expression of being actively unavailable.

Living in the illusion or the fantasy of the future or the past: Living in the exciting intention of the future or the nostalgia memories of the past means that this aspect of the Shadow Inner Adult is unavailable "in the present moment" where connected and sincere engagement is needed. This fantasy-generating behavior acts as a psychological deflection. As a result, you will find this aspect engaging in the "what if" potential of something or "wouldn't it be great if…" or "do you remember when…" focus.

The distinction between detachment and non-attachment: There is confusion about these two terms because they are unknowingly used interchangeably to describe the same state. They are not nearly the same.

Detachment: This term is an expression of actively separating from something, someone, a situation or a relationship. This retraction can be from one's own experience of their emotional state as a form of disassociation. The withdrawal here is motivated by fear and/or anger as an active choice to remove oneself from an undesirable or unwelcome inner or outer experience. It is expressed as a "cutting off" from a situation or individual as a reactive expression of protection or behavior of defensiveness.

"I really had to detach from the situation, It was too much for me to handle"
"I'm not playing anymore."
"I am taking my ball and going home."
"I have to disconnect from my feelings. It's overwehlming."
"I am totally cutting myself off from her. She does not deserve my love."
"I am so annoyed. He is not going to get anything from me."

Non-attachment: On the other hand, this term suggests a more objective or observational space of clarity. It retains an expansive experience of being connected without agenda. This state of being is not managed, manipulated or reactive in any way and one is not dependent on a specific desired outcome. In the experience of non-attachment, one is wholly connected and fully embracing the fullness of any given experience without expectation and accepts the outcome without judgment or fear, whatever it may be.

One can think of non-attachment as a place of conscious participation residing in the inner knowing that everything is simply unfolding. From an unconscious perspective, this behavior can be misunderstood as being disconnected because it is not overtly reactive, but the choice of "being with" whatever is happening is deeply nourishing.

Apathy: Psychologists have expressed the challenge in working with individuals who exhibit a prolonged behavior of apathy, because it can be difficult to not only stimulate a desire to connect but also address the initial trauma that is being suppressed in the emotional body. Apathy can be fueled by a deep, unexpressed and unresolved anger that manifests itself in this passive detachment.

The Child-Adult Complex "becoming a parent's parent": Emotionally stunted adults may consciously or unconsciously elicit nurturing to compensate for their own unresolved deficiencies from past traumas through their children. This creates the "child-adult." It forces a child to become adult-like and **emotionally independent before they're ready.** The child takes on the role of being "the parent's parent." The child must nurture the needy adult who is unwilling or unable to provide that role to the child.

This unhealthy dependency forms deep co-dependency along with a profound fear of security in the child. It promotes deep-seated anger and a sense of uncertainty, mistrust and loss of hope. In this unnatural role-reversal, the child-adult struggles to uplift the parent to garner approval. Without a parental role model, the child is put under immense psychological strain and are likely to develop a depleted sense of self-esteem. This will eventually spill over into future inner and outer relationships.

The quiet devastation caused by the Unavailable Adult: Unlike other aspects of the Shadow Inner Adult that openly control, manipulate or possess the child, this manifestation is quiet, passive and withdrawn in nature. As a result, the Unavailable Adult is not perceived as overt abuse, but it is equally devastating to the developing psyche of the child. The patterns of abuse as a child manifest in some of these issues later in life:

- **Emotional disconnection**
- **Unexplained neediness**
- **Feeling depressed, lost or being alone even with others**
- **An unexplained pattern of detachment**
- **Difficulty forming healthy, intimate connections**
- **No real sense of personal identity**
- **An unexplained fear of abandonment**
- **Low self-esteem**
- **Loss of hope, faith and passion**
- **Overwhelming sense of apathy**
- **Issues with various expressions of insecurity**
- **Unhealthy boundaries**
- **Issues of control, security and safety**

INTERNAL
CRITICAL PARENT

judgmental, critical, doubt
shame, disempowering,
dominating, persuasive

POSSESSIVE
INNER ADULT

ownership, possession,
property, objectification,
self-serving

ENABLER

co-conspirator, indulgent,
permissive, ednorsement,
denial, concede, co-
dependent, allowance

SHADOW
INNER ADULT

abusive, contractive,
immature, reactive,
unconscious, shame

CONTROLLING
INNER ADULT

dominating, manipulation,
gaslighting, forceful,
managing

INAUTHENTIC
HANDLER

uncompassionate,
dishonest, uncaring, vanity,
superfical, caculating

UNAVAILABLE
ADULT

unaccountable, checked
out, disengaged,
irresponsible

THE SHADOW INNER ADULT
The Controlling Inner Adult

*All controlling behavior is a contractive reaction and misuse of power
exacted to make another fulfill your conscious and unconscious needs.
People who control others are often protecting themselves from being controlled.
It is a survival mechanism ruled by fear.*

This aspect of the Shadow Inner Adult manipulates through instilling doubt, mitigating, and filtering all facets of the Wounded Inner Child by bullying it into a desired version that it can manage. There is a deep fear of the potential inability of the Controlling Inner Adult to adequately handle the circumstance. Therefore, the Inner Child needs to be subdued in a variety of ways into a comfortable level of expression, a position and a place where it can be managed effectively so there are no surprises. At the root of this abuse is a deep-seated fear and a sense of powerlessness. This translates into a need to create order.

Understanding the Dynamics of The Controlling Inner Adult:

People control out of a desire to feel safe and manage their own unconscious issues and fear. They often control through various means to uphold and embody their personal belief systems, conditioning or personal values. There are many variations and types of control, from external recognition, re-enforcement to suppression, threats and manipulation.

The relationship between control and the perception of power: The ideal of power is commonly defined as the capacity of an individual to influence the conduct or behavior of others. Control is the active use of that perceived contractive position of authority. Power is a perception. What is considered powerful for one person may not be for another person.

The distinction between powerful and empowerment: The word "powerful" means to be full of, having, characterized by, or containing power. The concept of power is directly associated to strength, force and scope of influence. In terms of an individual, a sense of personal power usually refers to an outward demonstration of this specific influence, and in most cases utilizing that influence in various ways "over or onto" another. Having power is a measurement of your ability to command that force, influence and control.

The common phrase of "taking back my power" is used to suggest that this power of personal influence can be oppressed, suppressed or dominated and even stolen. And to re-establish that sense of control, one must "reclaim that power" from the source that has threatened it.

123

Being powerful is also commonly understood in our society through an individual's social statue, wealth, popularity, affiliation or fame. This is especially true in the world of social media and pop culture. In this case, it is the strength of outer influence in the world that defines how powerful you are and how much influence you may have. (Example: look how many followers I have on social media)

But the term "empowerment" or "in-power-ment" literally translates to the "result or product of power within." Real empowerment truly has little to do with the outside world. It is the state of creating and sustaining power within. The real question is what aspect of you is executing influence within conditioning? Typically, empowerment does not refer to control, but rather something deeper and more expansive instead of the conditioning of the Shadow Inner Adult .

The Controlling Inner Adult is the Shadow Inner Adult's representative for all control: Control is an active expression of fear. As a result, it is a common theme that plays itself out through many overt and covert forms that are illustrated in the various archetypes of the Shadow Inner Adult. Consider the Controlling Inner Adult the archetype of all things associated with forms of control in the consciousness. If a controlling behavior is present, the Controlling Inner Adult has a hand in its formation and execution. For example:

The Enabler controls through manipulation, permissiveness.
The Unavailable Adult controls through withdrawal and neglect.
The Possessive Parent controls through domineering, dominance.
The Inauthentic Handler controls through hypocrisy, dishonesty and deceitfulness.
The Internal Critical Adult controls through manipulation, judgment, and doubt in the inner dialogue.

As this internal behavior of control becomes normal to an unsuspecting psyche, just like the voice of the Internal Critical Parent, it makes it exceedingly difficult to identify the abuse because of its familiarity. To varying degrees, these control dynamics play themselves out in the inner and outer relationships in many ways. Identifying different forms and varying behaviors associated with control is the first step to creating a more expansive inner relationship and breaking the ongoing pattern.

Identifying different forms and tactics of controlling behavior: While some forms of control are more obvious, many are subtle. This makes them difficult to unravel. Both forms of control play a powerful role in molding the conditioning of the Inner Controlling Adult. The expression of control can be broken down into two distinct forms of expression:

- **Overt control** (direct and forceful, also known as hard tactics): This form of control is performed openly, and it is readily apparent. **Overt is associated with the idea of "aggressive expressions of control"**

- **Covert control** (indirect and subversive, also known as soft tactics): The word covert is derived from idea of being "under cover." Because of its subtlety, it is more difficult to recognize. **Covert is associated with the idea of "passive-aggressive expression of control"**

Both expressions can be seen in all aspects of the Shadow Inner Adult. The Controlling Inner Adult will favor one of these forms of control through different methods, depending on individual conditioning. However, one can and will move in and out of these control expressions based on the what the circumstances are and how the Controlling Inner Adult is reacting to that specific set of circumstances.

There is a question about which of the two forms or styles of control is more difficult to handle. It really depends on the individual. There is no "less destructive or damaging" form of control; one is not superior to another. Both are always derived primarily from contraction and depending on the conditioning of the recipient, they will be internalized differently.

Some people are more triggered by passive-aggressive control if they have betrayal in their past, while others are terrified by overt aggression if they have been deeply humiliated. It is therefore important to intimately understand the Controlling Inner Adult's form of preference in every circumstance to understand your relationship to control in your inner and outer world.

The Controlling Inner Adult tactics of control can be rational or emotional:

Rational (logical): Rational tactics of control make use of reasoning supported by facts. This includes the ability to rationally convince through logic and sound judgment. Influence is gained by helping you to see that it makes sense.

Irrational (emotional): Irrational control attempts to access the emotional experiences of an individual to gain a position of influence. It relies on manipulating the psychology based on an individual's feelings. This can include persuasion, coercion, shame or guilt, bullying or blaming.

Trauma-based tactics of control: This is an attempt to induce trauma to gain control. This could include verbal abuse, threats, physical abuse or psychological abuse. The point of this approach is to destabilize an individual, throw them off balance and tap into their existing wounds to gain influence.

Examples of the behavior of the Controlling Inner Adult:

- **Threat of withdrawing love**
- **Intimidation and/or physical punishment**
- **Psychological manipulation through intentionally inducing shame or guilt**
- **Brainwashing, indoctrination and inception**
- **"Gas-lighting" (creating dependency through intense self-doubt)**
- **Praise, rewards, bribes and "positive" re-inforcement**
- **Oppression, suppression and domination**
- **Minimize your accomplishments and goals**
- **Using past mistakes and issues against you in the present**
- **Demand perfection for unreasonable expectations or unattainable standards**
- **Violation, manipulation and disrespect of your privacy**
- **Unwilling to admit or acknowledge fallibility or error in themselves**
- **Manipulation of the narrative, dialogue and thought process**

Manipulation: The deliberate attempt to intimidate, confuse or coerce. It is considered passive-aggressive because it is not direct. This contractive behavior from the Controlling Inner Adult deliberately takes advantage of desires, fears, and vulnerabilities in the intended victim for the manipulator to get his or her needs fulfilled in some way.

Psychological manipulation may take on many subtle or overt forms of lying, misleading, inauthenticity, guilting, shaming, feigning, brainwashing or "gas-lighting" but also positive reinforcement techniques such as using bribes and praise.

Emotional and psychological manipulation by inducing shame and guilt: The Shadow Inner Adult uses the Inner Child's innocence, unsophisticated psychology and need of approval to coerce behavior through guilt or shame to influence them to act in a specific manner. The Controlling Inner Adult uses this feeling of being "wrong" as an emotional manipulation tactic.

GUILT
is created through self-judgment + self-projected anger
Feeling wrong - directed inward at how you behave or act.

SHAME
is created through self-judgment + self-projected anger
Feeling wrong - directed at who you are.

Emotional manipulation using guilt and shame is usually solidified over time. The Inner Child is repeatedly given the message of being wrong until they eventually begin to believe the subversive conditioning and learn to feel wrong and project that anger and judgment on themsevles. This creates a sense of inner shame and guilt that lives in the subconscious. It affects self-worth, self-respect, boundaries and self-confidence as outer relationships become unconsciously motivated by this inner conditioning.

Manipulation of the narrative, dialogue and thought process: One of the most powerful tactics for coercing people is to dominate the narrative. By influencing their version of the event, the Controlling Inner Adult influences the ideas surrounding the event. When that happens, it can indoctrinate you into the version of the story that maintains its control.

Once the Controlling Inner Adult has gained influence, it can undermine and emotionally compromise an individual. To achieve this, the Controlling Inner Adult may use a combination of expressions of control through rational or emotional tactics. In this circumstance, the Controlling Inner Adult aligned with the voice of the Critical Inner Parent work hand in hand to subversively manipulate your inner dialogue.

On a larger scale, narrative control is used in the media, publicity, promotional materials, political propaganda, and leadership to gain influence.

> *"The best way to take control over a people and control them utterly is to take a little freedom at a time, to erode rights by a thousand tiny and almost imperceptible reductions. In this way, the people will not see those rights and freedoms being removed until past the point at which these changes cannot be removed."*
> *– Adolf Hilter (Mein Kampf)*

Gas-lighting: This now popularized term is in reference to a 1938 stage play and a 1940 and 1944 movie "Angel Street" that explores this devious form of exploitation. It refers to a calculated form of manipulation where the manipulator seeks to sow seeds of doubt in the hope of causing an individual to question their own memory, perception, and sanity. Using persistent denial, intentional misdirection, and lying, the manipulator attempts to destabilize the victim's sense of knowing and belief.

These tactics may range from the denial by an abuser that previous abusive incidents ever occurred, to more extreme methods where the manipulator may bend, fabricate and recreate certain happenings or events with the intention of completely disorienting the unsuspecting victim to keep him/her off guard and malleable for brainwashing and control. It is also seen in individuals (or groups) who attack others for the very things that have been accused of them. (For example, a racist politician calling others who find such beliefs abhorrent 'racists.')

The goal is to create unrelenting fear and deep self-doubt. The victim will therefore resort to an unhealthy dependency on guidance from the abuser coupled with an intense need for approval. This form of psychological abuse leaves deep trauma in an innocent child and damages their sense of self-worth. The child will then live in a falsely constructed illusion where they may censor their behavior out of fear of their own sanity.

Varying levels of this form of psychological manipulation can be seen in domestic abuse situations, cults, and the tactics of religious sects in order to control their congregation or disciples.

Signs of gas-lighting:

- **Second-guessing yourself**
- **You ask yourself, "Am I too sensitive?"**
- **You feel confused and even crazy**
- **You seem deeply dissatisfied with life for no apparent reason**
- **You frequently make excuses for others' behavior to yourself, friends or family**
- **You start lying to avoid the verbal disapproval and disappointment of others**
- **It is incredibly challenging to make even seemingly simple decisions**
- **You experience a general joyless feeling of hopelessness**
- **You believe that you cannot seem to do anything right**
- **You question if you are "good enough"**
- **Withhold information out of fear that you will have to explain, defend or justify your actions**
- **You sense something is terribly wrong, but you can never quite express what it is, even to yourself**
- **You feel like you used to be a very different person - more confident, more fun-loving, more relaxed**
- **You are always apologizing to someone: mother, father, boyfriend, partner, boss, children**

Unwilling to admit or acknowledge fallibility or error in themselves: A classic product of the psychological condition known as Grandiose Narcissism and one of the most powerful tools for oppression is the Controlling Inner Adult behavior of being absolutely unwilling to admit that they have made a mistake.

This unwillingness to be vulnerable usually stems from a deep fear of condemnation. In other words, they have a fear of being controlled, so they preemptively control to prevent that possibility. But the position of infallibility also maintains the power of the Controlling Inner Adult. This is a common tool used in gas-lighting, brainwashing, conditioning and oppressive or domineering behavior.

Minimizing your accomplishments and goals and expansive experiences: The Controlling Inner Adult minimizes potential expansiveness, joy, accomplishments and goals out of the fear of their potential transformational power. Goals represent change, growth and personal development.

Expansiveness and change terrify the insecure Controlling Inner Adult, because of its potentially unknown and unforeseen consequences. The Controlling Inner Adult will suppress the slightest expression of expansion if it fears it cannot control it. It feels powerless, so it attempts to diminish the experience of empowerment before it is beyond its control.

These various exterior forms of manipulation and control eventually become the foundation of the Inner Controlling Adult. These behaviors reflect how this Shadow aspect continues to control, manipulate and intimidate the relationship with the Inner Child. This conditioning will eventually surface in the dynamics of all outer relationships in some manner. Individuals ultimately become the Controlling Inner Adult because of their fear of being controlled, their perception of power, and the desire to gain influence using that perceived power.

A profound survival pattern emerges to control the Wounded Inner Child. This will eventually extend to your outer environments and potential relationships in a desperate attempt to create a feeling of safety. Since you may not be fully aware of the unresolved pain of that inner conditioning, the inability to relinquish this inner control creates a major barrier in accepting and loving not only different aspects of yourself but also those around you.

INTERNAL
CRITICAL PARENT

judgmental, critical, doubt
shame, disempowering,
dominating, persuasive

POSSESSIVE
INNER ADULT

ownership, possession,
property, objectification,
self-serving

ENABLER

co-conspirator, indulgent,
permissive, ednorsement,
denial, concede, co-
dependent, allowance

SHADOW
INNER ADULT

abusive, contractive,
immature, reactive,
unconscious, shame

CONTROLLING
INNER ADULT

dominating, manipulation,
gaslighting, forceful,
managing

INAUTHENTIC
HANDLER

Uncompassionate,
dishonest, uncaring, vanity,
superfical, caculating

UNAVAILABLE
ADULT

unaccountable, checked
out, disengaged,
irresponsible

THE SHADOW INNER ADULT
The Possessive Inner Adult

"Your children are not your children. They are sons and daughters of Life's longing for itself. They come through you but not from you. And though they are with you yet they belong not to you. You may give them your love but not your thoughts, for they have their own thoughts. You may house their bodies but not their souls, for their souls dwell in the house of tomorrow, which you cannot visit, not even in your dreams. You may strive to be like them but seek not to make them like you..."
– Kahil Gibran (The Prophet)

In this form of contractive behavior, the Shadow Inner Parent treats the Inner Child as an object of possession to be leveraged for its own selfish desires. The Possessive Adult does not acknowledge the inner child's autonomy and views the child as an extension of the Shadow Parent at the expense of the Inner Child's experience. This is deeply traumatic to the child's sense of freedom as the child will be exploited to the Shadow parent's unfulfilled desires and/or personal agenda.

Understanding the Dynamics of The Possessive Inner Adult:

The Possessive Inner Adult has an unhealthy relationship with one or more of the varying aspects of attachment: addiction, ownership, dependency, control, and objectification. The Possessive Inner Parent clutches on to the object of their desire, unwilling to share, as well as "needing" to control not only behavior, but the attention and love coming from that source as well.

This aspect of the Shadow Inner Adult is fueled by the fear of losing something it believes it desperately needs. This is expressed through a range of passive or aggressive conditioning, different behaviors and aspects of inner and outer relationships. It can be projected and played out on a child, sibling, partner, friend, parent, family member or spouse.

What Dynamics Create the Possessive Inner Adult?

Possessiveness is conditioned from insecurity and fear. The incidents of being controlled and manipulated as a child leave deep scars on the psyche of an individual. The Possessive Inner Adult needs to fill that void. They become obsessed, addicted to the attention from a specific person and fear losing their attention.

When the victim of the abuse creates boundaries and "takes a stand," the paranoia can intensify the obsessiveness of the already abusive behavior. When that fire of jealousy is inflamed, aggressiveness rises.

Examples of the behavior of the Possessive Inner Adult

- **Sexualization**
- **Being "espoused" or projecting surrogate partner**
- **Kidnapping a childhood (living vicariously through the child)**
- **Co-dependency**
- **Obsessive jealousy can be a symptom of possessive isolation tactics**
- **Creating a "parent-child" or "adult-child" through imposing inappropriate roles**
- **Unhealthy boundaries**
- **Using blame and guilt to create unhealthy dependency**
- **Taking ownership for a child's achievements**
- **Addictive behavior**
- **Defiles, dominates and possesses the notion of human sentience**
- **Attachment disguised or mistaken for deep devotional love**
- **The Possessive Inner Parent is never truly fulfilled through the violation**
- **Hypersensitivity and reactionary behavior**
- **Inappropriate, consistent and unjustified interrogation**
- **Dominating privacy and personal space**
- **Becoming inappropriately involved in others' lives**

Possessiveness defiles, dominates and possesses the expression of human sentience: Sentience refers to the ability to be self-aware, to recognize and ponder that existence. It is the capacity to feel, perceive or experience. It also includes the ability to govern discernment and the ability to distinguish through self-examination and introspection.

When any person, organization, governing body, parent, authority or individual in or out of this world possess a being as personal property it defiles the notion of human sentience. Any act of domination or possession of the life, desires or experiences of any being is an expression of a de-humanizing act abuse and personal violation. Slavery is an act of possession and degrades the notion of personal sentience.

> *"Probably the worst damage is done when parents*
> *lay their shadow on their children.*
> *This is so common that most people have to work very hard*
> *to throw off their parent's shadow before they can begin their own adult lives.*
> *If a parent lays his shadow on a young child,*
> *that splits the personality of the child*
> *and sets the ego-shadow warfare into motion."*
> *– Robert A. Johnson (Jungian Analyst)*

Different Forms of Possessive behavior

There are many manifestations of possessive behavior that express themselves through dominating, inappropriate and unsuitable behavior in relationships.

Co-dependency: This term describes unhealthy attachment and entanglements in different types of relationships. People who are in co-dependent relationships will resort to varying tactics of possessiveness as the boundaries between the people become blurred. They cannot differentiate where one person begins and the other person ends. As a result, this unhealthy entanglement can escalate into an obsessive sense of ownership over the other or over the relationship as a separate entity. One or both of the parties lose their individuality as they start to identify as a single unit.

In some cases, the individuals fight for control of the relationship. The willing sacrifice of individual personalities is consensual and both parties become comfortable identifying as a single unit at the expense of their personal individuality. This choice is driven by an unconscious longing for safety and comfort of the unit.

Kidnapping a childhood: This occurs when a child's experience is used to vicariously satisfy unfulfilled needs or desires. The Possessive Inner Adult dominates the life experiences, demanding participation in specific activities without any concern for the child.

For example, this can occur in regard to what school the child will attend, what subjects they will study, their career path, which instruments or sports they will play, which religion they will be indoctrinated into, who they will date… etc. As the parent becomes more identified to their child's opportunities or experience, the child's ability to be aligned with their own preferences becomes irrelevant under the shadow of the extreme possessiveness.

Once the childhood is effectively stolen, and the choice is gone, the Possessive Inner Parent may continue by vicariously living through this vehicle, mapping their feelings, experiences and wishes onto the child without concern. In many cases the parent will justify their actions. They will insist they are giving more opportunities while shuttering the child's voice and ability to follow their dreams.

Imposing inappropriate roles: A "parent-child" is a term given to a child that was forced to embody a parental role (to care for their own parent or sibling) at the expense of their own childhood. Regardless if they do this out of a sense of devotion or survival, it can cause deep trauma in the development of the child. This affects the boundaries of appropriateness moving forward into their adult lives, corrupting the foundation of their self-perception, and their (inner and outer) relationships.

Espousing an innocent child: This term refers to a care-giver who cultivates any form of inappropriate spouse-like relationship with their child. This can occur when there has been a death of a spouse, a divorce, a rift in the relationship or the parent is dealing with an unavailable partner.

This distorts the child's understanding of healthy roles and creates many potential psychological issues. Examples can be as unique as the personal dynamics of each case. Here are some common examples:

- **Exposing inappropriate overly mature information with an immature child.**
- **Demanding the child keep inappropriate and unhealthy secrets.**
- **Treating the child as a mature confidante with intimate and unsuitable problems or personal issues.**
- **Expecting the child to respond as an adult with maturity before they are ready.**
- **Creating an inappropriate emotional and psychological adult relationship**
- **Substituting romantic attention onto a child meant for a spouse or partner.**
- **Inappropriately complaining, bashing or discussing their partner with the child.**
- **Projecting unsuitable levels of intimacy onto your child, that should be reserved for a mature partner.**

In all of these examples, there is a self-centered choice to indoctrinate the child into a mature adult world they are psychologically unprepared to navigate.

In the above cases, the care giver is using the child as a means to satisfy their own insecurities, wounds, pain or desires. In many cases, the self-absorbed Possessive Inner Parent actually believes they have the right to demand this of their child.

Seeing the child as an object and to own their personal achievements: Society has programed most families to speak in a possessive manner in reference to their children. "My child" can suggest an expression of ownership. For most parents, the possessive sense of "my" is an innocent expression of a sense of pride for the child's accomplishments and a simple way to identify that the child belongs to a specific family, tribe or clan.

However, when it is taken literally the possessiveness supersedes a child's sense of personal identity. The contractive Possessive Inner Parent believes that their physical offspring belongs to them. Therefore, the child serves only as a physical extension of them, and all the child's achievements (or lack of achievements) are also theirs. The child is also expected to serve the needs in any way the Possessive Inner Parent sees fit.

Sexualization: This describes the destructive projection of sexuality (emotionally, mentally, energetically, psychologically and physically) onto an innocent child. The severe violation, shattering of roles, boundaries, betrayal and psychological trauma that is caused to a child when someone, especially a trusted parent or guardian, violates them sexually is horrifying.

There are varying degrees of this violation that can occur on different levels of consciousness. Because this abuse is often subversive, and the experience is so beyond the psychological maturity and understanding of the child, it can be very difficult to unearth the depth of the psychological damage.

This is especially true if the behavior was normalized. As the child develops and begins to consciously explore outer relationships, the patterns will repeat in unconscious expressions and they will not necessarily know why. Here are some examples of sexualized behavior on various levels of the consciousness:

Verbally and directly commenting on a child from a sexual point of view:

- Conversing about inappropriate personal sexual behavior with a child
- Projecting sexual commentary on a child
- Directly sexually propositioning the child
- Commenting on a child's sexuality

Verbally indirectly commenting on sexuality appropriately around a child:

- Describing inappropriate sexual fantasies
- Exposing a child to sexually explicit material
- Talking explicitly about sexual encounters, partners or past relationships
- Making sexual comments or lewd jokes in the presence of the child
- Over-sexualized language
- Implying sexualized conduct, offers or invitations by innuendo
- Allowing someone else to project sexuality on the child

Psychological sexually unsuitable behaviors:

- Objectifying a child as a sexual or romantic object
- Leering sexually at a child
- Buying sexually or romantic suggestive gifts for a child
- Lewd or suggestive behavior around a child
- Sexually suggestive games

Physically inappropriate or violating touch or any suggestive sexualized physical contact:

- **Groping, petting or fondling a child**
- **Extra-long hugs or embraces projecting sexual intentions**
- **Dominating or suggestive physical contact**
- **Invading a child's personal space, making them feel sexually uncomfortable**
- **Any sexualized physical behavior (including any or all sexual acts**

Many of the examples are subjective, making it difficult to understand and validate for a victim. But behind all of these inappropriate acts is the intentional projection of sexuality. These acts are often disguised as play and manipulated to seem like normal behavior. That is why these violations are not consciously acknowledged by the victim and may surface many years later as they are exploring intimate relationships.

Attachment and possessiveness disguised as deep devotional love: This form of possessiveness is justified as deep caring. Therefore, one may accept it as a loving act.

- **"I would never treat you this way if I didn't care so much."**
- **"He would never do this to me if he did not care so much. He is just overreacting and maybe I am not seeing how devoted he is to me."**
- **"Of course, I am concerned. Can't you see? I was just over-emotional and over-reacted in my behavior."**
- **"Don't you understand? Doesn't this just prove how much I love you?"**

Possessiveness is an expression of superficial and contractive emotions (fear, control, anger, jealousy…etc.) cleverly disguised as the expansiveness of love. In exploring any act or behavior, if the behavior feels contractive, then it is not a loving act.

True devotion empowers. In that humbled state of devotion, one only desires the object of adoration to be uplifted. The more expansiveness that the adored one feels, the more over-joyed the admirer becomes. Supporting the individual into growing into the most empowered and expansive version of themselves is the only intent.

Hypersensitivity and reactionary behavior: Possessive people will display varying degrees of hypersensitivity. Even the smallest action or comment can lead them to overreact. This emotional drama is a form of control. Because of the need to dominate their environments, an over-possessive pattern will exhibit behaviors that are manifestations of their deep insecurity and need to control.

Jealousy versus possessiveness: Obsessive jealousy left unchecked is destructive, but the foundational characteristics of possessiveness are far more sinister in nature than jealousy. Jealousy is usually fueled by some inner inferiority complex and insecurity that manifests as reactive acting out. Possessiveness reflects a belief in which an individual or group of individuals feel they deserve dominance over a thing or being. The violator believes themselves to be "the master" and therefore exacts a state of superiority.

With jealousy, the desire is to "be another person" or "take place of another person" because you covet their experience. Possessiveness is imbued with a deep sense of personal entitlement, narcissism, self-absorption and self-arrogance. It will be satisfied (by force if necessary) at the expense of another without concern what will happen to that individual during the process.

Becoming inappropriately involved in others' lives: This Shadow Inner Adult aspect does not understand the meaning of appropriate boundaries. It pushes its unsolicited perspective and opinions without regard and has the tendency to inject itself into someone's life in highly inappropriate manner. On the surface it can seem genuine, but closer inspection reveals the motivation to be a self-serving attempt to secure a personal need vicariously through the victim.

Dominating privacy and personal space: Privacy is a valued fundamental human right and allows an individual to create and maintain a sense of autonomy, individuality and personal expression. People explore and define themselves by exercising power over themselves, their experience and personal space. A healthy expression of privacy creates space for someone to investigate their own sense of personal expression and define their relationship to themselves. This is important for individual development that creates a sense of personal worth.

The domineering behavior of the Possessive Inner Parent will attempt to own the child by limiting their personal space and violating their right to privacy. They may even justify the control by saying "Being private is just an excuse for being sneaky and deceitful." Or "Why would you want to hide things from the people who love you?"

Isolation tactics: The Possessive Inner Adult demands complete attention. It will use different coercive methods such as emotional blackmail and subversive manipulation to isolate an individual when it does not receive that attention. It will minimize potential outside "distractions" because it believes the child belongs to them and does not deserve an individual experience.

Without access to a variance of opinion, the victim does not realize the depth of their own isolation or understand the lengths to which they have been dominated. If the child rebels against this imposed role or seeks to break the imposed isolation, the consequences can be very destructive and threatening.

Inappropriate and consistent and unjustified interrogation: The Possessive Inner Parent will cross the line of healthy inquiry until it turns into interrogation. The intent is domination. The assault keeps an unsuspecting victim off balance, and with enough intensity, can compromise an individual's ability to trust themselves.

The constant oppressive interrogation alters the psychological, emotional and mental suggestibility of the child which makes them more susceptible to imposed rules from the Possessive Inner Parent. At some point it may become easier to just submit to the control and accept the dominance rather than challenge it. In this case the victim may even confess to something that did not occur to keep the peace.

The Possessive Inner Adult is never truly fulfilled through the violation: The dynamics of the Possessive Inner Parent reflects a profound and unconscious weakness of inner nurturing because it seeks to satisfy and soothe itself through domination or possession. On a deeper level, the violator always has some level of consciousness that whatever they have stolen or possessed was not freely given.

All possessiveness requires a conscious and deliberate choice, even if it is compulsive. In other words, the abuser "knows on some level" what they are doing and understands the devastating nature of the action, even if they deny or justify the violation.

Possessiveness utilizes a collection of contractive Shadow Inner Adult archetypes working together to maintain domination.

- **The Controlling Inner Adult:**
  Utilizes various methods of overt and covert control

- **The Critical Inner Parent:**
  Instills guilt and shame in the child for not serving the ascribed role

- **The Enabler:**
  They enable themselves to indulge in their needs vicariously through the child

- **The Inauthentic Handler:**
  The sociopathic tendencies of objectification and lack of empathy

Your Personal Shadow Inner Adult Dynamics

_____ **INTERNAL CRITICAL PARENT**

_____ **ENABLER**

_____ **INAUTHENTIC HANDLER**

_____ **UNAVAILABLE ADULT**

_____ **CONTROLLING INNER ADULT**

_____ **POSSESSIVE INNER PARENT**

INTERNAL CRITICAL PARENT
judgmental, critical, doubt shame, disempowering, dominating, persuasive

POSSESSIVE INNER ADULT
ownership, possession, property, objectification, self-serving

ENABLER
co-conspirator, indulgent, permissive, endorsement, denial, concede, co-dependent, allowance

SHADOW INNER ADULT
abusive, contractive, immature, reactive, unconscious, shame

CONTROLLING INNER ADULT
dominating, manipulation, gaslighting, forceful, managing

INAUTHENTIC HANDLER
Uncompassionate, dishonest, uncaring, vanity, superficial, caculating

UNAVAILABLE ADULT
unaccountable, checked out, disengaged, irresponsible

After reading the chapters about **The Shadow Inner Adult,** take some time to consider which of the six archetypes best describe your personal conditioning. Rank them on a scale on the above list from 1-6 (1 being the most influential and active and 6 being the least).

Remember that all the Shadow Inner Adult archetypes exist within every individual's conditioning, but everyone expresses those dynamics in a unique way based on their specific life circumstances. Some of the dynamics are more prevalent than others in your inner and outer experience. The idea is to isolate the most active patterns so you can create more awareness and begin to work with those archetypes.

Consider the dynamics in your past and present (inner and outer) relationships. If you observe those relationships, you will begin to see the recurring patterns. Be honest. In many cases you will be delving into your unconscious patterns, and it will require self-analysis. One way to assist in processing your unconscious patterns is to journal your inner observations. Use the information in the six **Shadow Inner Adult** chapters as a guide to help you in your process.

Your Contractive Inner Relationship Feedback Loop

The self-perpetuating and dysfunctional relationship between **SHADOW** and **WOUNDEDNESS** activates the most destructive feedback loop. As the oppressive influence of the **Shadow Inner Adult** exerts dominance over the **Wounded Inner Child**, it locks you into a repetitive field of contraction. This includes different combinations of the Wounded Inner Child and the Shadow Inner Adult. These patterns have been perpetuated for so long, the behavior becomes normalized. They have become integrated into your inner conditioning through ongoing conditioning.

Every person has some form of "corrupted" inner conditioning. No one is exempt. Each of these contractive archetypes live within everyone. You are uniquely programed based on your unique upbringing, conditioning, culture and experience. No set of dynamics is better or worse than another. The way they play out along with their level of severity is unique to you. You cannot erase this conditioning, but you can actively examine, explore and shift your relationship to these existing inner conditions.

Until then, you will continue to repeat and project that familiar "normalized" inner relationship between aspects of the Shadow Inner Adult with the Wounded Inner Child in every relationship.

When you engage in a relationship, you will create your conscious connection with another from an aware, conscious maturity and a radiant childlike perspective. But you will also be attracted by the unconscious shadow and woundedness that already exists within you. (And that feels familiar in another.) As a result, you will unknowingly seek out your dysfunctional dynamics in all your relationships in the outer world that align with your existing conditions and the inner contractive feedback loop that is already playing out in your inner world.

Knowing your internal behavior dynamics can help you identify why you choose relationships that feed those dysfunctional patterns. This process requires you to explore the unconscious world of contraction, acknowledge its presence, be accountable for the existing patterns and consciously choose something different. Only then will you be able transform your inner relationship to these contractive elements. This awareness will give you the tools to allow you to break the unconscious contractive feedback loop that has continued to unknowingly bind you to the world of pain in all your inner and outer relationships.

Your Contractive Inner Relationship Feedback Loop

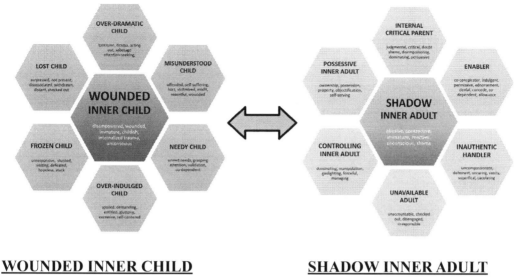

WOUNDED INNER CHILD

____ Over-Dramatic Child
____ Misunderstood Child
____ Needy Child
____ Over-Indulged Child
____ Frozen Child
____ Lost Child

SHADOW INNER ADULT

____ Internal Critical Parent
____ Enabler
____ Inauthentic Handler
____ Unavailable Adult
____ Controlling Inner Adult
____ Possessive Inner Parent

The contractive unconscious aspects of your **Wounded Inner Child** and **Shadow Inner Adult** consciously and unconsciously influence every relationship in your life. Transfer your observations and ranking for both contractive quadrants from the previous chapters. Pay close attention to the relationship between the different archetypes in the wounded and shadow expression of contractiveness. Examine the way each of the different dynamics fuels the contractive feedback loop in your relationships.

The seductive nature of this contractive feedback loop usually goes unnoticed in our inner and outer relationships because it feels so familiar. This can also become the basis for unconscious attraction that many people confuse as connection. That is why, it is so important to become aware with your contractive conditioning and understand the expression of these dynamics because these unexamined patterns are what often unwittingly sabotages most relationships. Until you truly know your shadow and your woundedness, you cannot have the ability to choose something different.

Exploring Your Unconscious, Contractive Outer Relationship Dynamics:

You are now delving in the mysterious inner world of the unconscious. You may have never ventured into your inner conditioning to examine these aspects of your being in this way. Remember to use the above chapters to familiarize yourself with the six different behavioral archetypes in each of the two contractive quadrants. Have patience with yourself as you begin to investigate the unconscious dynamics of the Wounded Inner Child and the Shadow Inner Adult.

1. If you cannot easily determine your internal dynamics, then begin by investigating your past and present relationship dynamics. What recurring behavior or dynamics do you notice? Pay attention to your existing and past roles, behaviors and repeating patterns in your outer relationships. What do you see? The recurring behaviors that show up in your different relationships are clues and invitations from the outer world to help you see the unowned and unexplored behaviors inside of you.

2. It may help to make a list of your past and present relationships and journal your initial observations. It may also assist you as part of your process to ask a close friend, existing partner, or family member for their observations about your patterns.

As long as you are unaware of your inner dynamics, you will ALWAYS unconsciously project the contractive element of the Adult/Child dynamics into every relationship.

Use the worksheet below to explore how you play out these relationship dynamics in the world. Explore different forms of relationships to get a better idea of how these patterns express themselves. For example, you may use your boss, co-workers, neighbor, siblings, past romantic partners, past or existing friends, extended family members and parents.

Explore the inner conditioning and which of the different expressions of the contractive relationships feedback loop that you play out when you react unconsciously. The deeper your awareness of your foundational conditioning, the more consciousness you will have in all of your relationships. Here is an example of how to use the below worksheet.

When you express a specific Wounded Inner Child or Shadow Inner Adult Dynamic:

In my relationship with my: *past girlfriend Katrina*
When I express the Wounded Inner Child dynamic of: *Needy Child*
She reacts by expressing the Shadow Inner Adult dynamic of: *Unavailable Adult*

When I express the Shadow Inner Adult dynamic of: *Critical Parent*
She reacts by expressing the Wounded Inner Child dynamic of: *Frozen Child*

How you react when someone expresses a specific Wounded Inner Child or Shadow Inner Adult Dynamic:

In my relationship with my: *best buddy Jack*
When he expresses the Wounded Inner Child dynamic of: *Over-Dramatic Child*
I react by expressing the Shadow Inner Adult dynamic of: *Controlling Inner Adult*

WHY: *I have a lot of judgment for drama, so I try to shut it down by controlling.*

When he expresses the Shadow Inner Adult dynamic of: *Inauthentic Handler*
I react by expressing the Wounded Inner Child dynamic of: *Misunderstood Child*

WHY: *It's really hard for me to deal with anyone who is inauthentic – I first get confused and then I feel unheard.*

Your Contractive Outer Relationship Feedback Loop Worksheet

(When I express a specific Wounded Inner Child or Shadow Inner Adult Dynamic)

1. In my relationship with: _____
When I express the **Wounded Inner Child** dynamic of: _____
He/she reacts with the **Shadow Inner Adult** dynamic of: _____

When I express the **Shadow Inner Adult** dynamic of:_____
He/she reacts with the **Wounded Inner Child** dynamic of:_____

(When someone else expresses a specific Wounded Inner Child or Shadow Inner Adult Dynamic)

In my relationship with: _____
When he/she expresses the **Wounded Inner Child** dynamic of:_____
I react with the **Shadow Inner Adult** dynamic of:_____
WHY: _____

When he/she expresses the **Shadow Inner Adult** dynamic of: _____
I react with the **Wounded Inner Child** dynamic of: _____
WHY: _____

(When I express a specific Wounded Inner Child or Shadow Inner Adult Dynamic)

2. In my relationship with: _____
When I express the **Wounded Inner Child** dynamic of: _____
He/she reacts with the **Shadow Inner Adult** dynamic of: _____

When I express the **Shadow Inner Adult** dynamic of:_____
He/she reacts with the **Wounded Inner Child** dynamic of:_____

(When someone else expresses a specific Wounded Inner Child or Shadow Inner Adult Dynamic)

In my relationship with: _____
When he/she expresses the **Wounded Inner Child** dynamic of:_____
I react with the **Shadow Inner Adult** dynamic of:_____
WHY: _____

When he/she expresses the **Shadow Inner Adult** dynamic of: _____
I react with the **Wounded Inner Child** dynamic of: _____
WHY: _____

(When I express a specific Wounded Inner Child or Shadow Inner Adult Dynamic)

3. In my relationship with: _____

When I express the **Wounded Inner Child** dynamic of: _____

He/she reacts with the **Shadow Inner Adult** dynamic of: _____

When I express the **Shadow Inner Adult** dynamic of: _____

He/she reacts with the **Wounded Inner Child** dynamic of: _____

(When someone else expresses a specific Wounded Inner Child or Shadow Inner Adult Dynamic)

In my relationship with: _____

When he/she expresses the **Wounded Inner Child** dynamic of: _____

I react with the **Shadow Inner Adult** dynamic of: _____

WHY: _____

When he/she expresses the **Shadow Inner Adult** dynamic of: _____

I react with the **Wounded Inner Child** dynamic of: _____

WHY: _____

(When I express a specific Wounded Inner Child or Shadow Inner Adult Dynamic)

4. In my relationship with: _____

When I express the **Wounded Inner Child** dynamic of: _____

He/she reacts with the **Shadow Inner Adult** dynamic of: _____

When I express the **Shadow Inner Adult** dynamic of: _____

He/she reacts with the **Wounded Inner Child** dynamic of: _____

(When someone else expresses a specific Wounded Inner Child or Shadow Inner Adult Dynamic)

In my relationship with: _____

When he/she expresses the **Wounded Inner Child** dynamic of: _____

I react with the **Shadow Inner Adult** dynamic of: _____

WHY: _____

When he/she expresses the **Shadow Inner Adult** dynamic of: _____

I react with the **Wounded Inner Child** dynamic of: _____

WHY: _____

(When I express a specific Wounded Inner Child or Shadow Inner Adult Dynamic)

5.   In my relationship with: _____

When I express the **Wounded Inner Child** dynamic of: _____

He/she reacts with the **Shadow Inner Adult** dynamic of: _____

When I express the **Shadow Inner Adult** dynamic of:_____

He/she reacts with the **Wounded Inner Child** dynamic of:_____

(When someone else expresses a specific Wounded Inner Child or Shadow Inner Adult Dynamic)

In my relationship with: _____

When he/she expresses the **Wounded Inner Child** dynamic of:_____

I react with the **Shadow Inner Adult** dynamic of:_____

WHY: _____

When he/she expresses the **Shadow Inner Adult** dynamic of: _____

I react with the **Wounded Inner Child** dynamic of: _____

WHY: _____

(When I express a specific Wounded Inner Child or Shadow Inner Adult Dynamic)

6.   In my relationship with: _____

When I express the **Wounded Inner Child** dynamic of: _____

He/she reacts with the **Shadow Inner Adult** dynamic of: _____

When I express the **Shadow Inner Adult** dynamic of:_____

He/she reacts with the **Wounded Inner Child** dynamic of:_____

(When someone else expresses a specific Wounded Inner Child or Shadow Inner Adult Dynamic)

In my relationship with: _____

When he/she expresses the **Wounded Inner Child** dynamic of:_____

I react with the **Shadow Inner Adult** dynamic of:_____

WHY: _____

When he/she expresses the **Shadow Inner Adult** dynamic of: _____

I react with the **Wounded Inner Child** dynamic of: _____

WHY: _____

PART IV
DYSFUNCTIONAL INFLUENCES

Dysfunctional Relationship Dynamics:
The Contractive Feedback Loop between Shadow and Woundedness

"We need to connect with this dark side for our own development,
and we have no business flinging it at others,
trying to palm off these awkward and unwanted feelings.
the difficultly is that most of us live in an intricate web of shadow exchange
that robs both parties of their potential wholeness."
— Robert A. Johson (Jungian Analyst)

It is important to consciously examine and understand the distinct traits and tendencies of the different Shadow Inner Adult dynamics in relation to Wounded Inner Child and learn to identify the ongoing reactive relationships. This will create a powerful awareness about how these different patterns operate. It will assist you in transforming dysfunctional relationships and transcending its influence in various aspects of your inner and outer relationships.

Below are some examples of the Contractive Feedback Loop between various aspects of the Shadow Inner Adult's influence on the Wounded Inner Child. More than one archetype can be triggered once the Contractive Feedback Loop has been activated creating a "cluster" of associated behaviors that all fuel the contraction.

Remember that the relationship between these different contractive archetypes always first occurs in your inner world and then plays out in your outer world. Understanding how the different contractive archetypes engage helps you better navigate this with others.

The Dysfunctional Influence of The Internal Critical Parent

The Internal Critical Parent is the most integrated, subversive and therefore most tolerated aspect of the Shadow Inner Adult conditioning. Though it can be easy to notice, it is also able to slip quietly into the background of the consciousness and remain undetected. Because it has had so much time and it has taken root within the inner dialogue, it fuels judgment, blame, and an ongoing cycle of self-doubt in the Wounded Inner Child. The Inner Critical Parent aspect of the Shadow Inner Adult is the most recognizable form of abuse that one can identify, because it is expressed as an "inner voice" of intense criticism.

An individual becomes so accustomed to this inner dialogue that they do not always recognize how it has fueled various aspects of the Wounded Inner Child dynamics. If the Internal Critical Parent is left unobserved, it has tremendous influence over the unsophisticated nature of the Inner Child. It covertly and strategically agitates the different wounds of all the various Wounded Inner Child archetypes.

The Internal Critical Parent and the Frozen Child: The voice of self-doubt instills a festering lack of confidence in the Frozen Child and keeps it transfixed in fear. The critical dialogue creates constant insecurity, bombards the Frozen Child with fearful consequences of not acting correctly, and creates terrifying "what if" scenarios. It questions everything until the Frozen Child is incapable of moving forward. The Internal Critical Parent's secret weapon to constantly trip up the Frozen Child will always be variations of fear, and it will always advise the Frozen Child that no action is the better choice.

The Internal Critical Parent and the Over-Dramatic Child: The Internal Critical Parent has an interesting relationship with the Over-Dramatic Child. This aspect of Shadow Parenting knows how to "push the right buttons" to ignite the dramatic nature of the Over-Dramatic Child.

The Internal Critical Parent will use the excessiveness and outrage of the Over-Dramatic Child's energy to its advantage to control the dialogue of the inner landscape. Quietly manipulating this aspect in the background, it will intentionally instigate the outburst and then direct the drama with a targeted dialogue. It will utilize the Over-Dramatic Child's unsophisticated nature and tendency toward immature explosiveness. As long as the Intneral Critical Parent, who is acting on behalf of all the Shadow Inner Adult aspects, controls the inner dialogue, it will keep the Over-Dramatic Child disempowered.

The Internal Critical Parent and the Misunderstood Child: The Internal Critical Parent has the capacity to create a profound level of self-doubt, mistrust, and shame through its inner dialogue. It is responsible for the much of the self-imposed pain and mistrust that manifests in the conditioning of the Misunderstood Child. It is calculated and sly in its ability to shift the inner dialogue to suit each of the different aspects of the Wounded Inner Child.

The Misunderstood Child defines itself by pain and by the pain it sees in others. This pattern is fueled by a self-perpetuating inner dialogue. The Internal Critical Parent constantly directs the dialogue to encourage self-doubt. It fuels the devaluing voice of shame and guilt, creates mistrust in the ability to change, and inflates the false story that it will never be understood. (And cannot be properly loved.)

The Dysfunctional Influence of The Enabler

Depending on the archetype it engages with, the dynamics of the Enabler can take on many manifestations. The Wounded Inner Child lacks the maturity to understand its own needs, and the Enabler entices the childish and superficial desire for what it wants.

The Enabler and the Over-Indulged Child: This aspect of the Wounded Inner Child is conditioned by the Enabler to feel entitled and creates the foundation for addictive patterns. The differences between a "need" and a "want" has never been modeled for this aspect of the Wounded Inner Child. Therefore, this over-indulgence creates a desperate need for constant attention. This unbalanced pampering combined with instant gratification forms the basis for highly narcissistic tendencies. The Over-Indulged Child has not been exposed to healthy moderation, and therefore becomes willing to disrespect boundaries to get what it wants.

Underneath the superficial flow of excess and gratification, the Overindulged Child still feels deep insecurity. If the contractive collusion remains intact, the Overindulged Child will remain disempowered, accountable and co-dependent.

The Enabler and the Over-Dramatic Child: The Enabler refuses to draw boundaries, demonstrate discipline, and is unwilling to model the difference between true needs and desires. As a result, this state of perpetual high drama, chaos and inflated excess have been conditioned in the reactive survival mechanism that the Overdramatic Child now habitually uses to demand attention.

Enabling prevents an individual from experiencing the natural consequences of their own behavior. The Over-Dramatic Child will create whatever drama it needs to satisfy its desires. The Over-Dramatic Child has been conditioned to seek attention without consequences of their behavior. The Enabler feeds this damaging cycle.

The Enabler and the Needy Child: The indulgence of the Enabler is terrible for the Needy Child. The focus of the over-generosity is at the expense of the deeper needs of the Wounded Inner Child. Indulgence without substance leaves the fundamental, deeper needs unmet. This perpetuates the woundedness of the Needy Child's conditioning. They feel neglected in the midst of the indulgence and ache for a deeper connection that the Enabler is unable to provide. The continued excess without substance keeps the co-dependent Needy Child grasping for more.

The Dysfunctional Influence of The Inauthentic Handler

The driving force behind this aspect of the Shadow Inner Adult is its capacity for deceit and perpetual lack of integrity. As a result, the Inauthentic Handler superficially manages the Wounded Inner Child while it creates a misrepresented outer persona.

The Inauthentic Handler offers nothing but a collection of broken promises, mistrust and shifting loyalties. This pushes the Wounded Inner Child into a false sense of longing, only to be continually disappointed. This ongoing betrayal fuels insecurity, fear and self-loathing.

The Inauthentic Handler and the Over-Dramatic Child: Because the Over-Dramatic Child acts out on behalf of the repressed needs of all the other aspects of the Wounded Inner Child, it functions as the unconscious and reactive "cry." The Over-Dramatic Child's reaction can take varying forms, but it is always challenging deception, inattentive behavior and insincerity. The Inauthentic Handler is willing to maintain the disingenuous posturing by investing in its own illusions. It will dismiss, reject, and ignore the repeated cries for help. As a result, the Over-Dramatic Child will shift to covert tactics like self-sabotage as it acts out.

The Inauthentic Handler and the Misunderstood Child: The Inauthentic Handler spends most of its time managing its outer perception. This conflict between the reality of how the Inauthentic Adult functions and the façade it creates and invests in is a profound source of trauma for the Misunderstood Child. It feels completely unrecognized and unvalidated and is devastated by the lack of commitment.

When the Inauthentic Handler defends its illusions at the expense of the child, it manifests as a feeling of isolation, mistrust and disconnection that is projected on the outer world. Tragically, because of the mixed messages of inauthenticity and insincerity, the Misunderstood Child lives in its own self-generating prison of unworthiness fueled by the pain of mistrust and isolation.

The Inauthentic Handler and the Needy Child: Attention seeking in the Needy Child is manifested when the Inauthentic Handler invests more in outer perception than genuine emotional and psychological investment. The Needy Child feels this lack of attentiveness and craves sincere, devoted attention. However, it does not know how to sustain itself and manipulates to get attention in the outer world but feels guilty when it receives it.

How can the Needy Child create a sense of inner confidence or self-worth when the conditioning of the Inauthentic Handler offers disengaged and fleeting appreciation and approval and is deceptive and hypocritical in the process? The Needy Child feels no inner security or sense of self-respect. It grasps for approval in its engagements because it does not believe in its own value.

The Inauthentic Handler and the Lost Child: Rather than live with the constant pain of rejection and shifting values of the Inauthentic Handler, the Lost Child disassociates itself from its own feeling of woundedness and "checks out" of the entire process. It unconsciously chooses not to participate in the ongoing masquerade because the pain of it is just too much to for the innocent child to bear. It is especially difficult to feel so neglected and unloved while the self-invested Shadow Adult seeks to present a false story for the sake of its narcissistic ego. As long as the Inauthentic Handler is active, the Lost Child will never feel safe or protected enough to face its pain and remain disempowered.

The Dysfunctional Influence of The Unavailable Adult

The lack of consistent attention, caring, neglect and irresponsibility from the Unavailable Adult is a form of passive, covert abuse that has a deeply traumatic effect on the Wounded Inner Child. On the spectrum of abuse, it is as devastating as other forms of more aggressive, overt forms of abuse. Through the ongoing lack of attention and neglect, it creates irreversible undertones of deep abandonment in the different archetypes of the Wounded Inner Child. The lack of loving attention and validation is deeply hurtful, causes great harm and has lasting effects.

The Unavailable Adult and the Over-Dramatic Child: The Over-Dramatic Child acts out in an attempt to garner attention. In its unhealthy relationship with the Unavailable Adult, the neglect and indifference of the Unavailable Adult creates a sense of abandonment. This activates the reactive conditioning of the Over-Dramatic Child. Even though the Unavailable Adult may be physically present, the lack of engagement keeps the Over-Dramatic Child grasping for some sort of unavailable connection. Because the Wounded Child cannot comprehend the apathy, it will continue to react feeling the loss that it cannot articulate.

Over time the patterns may shift, expressing various forms of passive aggressive disgust. If the Unavailable Adult continues to ignore these desperate cries, the Over-Dramatic Child may resort to more self-destructive patterns, directing the outrage and anger inwardly on itself where it will remain deeply hurt and disempowered.

The Unavailable Adult and the Misunderstood Child: The apathy of the Unavailable Adult is difficult to resolve for the Wounded Inner Child, especially since there is no apparent or obvious form of abuse. This fuels the Misunderstood Child's conditioning of turning the blame inward. It will manifest a self-imposed exile because of the shame and become deeply identified to the wound. The painful feedback loop is a direct result of the external neglect and the inability to understand the reason for it. It begins to mistrust itself and refuses to believe in a life without self-inflicted pain.

The Unavailable Adult and the Needy Child: The Unavailable Adult creates a deep emotional void in the Inner Child. The wound of unmet needs will manifest in reactive conditioning. When the Wounded Inner Child lacks mature, healthy parenting, the void is deeply felt.

Since the Needy Child craves connection from the lack of nurturing in its present environment, it attempts to counteract this sense of inner loss. However, its low self-esteem makes the Needy Child susceptible to emotional manipulation and varying levels of abuse. It prompts the Needy Child to be clingy, take unnecessary risks and willingly compromise self-respect to receive the unfulfilled love.

Without sincere caring, the Needy Child will remain in a disempowered sense of scarcity. This contractive feedback loop between the Shadow and disempowered will remain active as long as the Unavailable Adult continues its thoughtless, delinquent form of Shadow Parenting.

The Unavailable Adult and the Over-Indulged Child: The apathetic nature of the Unavailable Adult creates a massive void of accountability. This lack of caring has helped to perpetuate the reactive, out-of-control conditioning of the Over-Indulged Child. And it has filled the gap left by the Unavailable Adult with it its immature need for indulgence.

The lack of accountability in the Shadow Parenting has fueled an entitled and manipulative Over-Indulged Child with no consequences for its actions. This self-pampering combined with instant gratification and an unhealthy self-centered focus forms the basis for highly narcissistic tendencies.

Underneath the nonstop flow of excess, there is a deep desire to fill the void of caring with anything that will numb the pain of the abandonment. The overindulgence is an attempt to soothe the emptiness. The Over-Indulged Child will continue demanding attention from anywhere it can get it. And this never-ending contractive feedback loop will keep the Wounded Inner Child locked in the pattern of being unaccountable and owned by its disempowered need to be satisfied until a responsible boundary can be drawn.

The Dysfunctional Influence of The Controlling Inner Adult

The Controlling Inner Adult expresses many different patterns of manipulation that are channeled through all the various voices of the Shadow Inner Adult. The oppressive and dominating relationship between every aspect of the Shadow Inner Adult and the Wounded Inner Child is perpetuated through the ongoing control mechanisms that embody the archetype of the Controlling Inner Adult. The pattern of control always keeps the Wounded Inner Child fearful, unconsciously co-dependent and therefore disempowered.

The Controlling Inner Adult and the Over-Dramatic Child: The Over-Dramatic Child will always rebel against the patterns of the Controlling Inner Adult. It instinctually reacts to this oppressive powerplay like it does with any of the other Shadow Inner Adult Archetypes: with drama. The degree and form of it is dependent on the type of control and the specific conditioning of the Over-Dramatic Child. This expression of drama can take many forms.

Although the Over-Dramatic Child does not have enough of a maturely developed psychology to comprehend the entire scope of the abuse, especially if the control is covert, it does feel and react to this violation of power. The Over-Dramatic Child is not built to respond in a strategic or conscious manner. It is more like a natural eruption of pressure when something is suppressed long enough. The response is immature, but it does not know how to react in any way except through its dramatic nature.

Unless something more mature and conscious is introduced, the Over-Dramatic Child will ultimately stay disempowered while it is locked in this reactionary contractive feedback loop with the Controlling Inner Adult.

The Controlling Inner Adult and the Frozen Child: The Inner Child is psychologically unprepared to navigate the oppression and bombardment of abuse from the Controlling Inner Adult. In response, the Frozen Child reacts in the opposite manner of the Over-Dramatic Child. It will cower and freeze because it is completely overwhelmed and consumed by fear. This instills a deep sense of shame and guilt, because it knows that it is too scared and not mature enough to move through the fear. The Controlling Inner Adult utilizes this frozen state to continue its violation, and keeps the Frozen Child transfixed by a cycle of fear, shame and self-doubt.

The Controlling Inner Adult and the Lost Child: When the intensity of Controlling Inner Adult becomes too traumatic, the Wounded Child reacts by going into deep survival mode. As a result, it begins to exhibit the conditioning of the Lost Child.

The Lost Child finally splinters the trauma into smaller pieces and disperses them beyond its own awareness, so they are more difficult to access. This form of unconscious detachment is a result of profound trauma. The level of conscious or unconscious withdrawal of the Lost Child is in direct proportion to the degree of the control imposed. Eventually, this pattern of the Lost Child becomes an ongoing reaction to dealing with any possibility of conflict, even if the circumstance is not as severe. The potential pain is being preemptively managed, and the now habitual Lost Child patterns of escape become normalized.

The Dysfunctional Influence of The Possessive Inner Adult

The Possessive Inner Adult exhibits domination over the different aspects of the Wounded Inner Child. If the possessive patterns remain unaddressed, the oppressive behavior will continue.

This pattern exerts unwanted influence, ignores appropriate boundaries and forces the Wounded Inner Child into co-dependent and unhealthy roles to satisfy its own selfish desires. This shadow form of parenting can involve varying aspects of addiction, ownership, and objectification. It causes deep trauma and disempowerment in the different archetypes of the Wounded Inner Child.

The Possessive Inner Adult and the Over-Dramatic Child: When the Possessive Inner Adult begins to exert its possessive tendencies, the first survival reaction is from the Over-Dramatic Child. Through its various forms of "childish" drama, it communicates in every way imaginable to command the necessary attention and support.

This can take the form of passive-aggressive behavior, overt temper tantrums, and self-destructive behavior, depending on the nature of the violation. At some point, if the overt and direct expression of alarm becomes dangerous, it will revert to more covert drama for survival. As long as the dominating behavior from the Possessive Parent continues, the Over-Dramatic Child will "sound the alarm" in order to call out for support.

The Possessive Inner Adult and the Misunderstood Child: This Shadow Parent's dominating and possessive behavior is motivated by self-absorption. This aspect of the Shadow Inner Adult is devoted to easing its own pain and serving its own desires at the expense of the needs of the Wounded Inner Child. The ongoing possessiveness creates the Misunderstood Child's identification and attachment to suffering. This disempowered aspect of the Wounded Inner Child becomes accustomed to living in the wound.

The tendency for the Misunderstood Child to manifest self-imposed exile is a direct result of external oppression. The pain and suffering of the contractive feedback loop are a desperate and silent cry for help, even though the Misunderstood Child has convinced itself that it does not deserve the loving assistance. This creates the "unsolvable problem" that overshadows the Misunderstood Child's conditioning.

It also creates the pattern of hyper-sensitivity as it begins to identify to the pain in others. The identification to the wound has created a lasting effect on the Misunderstood Child, as it now tends to experience life by internalizing the pain of outer situations and relationships as its own. The attachment to pain and isolation is now deeply rooted in its conditioning.

The Possessive Inner Adult and the Needy Child: The Possessive Parent does not provide for the needs of the Wounded Inner Child. Instead, it imposes its agenda, dominates the child's experience and exploits the child's needs. This selfish pattern of Shadow Parenting is manifested in the wounds and patterns of the Needy Child. Broken, hopeless and downtrodden, the Wounded Inner Child has adapted by relentlessly seeking outward to have its needs met. The betrayal of the Possessive Parent creates a constant fear to get those needs met at any cost, and that healing and wholeness will only come from an outside event, person or experience.

Because of a deep lack of trust, the Needy Child believes that it can lose its position or safety at any moment so it will do whatever it takes to maintain that security. The Needy Child conditioning has not developed the confidence of self-reliance. Instead it models the grasping, scarcity and manipulation of the Possessive Inner Adult.

The Possessive Inner Adult and the Frozen Child: If action creates abusive attention, then maybe the violator will lose interest or see nothing it can exploit from the paralyzed inactivity. If there is a threat of abuse and the contractive feed-back loop of abuse from the Possessive Inner Adult is engaged, then the disempowered and terrified Frozen Child conditioning remains active. Unfortunately, even after the threat is gone the imprint of the terror remains and the frozen condition has now become a habitual reaction to the possible threat of any confrontation.

The Possessive Inner Adult and the Lost Child: The Lost Child is a disempowered aspect of the Wounded Inner Child pattern that is caused by the profound trauma inflicted by the Possessive Inner Adult. The level of withdrawal of the Lost Child is dependent on the degree of overbearing behavior from the Possessive Inner Adult. When a parent selfishly seeks to dominate a child's experience to satisfy their unmet desires for their own agenda, the level of betrayal is profound.

Because the Lost Child was psychologically unprepared for this dominating, contractive behavior, it fragmented painful memories, emotions, and aspects of itself into an untouchable space within its consciousness. To further protect itself, the Lost Child will also disassociate from its own fragmented memories to cover the trail. It is only when it represses the trauma, or the source of the trauma, that it can continue functioning.

This is especially painful for the child because the abuse is inflicted by a supposedly "trustworthy" adult. If the possessive patterning continues, the reactive feedback loop of escapism stays intact and the (inner or outer) Lost Child continues to feel dominated and disempowered.

PART V
EXPANSIVE CONDITIONING

AVAILABLE ADULT

attentive, engaged, beingness, holding space avaialble, present

PROTECTOR

boundaries, guardian, integrity, security, discipline, dicernment

COMPASSIONATE ADULT

tolerance, loving-kindness, sensitivity, caring, empathic, concern

MATURE INNER ADULT

conscious, mature, responsiveness, awareness, empowered, accountable, expansive

RESPONSIBLE ADULT

capable, responsive, accountable, trustworthy, action-oriented, pragmatic

NURTURER

tenderness, warmth, gentleness, affection, caring, support, cherishing

HONORING ADULT

acknowledgement, appreciation, recognition, grateful, respectful, celebration

The Mature Inner Adult

The Mature Inner Adult is the powerful, transformational aspect of expansiveness. It is the conscious flipside of the contractive Shadow Inner Adult. This maturity is not determined by age. It is a development of intentional, aware and responsive behavior that is rooted in conscious expansiveness. It only evolves with practice, cultivation and refinement. Without it, people default to their past unconscious conditioning of maturity.

The Mature Inner Adult is the embodiment of the "ideal parent, role model or adult" that you may never have experienced. That is why it is vital to continue the intentional ongoing development. Learning how to maturely re-parent yourself offers you the opportunity to re-create the inner relationship into the loving example that you have always wanted. You will not be able to sustain this example of maturity in your outside relationships until you know what it feels like to create a level of awareness of this relationship in your inner relationships.

Everyone has some level of empowerment, awareness or a strength in one of the specific Mature Inner Adult archetypes. Some people are highly responsible yet lack development in the area of inner and outer compassion and nurturing. Some are deeply caring but are unable to draw boundaries and lack inner and outer conviction and discipline. Most people settle for a certain degree of mastery in one or two of the most comfortable archetypes for themselves.

But what they do not realize is that this limits their capacity for experiencing and creating maturity in their outer relationships. They are unaware of the inactive archetypes of the Mature Inner Adult within themselves. This is the unconscious influence that causes them to seek those empowered archetypes in others. To create an effective and highly responsive Mature Inner Adult, you want to cultivate a balanced and ever-evolving relationship of deepening awareness in each of the six archetypes. Everyone has the access and ability to develop every one of these mature archetypes within them if they are committed to the process of ongoing refinement.

Society is rampant in the unconscious reactivity of the Wounded Inner Child and the Shadow Inner Adult. Conscious "maturity" is a rare and much needed commodity in relationships. The mere concept of the pop-culture phrase "Adulting," demonstrates how deeply the majority of the culture lives through the lens of the Wounded Inner Child. This fuels the resentment to behave as an emotionally aware and empowered adult.

Growing up, you are presented with many opportunities and experiences to inspire maturity. But that does not mean those invitations are realized within an individual. Maturing naturally happens as we grow up, but psychological, emotional and behavioral maturity needs to be developed and integrated through conscious introspection and empowered action. Without the practice of mature conscious behavior, it will remain unevolved and unintegrated in your daily life.

The Archetypal Conditioning of the Mature Inner Adult

Growing up is not synonymous with maturing.
Becoming an adult is a matter of age, not maturity.
Being an adult does not ensure "adult behavior."
Adult behavior is a cultivated choice and a ongoing practice.
There are too many so-called adults who are nothing more
than "grown up" disempowered children living under the guise of maturity.

The quality of mature expansiveness allows you to have engaging inner and outer connection. Maturity supports all of the other archetypes to grow and evolve. Without these qualities, it is impossible to create healthy inner and outer relationships. The understanding of which archetypal medicine of maturity is required for the Wounded Inner Child, Shadow Adult and Radiant Inner Child in any given circumstance is only learned through trial and error and by directly experiencing that remedy in action.

You cannot empower the different expressions of the Radiant Inner Child without the support of maturity. The expansive expression of maturity aligned with the "child-like" qualities of the Radiant Child, can sustain a highly evolved degree of expansiveness in your consciousness. This creates the synergistic Expansive Feedback Loop that integrates both qualities of expansiveness in an interconnected, self-regulating system.

The Available Adult: This aspect is emotionally connected and available. It "holds space" without controlling, manipulating or dominating. Considerate and respectful, it is a master in the art of observation and witnessing without interfering. It is more than simply being present. It being ready, engaged, and present if and when you are needed. The neutral acceptance and active availability support the space for powerful transformation. Availability is the first stage in the process of self-awareness.

The Compassionate Adult: This aspect of the Mature Inner Adult approaches each engagement with a sense of kindness and sensitivity. This is the expression of deeply empathic understanding of human suffering. It allows any individual to feel loved, heard and ultimately safe. True compassion is more than just tolerance. But tolerance can lead to deeper compassion. Compassion opens the heart and allows vulnerability and connection.

The Nurturer: This aspect of the Mature Inner Adult knows how to encourage a loving environment. It promotes growth and safety through expansiveness. The feminine energy of nurturing is illustrated through the archetype of the Universal Mother who stimulates evolution through nourishment, sensitivity and loving support. It embodies the feeling of being loved, adored and cherished.

The Honoring Adult: So many aspects of ourselves and our experiences are undervalued, unappreciated and therefore dishonored. This aspect of the Mature Inner Adult acknowledges and validates your inner or outer world with genuine respect and appreciation. To hold something in high esteem demonstrates reverence, respect and humility. This cherished admiration uplifts the subject of attention to a treasured position so that it is praised, strengthened and honored.

The Responsible Adult: Responsibility means the ability to respond. This aspect is never fueled by obligation or guilt. It understands responsibility as a privilege. This allows it the ability to focus on any given situation with a grounded awareness and responsiveness that results in clarity of action. This aspect embodies "practical maturity" and executes action though pragmatic sensibility.

The Protector: This aspect of the Mature Inner Adult is regarded as the eternal champion of the being. The Protector is the vigilant, discerning sentry and safeguards all facets of the Inner Child. This archetype is concerned with preservation, security and shelter. And as the keeper of the inner sanctuary, it always defends the vulnerable and valued aspects of the being. The Protector is the honorable custodian of boundaries, grounded in virtue, sustains personal integrity, and lives by a strict conduct. Empowered by duty, this loyal advocate is watchful, steadfast and confident. And like any responsible guardian or true warrior, it is a peacekeeper first and will only be fierce as a last line of engagement.

AVAILABLE ADULT

attentive, engaged, beingness, holding space avaialble, present

PROTECTOR

boundaries, guardian, integrity, security, discipline, dicernment

COMPASSIONATE ADULT

tolerance, loving-kindness, sensitivity, caring, empathic, concern

MATURE INNER ADULT

conscious, mature, responsiveness, awareness, empowered, accountable, expansive

RESPONSIBLE ADULT

capable, responsive, accountable, trustworthy, action-oriented, pragmatic

NURTURER

tenderness, warmth, gentleness, affection, caring, support, cherishing

HONORING ADULT

acknowledgement, appreciation, recognition, grateful, respectful, celebration

THE MATURE INNER ADULT
The Available Adult

It is only when you learn to be present and available with non-judgment and compassionately hold space for the wounded and broken fragments of yourself, that you are able to truly hold space for another.

Understanding the Dynamics of The Available Adult:

This aspect of the Mature Inner Adult is a truly supportive presence and offers counsel through embracing receptive non-interference. That does not mean that the Available Adult is non-engaged, uncaring or uninterested. The Available Adult expresses its caring through inconspicuously being available and lovingly observing from the background.

This conscious and expansive aspect of the Mature Inner Adult is deeply respectful and allows for individual exploration. It honors the importance of personal discovery through direct experience without interference, manipulation or influence, while offering a safe space for this to unfold naturally.

> *"Out beyond ideas of wrongdoing and rightdoing*
> *there is a field. I'll meet you there.*
> *When the soul lies down in that grass.*
> *the world is too full to talk about."*
> *– Rumi*

Whereas, the Responsible Adult is engaged in the practical action of life, the Available Adult expresses a connected beingness by holding space as a non-intrusive, overseeing but mindful advisor. This aspect of the Mature Inner Adult has mastered the balance of embodying whole-hearted availability without disruption or interference.

Being available means that your presence is indirectly felt and seen but never feels imposing. Being there as a guardian of safety and support also does not mean that any action is required. You know the Available Adult is present when its support is never consciously felt because it feels so integrated with the entire container of safety that was created. This requires deep humility to step out of the limelight and not require some sort of validation for all that is done on behalf of upholding that expansive space. There are many vocations that practice this humble and silent devotion and many people never even notice their contribution or influence, despite its importance.

The Qualities of the Empowered Available Adult:

- **Engaged, connected and present but non-attached**
- **Approachable, welcoming, receptive when asked**
- **Remains a present, but noninvasive guide that is on-hand when called upon**
- **Does not interfere, dominate, control or push their own agenda**
- **Offers non-intrusive suggestions, supportive guidance and loving invitations**
- **Allows people permission to trust their own intuition and wisdom**
- **Gives guidance and help with humility and thoughtfulness**
- **Creates a supportive, nonjudgmental container for exploration**
- **Allows people to have their own opinions and make their own decisions**
- **People feel safe, expansive, vulnerable and open in their presence**
- **They are peacefully aware, connected and perceptive of their surroundings**
- **Deeply empathic and considerate and accommodating of the needs of others**
- **Adaptable to change, goes with the flow, is agreeable and flexible**
- **Available Adults tend to be present in the "now" moment (not the past or future)**
- **Skilled at watchfulness, witnessing, observation and mindful presence**
- **Adept at holding space for another without needing acknowledgment**
- **Empowers self-discovery, autonomy and confidence through supportive supervision**

Being available is the foundation of all healing and transformation: No transformation can occur without some level of inner availability. To shift your relationship to any of the fragmented aspects of your corrupted psychology requires an empowered Available Adult. The balance of non-interference and presence empowers space for potential transformation. Being "willing to be willing" creates an open field of receptivity that allows for all possibilities of growth. Being available as an objective and accepting witness to transformation creates the validation and safety the uncertainty of the healing process requires.

The delicate balance of being available but not interfering: The Available Adult delicately balances the experience of being present and available through non-interference. For some, this is natural and effortless. But for others it requires a constant check on personal preferences and agendas to serve the needs of the greater good and the bigger picture.

Cultivating safety through a neutral expression of presence: One of the most profound gifts that the Available Adult can offer is the gift of acceptance in a container of non-interference and non-judgment. This allows any fragmented aspect from your psyche or another to feel secure. The state of feeling "safe" is the condition of being shielded from harm or outer influence. The Available Adult cultivates the space that allows for safety to flourish because of its neutrality. That sense of presence and availability cultivates the perfect environment for connection without interference.

Being available to experiencing inner and outer radiance: Our familiar conditioning defaults to the small version of ourselves that does not allow us to be available to our own radiance. We do this for reasons of comfort and predictability. It can be exceedingly difficult to be present to the expansive expressions of the Radiant Inner Child.

If you are going to develop a deeper relationship to your own radiant nature, then you need to be willing to bask in your own beauty. There is no bypassing availability. At some point, if you want to evolve, you must "let go" and be present with the direct experience of yourself. The Available Adult unravels the outdated survival pattern of conditioned unworthiness as well as the false modesty that prevents people from evolving. Once you can stabilize the process of holding space and allowing for the permeation of your own Radiant Inner Child, you will then also be capable to hold space for those evolving expressions of radiance in others.

Availability is expansive but not always comfortable: Sincerely holding space for any process of resolution can be uncomfortable. Conscious neutrality allows for everything to unfold without interference. Everything. But being deeply connected increases sensitivity, which can also mean that you can be deeply affected by the unfolding drama of the circumstance. The maturity of the Available Adult allows you to be present and be affected but not thrown off center. Availability centers your presence in the eye of the storm.

> *"When listening to another person, don't just listen with your mind,*
> *listen with your whole body. Feel the energy field of your inner body as you listen.*
> *That takes attention away from thinking and creates a still space*
> *that enables you to truly listen without the mind interfering.*
> *You are giving the other person space —space to be.*
> *It is the most precious gift you can give."*
> – Eckhart Tolle

Holding space: To truly be available requires sincere intention, clarity and compassionate presence. To cultivate this container, the Available Adult must be willing to set aside preference, personal opinions, judgments, and agendas. Only then can you offer genuine love and support, give gentle guidance when it is needed, and make an individual feel safe especially when they falter or make mistakes. Holding space is not martyrdom. This is not the same experience as "giving away your power" out of personal sacrifice. Availability is never contractive or disempowering.

Holding space is something that we need to develop in ourselves before we can genuinely be available for others. The experience is also referred to as holding "sacred" space. This sense of respect and reverence refers to the quality of the presence that is offered by the Available Adult.

This experience of holding sacred space can be applied to any aspect of your being (Wounded Inner Child or the Radiant Child) or to an individual in the outer world. The experience will only be as transformative, safe and sacred as the Available Adult's depth, clarity and intention which will vary in different individuals and also in different circumstances.

Some advice, perspective and techniques for effectively holding space:

1. **Cultivate a supportive container:** What is a supportive container? This idea will differ from person to person. It is important to consider the qualities that define a supportive container for you. What are the values that you consider when holding space for yourself or another? Consider qualities like receptivity, compassion and safety.

   What is important to you may not be as important to another. Clarifying those specific values of what you need the container to look and feel like engenders trust and honesty. This will make a significant difference in the quality of holding space. Be clear with your intentions. These intentions and qualities are the foundation that supports the framework.

2. **Give permission for an individual (or an aspect of self) to express the range of emotional experience:** When people feel genuinely respected, they feel safe to allow their emotional world to surface. The Available Adult not only allows this expression but nurtures it. The depth to which an individual will be vulnerable is determined by their level of inner clarity and ability to "go there."

3. **Gently offer new information at a pace and quantity that can handled:** This level of vulnerability can be overwhelming to anyone who has not experienced the supportive expansiveness of this kind of space. One may not be able to handle a significant amount of information or be able to receive and integrate that data at an accelerated pace. Relax, slow down, tune in and pay attention to what is in front of you, what is needed and what can be handled. Less is more. A wise space holder knows when to temper guidance because it can make a person feel inadequate. This same kind of attentiveness applies within.

4. **Allow the individual to lead the process:** When we take personal decision-making power out of people's hands, they become disempowered. If you are truly listening, you will see that the individual is offering cues to what they need. Allow those indicators to guide the way. It is their process, and you are the non-invasive, receptive guide. There will be circumstances when you need to offer differing opinions, but it is important that you allow them to lead the way.

5. **Allow people's perspective to be based on their own direct experience:** Every person's life experience has shaped their perspective. This may lead them to make choices or have beliefs that you would never consider. Everyone should be allowed to have their own view of their experience, even if you do not agree with it. They may make choices based on family, generational or cultural norms that you may not have the context to understand. When holding space, release the need for everyone to behave in the same manner. Honor those differences. This unique perspective is what creates diversity. Holding space is not about conformity.

6. **Feel safe enough to allow yourself and others to "fail":** Whenever anyone is actively engaged in self-exploration, it is inevitable that there will be mistakes. Failure is not only healthy, but essential to the process of evolution. It means that you are actively engaged in the process. This experience allows for internal feedback which can open deeper introspection, an adjustment of perspective, more refinement and modification of behavior.

Knowing what does not work is as important as knowing what works. If seen from an expansive perspective, failure can offer some profound insight. Therefore, when holding space, we give permission to fail without offering judgment or potential shaming. Have the tenacity to keep going even when falling short of a goal or desired outcome. Many people have unrealistic expectations for themselves and choose to be unforgiving of their mistakes, but it is all part of the learning process.

7. **The necessity of ongoing self-purification:** In holding space for others, it is inevitable that your unresolved issues will be triggered by what is being mirrored in the other person. It is imperative that you are conscious of your conditioning and engaged in self-purification to "clean up" what was brought up for you. You become effective at holding space when you relate to the experience of being triggered. You must practice what to do for yourself to get back to center before, during and after holding space with another. How can you be expected to help someone else go through their process of self-purification by creating a supportive "sacred" space if you are unable to work out your own issues in the process?

    If you ever find holding space to be exhausting, or you feel a sense of resentment, it is because something unconscious is arising within you that needs to be resolved. Many people spend a lot of time holding space for others as a distraction for their own issues. They believe they are in alignment and in a clear state of mind but are subversively repressing their own issues because they have resistance to facing their own dysfunction.

8. **Holding space without distraction, self-sacrifice, or personal agenda:**
    When you are consciously or unconsciously sacrificing your own time, repressing or denying your own process, or giving away your vital life energy, you are not helping anyone, no matter how it appears. That is not holding space. You might fool yourself into believing that your self-sacrifice is helping another, but neither will benefit when you give up on yourself.

    Of course, it is always affirming and fulfilling to help someone – it feels good. But that should not be the sole motivation, especially if it is secretly disguising a coping mechanism. This is an unconscious, self-serving agenda.

    When you are truly acting without agenda you will not become exhausted. You will not be overcome with the drama of an individual's process. When you radiate this authenticity, you will cultivate a powerful atmosphere for safety, healing, transformation and personal exploration.

Watchfulness, witnessing, overseeing, observation and mindful presence: True observation is paying attention to everything that is happening without the need to judge. This mindful presence creates the neutrality that is necessarily to be non-attached to any unfolding process.

When a level of authentic acceptance is present, there is no need to "tolerate" anything. Practice accepting "what is" and explore the idea of observation without preference or emotional charge. This skill allows the Available Adult to be connected to what is going on without having to be actively engaged in a contractive way.

*"To me, holding space is about stopping and absorbing the environment
or the information I am receiving, not thinking about the future or the past
but sitting in the 'now.' To hold space, or to 'deep listen,'
is to be in a space of healing or deep connection."*
— Jamie Marloo Thomas

Being "available" is deep listening in the present moment: You can never be truly available if your attention is lost in the past or projected into the future. Being present in the present moment is the essence of availability. Everything that is unfolding in the moment can only be supported by an empowered, expansive presence. Once that centered presence has been established, that receptive space ("deep listening") allows for this aspect of the Mature Inner Adult to be responsive to what is needed. Never underestimate the potential of what can naturally unfold by holding this sacred space in the inner and outer world. The profundity of life is available to you when you are in the moment.

Being flexible, adaptable to change and going with the flow: This "deep listening" is what allows the Available Adult to be flexible to what is needed and respond accordingly. The only constant in the universe is change, and therefore no supportive space is ever static. An ineffective "space holder" may get into trouble if they become attached to the space that they created.

Being available to any situation is never going to be linear or predictable. Tap into the direct experience of what is suitable for that particular person or circumstance. Any inflexibility only gets in the way of the Available Adult being an effective custodian. Being available means being "available to accept organic change" and going with the flow of the unfolding natural evolution. This change could take many forms. It could be an expression of shifting the dynamics support, offering new invitations, coming forward or stepping back… Whatever happens or however that manifestation occurs, the Available Adult is always responding to the environment and the people within it. The Available Adult will adapt how it needs to show up to keep the container as expansive as possible without interference.

Like any devoted caretaker, meeting these potential challenges is never a burden because the Available Adult has lovingly accepted its responsibilities and understands the importance of its role in the bigger picture.

The gift of being available to yourself: Being available to yourself is imperative before you can be truly available for another. When you are a truly sovereign being, you are independent, self-governing and self-sufficient. When you are available to another, you radiate the depth of that quality.

The expression of availability can take on different forms: paying attention to your inner and outer needs or experiences, your changing internal states, emotions, unprocessed pain, trauma, inner dialogue and anything else occurring within your inner ecosystem.

In some cases, you may allow yourself to be available for an aspect of your Wounded Inner Child, an unowned belief or even a reclaimed memory. You may also allow yourself to honor an intuitive feeling that emerges from within. You can hold yourself in a loving space of acceptance as you go through the different internal processes of growth as you continue to evolve.

Examples of Affirmations that Empower the Available Adult:

"I give myself permission to be lovingly available to all aspects of myself."
"I am always present, available and respectful to all of my emotions, feelings and thoughts."
"I am always available to myself before I am available to another."
"I am present with what is happening in me, around me and through me right now."

AVAILABLE ADULT

attentive, engaged,
beingness, holding space
avaialble, present

COMPASSIONATE ADULT

tolerance, loving-kindness,
sensitivity, caring,
empathic, concern

PROTECTOR

boundaries, guardian,
integrity, security,
discipline, dicernment

MATURE
INNER ADULT

conscious, mature,
responsiveness, awareness,
empowered, accountable,
expansive

RESPONSIBLE ADULT

capable, responsive,
accountable, trustworthy,
action-oriented, pragmatic

NURTURER

tenderness, warmth,
gentleness, affection,
caring, support, cherishing

HONORING ADULT

acknowledgement,
appreciation, recognition,
grateful, respectful,
celebration

THE MATURE INNER ADULT
The Compassionate Adult

"Love and compassion are necessities, not luxuries.
Without them humanity cannot survive."
– Dali Lama

Understanding the Dynamics of The Compassionate Adult:

The Compassionate Adult embodies the most expansive qualities of selflessness, compassion, and altruism. Compassion has been explored worldwide in almost every religious tradition because its principles are considered to be some of the greatest of all human virtues.

This powerfully expansive expression has been studied by a wide range of scientists, psychologists, philosophers, spiritualists and metaphysicians throughout the ages. In our modern culture and society that continues to become more desensitized and disconnected to the essence of our inherent humanity, this vital aspect of the Mature Inner Adult is more important than ever.

The word "compassion" is derived from ancient Latin roots: com (with) + passus or patiens (one who suffers) meaning to be "in love together with or for the one who suffers." Compassion is experienced through a connected equality of "feeling with another." It is the precursor to empathy which refers more to "feeling as another."

Compassion is an altruistic expression of our natural human state. It is not so much something that we need to acquire as much as it is something we need to realize. It has been said that the greatest experience of inner tranquility comes from the development of love and compassion.

The Key Components of Compassion:

1. **A sincere awareness of suffering:** For sincere compassion to occur, there must be a cognitive (mental understanding) and empathic (emotional connection) awareness of the suffering. Without this openness, compassion cannot arise. In many cases, an individual will be so desensitized to their own or another's suffering that it makes it extremely difficult for a sincere connection to occur. They may cognitively acknowledge this pain but remain emotionally distant.

2. **Being sympathetically affected by suffering**: When an individual is "affected," it is another way of saying that one is having a direct experience of empathy relating to the suffering or pain before them. It has been proven that the more direct personal experiences that one has, the more difficult it becomes to ignore the natural human expression of compassion.

3. **The desire to see the relief of pain or suffering:** Even with the above components in place, one can acknowledge suffering and still not have enough resolve to do things differently. Compassion resolves itself to see the relief of suffering.

4. **The ability to actively respond to suffering:** This is the final stage in the full expression of compassion. This combines the emotional and mental acknowledgement and the intention to act. There is an integrity in the responsive action because it authentically reflects the now personalized experience.

The human need for love and compassion through interdependence:
Interdependence is a fundamental law of nature. All forms of life survive by some form of mutual co-operation based on an inherent recognition of their interconnectedness. The most subtle level of material phenomena is also governed by this principle. From this innate interdependency, an instinctual level of compassion naturally arises.

The need for compassion is the foundation of human existence. Under normal circumstances, any individual who is isolated from human connection for too long can become psychologically traumatized. The support and compassion of others is imperative to thrive. Compassion through interdependence is at the very core of our continued human development.

The Qualities of the Empowered Compassionate Adult:

- **Demonstrates a sincere expression of loving-kindness, gentleness and tenderness**
- **Does not attempt to convert, change or manipulate another's perspective**
- **Holds a general sense of equality and equanimity for all things**
- **Expresses a high degree of sensitivity, empathy and connection to others**
- **Does not exhibit a superior, patronizing or condescending position**
- **Open-hearted, vulnerable and authentic**
- **Practices inclusion and inter-connectedness instead of exclusion and separation**
- **Exhibits a welcoming, accepting and non-judgmental persona**
- **Motivated by altruistic, unselfish attitudes and beliefs**
- **Does not expect payment, acknowledgment or validation for their behavior**
- **Cultivates an attitude and behavior of sincere appreciation and gratefulness**
- **Expresses a sense of selflessness and willingness to give assistance to alleviate suffering**

The difference between empathy, sympathy and pity: When examining the qualities of compassion, the terms sympathy, empathy and pity are interchanged and misunderstood.

- **Empathy:** The ability to fully experience, feel and share another person's emotions. It is also the action of vicariously experiencing those feelings in an objectively explicit or direct manner. The ability to imagine oneself and/or relate as another person is a somewhat sophisticated intuitive process. The basic capacity to recognize emotions is inherent in the human condition and can occur unconsciously or consciously through connection.

- **Sympathy:** This occurs when you are sorry about someone else's grief or misfortune, and while you can relate to their pain, you do not share their experience as you would with empathy. Sympathy involves a level of emotional distancing. In order for the experience of sympathy to occur, certain conditions must be present. There must be a belief that the individual is in a varying degree of pain.

- **Pity**: It is the least engaged and connected experience (far less than empathy, sympathy, or compassion), amounting to little more than a conscious acknowledgement of someone's pain. It can be described as a feeling of internal discomfort at the distress of an individual and can have insincere and condescending overtones. When you feel pity for someone, you feel superior to them or their situation. There is a subtle or not so subtle element of "looking down" or "feeling sorry" for the plight of that particular individual, group or circumstance.

Compassion is always non-violent: Compassion is always peaceful, gentle, non-violent and non-aggressive. It is vital for the healing process. It allows one to feel supported by tenderness and loving nourishment. Contraction never heals contraction. You can never truly heal a wound created from toxicity or violence with more aggression or violence. Everyone longs to feel the expansive, heartful solace that only gentle loving-kindness can provide.

The relationship between courage, vulnerability and compassion: It takes courage to be compassionate. It is easy to become jaded, desensitized and comfortably numb. This "deadened state of caring" is a protective mechanism to manage the relentlessly broadcasted pain and suffering in the world. Anyone can instantly access countless examples of human suffering. To be compassionate, you must boldly challenge the collective denial of suffering.

> *"From caring comes courage."*
> *— Lao Tzu*

When you allow yourself to connect, feel and empathize with suffering, you must become vulnerable. And it takes a tremendous amount of courage to do that and take empowered compassionate action.

Compassion is more than simply tolerating: When someone "tolerates" something, it implies temporary patience in enduring a particular circumstance. (It can also suggest a subtle level of arrogance as you are tolerating a less evolved or immature behavior.) And though it is true that cultivating tolerance can open the door to feeling true compassion, they are not the same thing. Authentic compassion does not require strained effort. It does not require struggle to maintain. It resonates from a deeper expression of empathy from within. Tolerance is always cultivated through personal will, while inherent compassion arises effortlessly through sincere empathetic human connection.

Compassion is beyond emotions: The profoundly intuitive aspect of authentic compassion is deeper than emotion. It is an unprompted, and completely organic expression of human connection that can include but also transcend the emotional plane. This feeling arises from deep within the being, beyond the relative human psyche or the individual personality. And although it can include the empathic experience of the emotional suffering of another, true compassion can also transcend that. It takes place beyond the concept of individual separation. It is completely effortless without planning, assessment, strategy or a plan, as an individual simply and organically acts in the situation with the appropriately humane response.

Even though one can create a container to facilitate compassion, the act itself is instinctual. All beings can relate to the experience of suffering and have a desire to alleviate that suffering for themselves or another.

Authentic compassion does not require outer acknowledgement: We respond to the suffering of others because we recognize that we are not separate from them. If there is a personal agenda, the expectation of gaining something in return, some sort of debt owed, or future favor expected, then it is not compassion. If this is the case, a personal agenda is present, and the ego is involved. As the Compassionate Adult, the expression of generosity to yourself or another has no hidden expectation of payback, because alleviating suffering is the reward.

"Selflessness is self-benefiting… It is one of the most beautiful compensations of life that no man can sincerely try to help another without helping himself."
– *Ralph Waldo Emerson*

Self-sacrifice vs selflessness: Sometimes the merit of a compassionate act is mis-measured by the extent of the personal sacrifice. Somehow the level you are willing to sacrifice elevates the act as a more noble, unselfish deed. But an unselfish act does not require sacrifice to qualify as a compassionate one. Acting compassionately towards another may be inconvenient, but if you have acted at the expense of yourself, then you are giving your Wounded Inner Child the message that concern for another's wellbeing is more important than your own.

Compassion is an expansive act of responsiveness. Self-sacrifice, regardless of justification, is always fueled by scarcity. If you give at the expense of yourself and create suffering for yourself, then you have not alleviated suffering. Instead, you have simply "taken on" the suffering of another.

Compassion is not delusion or denial: There is no requirement that you have to "like" everyone to be compassionate. Being compassionate is a benevolent expression of empathy towards another despite their flaws, but it does not mean denying or minimizing the existence of those flaws. You can actively dislike someone and at the same time feel great compassion for them. You don't have to pretend that you are unaffected by the behavior of another, nor do you have to establish a personal friendship or relationship with someone to feel compassionate towards them.

You also do not need to romanticize the illusion that all people behave lovingly with a sense of morality and kindness. Acceptance and compassion are not the same as delusion or denial. It is powerful to be compassionate towards another and still acknowledge their capacity for non-loving behavior. That does not diminish your experience of caring.

Strength and compassion are not mutually exclusive: The thought that one must trade in their personal strength for compassion is wrong. Compassion does not require an all-pervasive demeanor of passivity that expresses gentle loving-kindness at all times. Though there is no denying that these are beautiful qualities of compassion, this misconception can lead to an insincere, idealized expression.

Compassion can also be expressed with a sense of stern determination, fortitude and unwavering "tough love." True strength requires vigor, durability and moral empowerment. And a form of that is the necessary drive to sustain compassion.

Self-kindness is necessary to further develop deeper compassion: Self-kindness leads to self-compassion. Those who practice this principle are more motivated to not only improve themselves, but assist others. Self-compassion is the first step in changing any destructive or contractive behavior within. There is only a certain level of compassion an individual can express if they do not acknowledge their own pain and suffering. To deepen compassion, one must be introspective and self-examining, or they become inauthentic in their outward expression of compassion.

> *"Self-compassion is the key to becoming a more compassionate person overall. It's hard to feel for other people something we don't feel for ourselves."*
> *– Lisa Firestone, Ph.D.*

The Compassionate Adult holds great empathy and love for the dysfunction and contractive behavior of the unconscious, immature and contractive aspects of the Shadow Inner Adult. True healing can only take hold and be sustained when true compassion is present.

Compassion requires an awareness and presence in the moment: When you're exercising compassion, you are always expressing yourself in the moment. You must be present to be responsive and connected in order to do so. This presence is crucial because it allows one to be "in compassion" rather than being reflective or analytical. Intellectualizing distracts you from the moment. Being fully present allows an individual to develop an intimate relationship to the direct experience without losing consciousness. It is highly unlikely that any individual would "react" unconsciously from a true place of compassion because a full and conscious awareness is required to inspire the experience.

Compassionate people act on their empathy: The next important step in a compassionate life is action. Or "giving back." A small act of kindness can turn a life around. Our words and actions have consequences that we can never wholly foresee for ourselves and for others. Compassionate people instinctively and intuitively act on their kindness, through volunteering, just being there for someone, or by offering help. This generates deeper expansion and creates an innately human connection.

> *"If you want others to be happy, practice compassion.*
> *If you want to be happy, practice compassion."*
> *– Dali Lama*

Examples of Affirmations that Empower the Compassionate Adult:

"I always respond to my inner and outer world with loving-kindness."
"I give myself permission to give and receive gentle and supportive compassion."
"I have compassion and patience for my perceived faults."
"I am always open and tender with my own woundedness."
"I allow myself to recognize the strength and courage in my vulnerability."

MATURE
INNER ADULT

conscious, mature,
responsiveness, awareness,
empowered, accountable,
expansive

AVAILABLE ADULT

attentive, engaged,
beingness, holding space
avaialble, present

PROTECTOR

boundaries, guardian,
integrity, security,
discipline, dicernment

COMPASSIONATE ADULT

tolerance, loving-kindness,
sensitivity, caring,
empathic, concern

RESPONSIBLE ADULT

capable, responsive,
accountable, trustworthy,
action-oriented, pragmatic

NURTURER

tenderness, warmth,
gentleness, affection,
caring, support, cherishing

HONORING ADULT

acknowledgement,
appreciation, recognition,
grateful, respectful,
celebration

THE MATURE INNER ADULT
The Nurturer

The conscious practice of nurturing inspires and activates the recognition of our innate capacity. The experience awakens a biological, emotional, psychological and spiritual memory of our natural tendency.

Understanding the Dynamics of The Nurturer:

The word "nurturing" is derived from the Latin verb *nutrire* which means "to suckle" or "to nourish." Almost all mammals in the animal kingdom offer their offspring the option to breast-feed. This physical act of nourishment also offers the newborn a feeling of connection, safety, emotional and psychological nurturing. It is an inherent expression of devotion and sustains survival at the most basic level.

Not only does the Nurturer provide a sense of sustaining nourishment on all levels, it includes the more abstract idea of providing support. For example, the concept of nurturing a child's creativity and development. The idea of nurturing can also apply to cultivating something in your mind or consciousness by holding or being with it for a period of time (like nurturing an idea or dream, for instance) in order to allow for its healthy manifestation and full maturity.

The idea of nurturing may seem like common sense to most, but the concept of nurturing can be subjective. What may be nurturing for one is not necessarily nurturing for another. Each person has unique personal conditioning, history, personality, body, emotional experiences, thought processes, humor, imagination… etc. Therefore, the way each person expresses and experiences personal nurturing will also be unique. It is important to connect to the personal expression of nurturing that is authentic to you. Knowing what nourishes and revitalizes you is imperative for any individual to know and give conscious nurturing to themselves or another. Honoring this unique experience is an act of self-respect and self-love.

There can be no true growth without nurturing: The inherent nature of any form of growth is always expansive. And expansion inspires more expansion. Any real and sustainable personal growth will only ever be achieved with genuine expansive and uplifting nourishment. The different forms of nurturing are the active ingredients that support, encourage and inspire evolution.

Though it is true that toxicity, negativity and contraction can inspire someone to pause, reflect and make a different decision or choose a new course of action, even that new alternative or choice still requires active, expansive nourishment in order to reach its full potential.

The Qualities of the Empowered Nurturer:

- **Exhibits sincere loving attention, encouragement and supportive feedback**
- **Exhibits and fosters emotional awareness and emotional intelligence**
- **Focused on spending quality time with people**
- **Shares genuine warmth, gentleness, and kind demonstration of caring**
- **Nurturing is inspired from a space of empathy and compassion**
- **Openly and frequently voices expression of care, concern and love**
- **Openly shares nurturing physical attention and care**
- **Expresses an overall uplifting and expansive attitude towards people and life**
- **Shows kind, consistent and honest communication**
- **Openly expresses emotional support, validation, and compliments**
- **Encourages your dreams, goals and visions**
- **Shares love through emotional and physical intimacy**
- **Exhibits an authentic, warm pleasant demeanor**
- **Is present and connected in the moment**
- **Able to adapt to the unique individual needs of different people**
- **Is able to offer "mothering without smothering"**
- **Demonstrates and cultivates active listening skills, and allows be people to be heard**

Feeling your own pain is an act of nurturing: One of the most profound forms of self-nurturing is giving yourself the permission and space to process your pain. All healing is sustained through nurturing and support. One of the most potentially uncomfortable but devoted expressions of self-love you can offer yourself is to be fully available for this level of support. By holding space (through the Available Adult) combined with loving nourishment (through the Nurturer), this beautiful act of self-love can create the secure and safe environment and the kindhearted nurturing to heal all wounds.

It should be noted that you will find it difficult to authentically support this process in another if you have never given yourself permission to experience this depth of inner self-nurturing.

Nurturing is empowered by conscious choice: Your default conditioning may not be loving-kindness and self-care. As a result, an unhealthy interpretation of nurturing rules the consciousness. At first, it can be devastating to acknowledge the corrupted relationship to what you thought was nurturing.

But a healthy inner and outer expression of nurturing will only become an integrated behavior in your life through recognition, practice and refinement. The expansive experience of it must be re-established as an ongoing, conscious choice.

Like any new behavior, you do not wake up one day and instantly become masterful at nurturing yourself or others because you have decided that you will be this way. It must be cultivated. A conscious choice that you repeat again and again until it becomes integrated as part of your behavior.

Practicing being nurturing teaches you how to nurture more deeply. You begin to realize that the practice of nurturing inspires and activates the recognition of our innate capacity to do so. The experience awakens a biological, emotional, psychological and spiritual memory of our natural tendency.

Understanding the Different Forms of Nurturing

This aspect of the Mature Inner Adult is essential for healthy inner and outer development. Your level and experience of nurturing will deeply impact the nature of all the relationships throughout your life. It occurs on various levels of consciousness and is deeply empowering for your growth. Below are some of the examples of nurturing that can be applied to all the different aspects of your whole being:

Physical Nurturing: This form of nurturing is the most obvious because it involves all aspects of the physical experience. Some examples of the physical world of nurturing include:

- **Physical touch** (all forms of loving human connection)
- **Food and meals** (gardening, farming and crop cultivation)
- **Physical health** (physical diet, stress, sleep, activity and exercise)
- **Animals and pets** (wild and domesticated, relationships with different animals)
- **Re-connecting to the Earth** (nurturing through nature)
- **Creating your physical sanctuary** (the personal expression of your physical environment)

Mental Nurturing: This form of nurturing focuses on all things relating to the mind or to your mental functioning. Examples of mental nurturing include:

- **Choosing an expansive mindset** (positive baseline from which you think)
- **Healthy and frequent exercising of the mind**
- **Maintaining an expansive and nurturing "mind-diet"** (what you feed your mind)
- **Cultivating your expansive internal voice**
- **Fostering your creativity** (a creative outlet that allows you to focus the mind)
- **Nurturing your intellectual curiosity** (exploring new engaging ideas)

Emotional Nurturing: Your emotional experience is one of the most powerful sensory tools you have as a human to empathically connect to yourself and to your experience in the outer world. Nurturing this aspect of your being is vital for healthy relationships. It has also been proven that the degree of emotional awareness and your ability to use that experience heavily impacts your choices and decision-making process. In a world that offers the bombarding temptation to distract yourself from how you feel, nurturing this aspect of your being can create unprecedented empowerment.

- **Allow yourself to feel the full spectrum of your emotional experience**
- **Develop an emotional language** (learn to speak using feeling-based language)
- **Practice articulating your emotional experience** (describing the expereince)
- **Connect to the emotional body-sensory experience** (somatic or body sensations)
- **Do not judge what you are feeling** (your feelings are all valid – even though they may be uncomfortable)

One of the most powerful and emotionally nurturing things you can do for yourself is allow yourself to feel your own pain.

Cultivating your emotional awareness
through your authentic and direct experience of feelings
is one of the most powerful means to access and awaken your innerconnection.

Psychological Nurturing: Your psychological state refers to your inner and outer behavior that is associated to your conditioning and your beliefs. There is a simple formula: (thought + emotion = belief). In this formula, the thought and the emotional charge or association can be either contractive or expansive (negative or positive). Those building blocks of belief make up the patterns that define your behavior.

Everyone has some level of foundational conditioning that they have acquired through their development and powerful associations to those patterns. But many have never examined if their existing programming is serving them in an expansive manner. A big part of psychological nurturing is to, without judgment, cultivate a conscious awareness of those beliefs and begin to discern what part of the "conditioned software" serves and then adjust your behavior accordingly to match that inner relationship. Here are some ways to nurture the psychological aspects of your being:

- **Nurture awareness of your present inner conditioning and existing behavior**
- **Observe inner conditioning without judgment**
- **Nurture new patterns that are more supportive and expansive**
- **Be gentle with yourself as you let go of the outdated conditioning**
- **Be patient and nurturing as you practice new inner and outer behaviors**

Spiritual Nurturing: Nurturing your connection to your source is a profound experience. When you do this, you are making a conscious intention to access the deepest aspects of your being. When you engage in spiritual pursuits or practices that access this potential within, you are engaging in the purest form of self-love. It is impossible to access and cultivate your spiritual awareness without nurturing.

For example, you cannot make a rose open faster by yelling at it. The rose will flower into full bloom in its own time. What you can do is cultivate a nurturing environment to offer the supporting elements it requires by adding nutrients to the soil, pulling the weeds, watering, pruning and so forth. And in time, the flower will bloom. If you fail to nurture the process, the environment and provide the nutrients it requires, you may damage or even kill the plant or cause stunted growth that does not express the inherent potential of the bloom.

Spiritual nurturing can look different for everyone, because everyone has a unique relationship to accessing their inner world. There are some things that can be done to nurture this experience, to promote a natural unfolding of consciousness instead of unconsciously sabotaging and disallowing your inherent spiritual development.

- **Be understanding that you are nurturing a journey and a process**
- **Acknowledge and invite a deeper spiritual reality**
- **Listen to and follow your inner voice or intuition**
- **Nurture spiritual practices that are in alignment**
- **Allow your relationship to your spiritual reality to change as you evolve**
- **Allow your inner and outer behavior to authentically reflect your process**
- **Allow your direct experience to be your guide**
- **Nurture your dreams and vision**
- **Seek assistance from a guide or teacher that you feel is in spiritual alignment with you**

Examples of Affirmations that Empower the Nurturer:

"I give myself permission to be kind, gentle and supportive to all aspects of myself."
"I accept, receive and embrace nurturing from everywhere."
"I lovingly nurture all of my perceived faulty, broken and wounded parts."
"I deserve to be nurtured and accepted without judgment or conditions."
"I allow myself to be tender and gentle to myself and others."

AVAILABLE ADULT

attentive, engaged,
beingness, holding space
avaialble, present

COMPASSIONATE ADULT

tolerance, loving-kindness,
sensitivity, caring,
empathic, concern

PROTECTOR

boundaries, guardian,
integrity, security,
discipline, dicernment

MATURE
INNER ADULT

conscious, mature,
responsiveness, awareness,
empowered, accountable,
expansive

RESPONSIBLE ADULT

capable, responsive,
accountable, trustworthy,
action-oriented, pragmatic

NURTURER

tenderness, warmth,
gentleness, affection,
caring, support, cherishing

HONORING ADULT

acknowledgement,
appreciation, recognition,
grateful, respectful,
celebration

THE MATURE INNER ADULT
The Honoring Adult

*Honoring is a conscious form of respect. It uplifts, values and celebrates
with magnanimity, deep appreciation and dignity.*

Understanding the Dynamics of the Honorable Adult:

The word "honor" is derived from a Latin word which refers to a perceived quality
of worthiness and respectability. This affects both the social standing and the self-
evaluation of an individual or a group. It relates to one's personal dignity and
character. The idea of self-honoring is closely related to the idea of self-esteem. The
word "esteem" finds its roots in the meaning of "value" and "worth."

Honoring is about celebrating value through acknowledgement. This expansive
expression is a form of treasured recognition. It can also be an elevated form of deep
respect. Most people do not recognize the importance of honoring themselves, their
Inner Child, their experiences, their achievements, and their time with any conscious
intention.

In a society that does little self-honoring, as a result, few people have an empowered
Honoring Adult that consciously uplifts, upholds and strengthens qualities and aspects
of the being. This results in a lack of self-respect and low self-esteem.

Living an honorable life: The idea of an honorable character is not as acknowledged
as it was in the past. Because of a growing "casualness" and a relaxed approach
to life, combined with the disconnection to the ideals that honor represents, the
Honoring Adult is undervalued. As a result, this aspect of the Mature Inner Adult goes
unrecognized and is disempowered as an active and conscious "code of upstanding
moral conduct" in the inner and outer worlds.

Being honorable can be defined as someone who believes in telling the truth and
doing the right thing because it is right. An honorable person is also decent, kind,
humble, noble, dignified, self-assured, compassionate, courageous and a walking
example of honoring their word and living their truth.

The qualities of the empowered Honoring Adult:

- **Consciously honors and accepts compliments**
- **Offers sincere acknowledgements and compliments to others**
- **Respectful and honoring of the different aspects of their being**
- **Consciously listens with attention and respect**
- **Apologizes and makes amends where appropriate**
- **Sincerely celebrates accomplishments**
- **Exudes self-esteem, composure and confidence**
- **Can appreciate and respect differences without making them wrong**
- **Accepts defeat gracefully**
- **Less affected by others' opinions or perceptions**
- **Demonstrates a high degree of integrity and honesty**
- **Keeps their word and is trustworthy**
- **Practices self-compassion and self-appreciation**
- **Not prone or seduced by comparison**
- **Lives by a set of internal and external principles**
- **Embraces faults, past mistakes and errors**
- **Does not focus on expectations and the illusion of perfection**
- **Appreciates the inherent value in all people**
- **Demonstrates a conscious level of self-respect**

Recognizing your own uniqueness: The key to developing self-respect begins by acknowledging your own uniqueness. When you realize that you are completely unique you can appreciate how truly special you are. This also applies to your contractive conditioning, wounds and survival patterns. All these fragments, facets, qualities from the unique expansive and contractive combination creates the diverse multi-verse of you. All aspects of you are worthy of appreciation and self-honor:

- **Your unique physical body is the vessel and vehicle to express yourself**
- **Your thoughts are unique to you and deserve attention and examination**
- **Allow your ideas to be considered, appreciated and explored**
- **Investigate, acknowledge and value the full spectrum of your emotional body**
- **Your wants and desires deserve to be felt, examined and explored**
- **When you value your needs, you are acknowledging a deeper message from within you**

"When self-esteem is the problem;
self-respect is the solution."
– John Rosemond

Honor your word: Building a relationship with yourself or others involves making agreements or renegotiating those agreements in a respectful manner. Honoring your word is the foundation of all agreements. It creates trust and allows for deeper respect and intimacy. If you cannot keep your word, then how can you be trusted? How can you trust yourself? Keeping your word is the demonstration of your character. "Walking your talk" means that you will do what you say, and you say what you will do.

There are plenty of examples in this world of people casually promising things without ever having the intention of following through. This lack of accountability has become a socially accepted habit of communication. For example, when someone says, "I will call you" or "I will get back to you on that" and they never had any intention of connecting with you. Or when someone says, "I promise I will take care of that next time," and they never follow through. These seeming simple infringements seem harmless, but they dissolve trust and breed doubt about your dependability. It diminishes your word. The foundation of character always begins with honoring your word.

Authentic self-honoring is expressed individually: Even though the dynamics of appreciation are universal, every individual's method, practice and form of honoring will be unique to them. The Honoring Adult is always responding to the individual needs of everyone differently based on what they need and their history, conditioning and culture. What is honoring to one may not be honoring to another. It must resonate with you. The powerful level of responsive attentiveness that is offered through the Honoring Adult recognizes those unique needs and allows an uplifting and expansive experience.

Exudes self-esteem, composure and confidence: A deeper level of self-acknowledgement offers the opportunity for deeper acceptance. This includes the ability to accept and appreciate all the different aspects of your being. This genuine and realized self-appreciation therefore helps develop self-confidence, composure and self-esteem.

Less affected by others' opinions or perceptions: As a result of this inner relationship of developed self-value, the empowered Honoring Adult is less likely to be affected by someone else's opinion. Genuine appreciation creates a steadfast centeredness that comes from knowing, recognizing and cherishing the different aspects of you.

If you have done this inner acknowledgement and have explored your own value, then another perspective (even though it may offer more invitations for introspection) won't matter. You may take the outer perspective under consideration, but it will not sway your inner experience of yourself.

Does not focus on expectations and the illusion of perfection: Expectations are based on an idealized picture of the future. Perfection is defined as being free from all flaws or defects. The idea of perfection is just that, an ideal. If you are truly honoring something as it is, you will also have to be willing to acknowledge existing flaws. The Honoring Adult celebrates accomplishments but does not build grandiose expectations. The Honoring Adult has the ability to assess value outside the unattainable lure of perfection. It is grounded in reality.

Embraces faults, past mistakes and errors: The Honoring Adult recognizes that faults, errors and past mistakes are essential in the process of conscious evolution. Without these mistakes, you would have nothing to learn from or improve. When you embrace those past errors in judgment, you are recognizing the process of growth and development. When you honor past mistakes, you are doing it from an already refined consciousness that can now recognize the error of your ways.

It is completely unfair to judge your past based on your present awareness. You are not honoring the consciousness you were in when you made the mistakes. You are also unwilling to accept your present awareness. If you are unwilling to honor your journey in that way, then you are falling into a deeply contractive feedback loop that sabotages and minimizes all of your achievements.

Honoring the whole process with all of its contractive elements gives you permission to recreate yourself anew. When you embrace, accept and forgive the errors, you can move forward. Your mistakes are your experience. Past failures become wisdom when they are honored, so embrace your whole story but do not allow the story to define you in the present.

Apologizes and makes amends where appropriate: Part of embracing your human infallibility is also knowing when it is appropriate to make amends and apologize when you have been out of alignment with yourself or another. An honorable person is mature enough to acknowledge the error of their ways, recognize their mistakes and do what is necessary to restore balance in themselves or with another person. There is sincere humility in this accountability which gives permission to recreate yourself (and also allow another to recreate themselves).

An apology is not exclusively offered for another to make them feel better or to soothe their pain. From this perspective, your apology is at risk of becoming insincere. Without that introspection and inner referencing, your unexamined apology can become nothing more than habitual social protocol or obligation. A conscious apology is a powerful aspect of honoring because it is an honest recognition of a misaligned behavior with heart-felt remorse. The process of making amends always creates the opportunity for inner and outer restoration.

The Honoring Adult practices an "attitude of gratitude": Sincere gratitude is the natural expansive disposition of the Honoring Adult. The empowered Honoring Adult realizes that it is always a conscious choice to be in gratefulness because it requires consciousness, presence or awareness.

When you examine the complex nature of gratitude, you will realize it combines many different aspects of expansiveness: Consciousness (presence) + Expansive mindset + conscious contentment through recognition + a sense of peacefulness through appreciation.

The Honoring Adult consciously listens with attention and respect: Someone who listens with respect (to themselves and others) is not only honoring the exchange but also acknowledging its value. Many commonly regard the words "hearing" and "listening" as synonyms. But the truth is they are not the same at all. Though "hearing" is the sense by which sound is perceived, "listening," on the other hand, is defined as making a conscious effort to carefully absorb what is being said. This is an important distinction.

The art of conscious listening is a developed empathic skill that is inspired by respectful awareness because it validates what is being "received." This is particularly powerful when you are relating to an aspect of your Wounded Inner Child or Radiant Inner Child. Someone who feels valued and acknowledged is inspired to offer their best to you, because they feel valued. The same is true of ourselves.

The Honoring Adult consciously honors and accepts compliments: Someone with an empowered Honoring Adult understands that consciously accepting a compliment is important. How you receive a formal expression of admiration or respectful recognition can offer valuable insight into your personal relationship of self-love.

At first, it may feel uncomfortable. When you begin this practice, it may challenge your familiar and unhealthy internal software in exchange for an expansive upgrade. Here are some things to consider:

- **Accept recognition without the need for justification:** Many feel the need to justify a compliment with expressions like "You would have done the same thing if you were in my shoes" or "I was just doing my job." Some belief systems indoctrinate a subtle form of false humility that insists this deflection is well-mannered. But this accepted social behavior illustrates a lack of self-honoring and lack of self-worth.

- **Do not minimize acknowledgement from another:** Expressions like "It was nothing, it's not a big deal" or "anyone could have done this..." are examples of minimizing recognition. Not only does this choice dishonor another's experience, but it also is an attempt to minimize the act for which you are being appreciated. Diminishing a compliment into a lesser, more comfortable version that you are now willing to accept dilutes the gift and invitation to expand your sense of self-love.

- **Accept a compliment without suspicion or disbelief:** Many choose to deflect recognition because they are suspicious of an ulterior motive on the part of the giver. "Why are they being so nice?" "What is their intention?" "What is the hook?" Do not be distracted by "trying to figure it out."

  Remember, that accepting recognition does not mean you condone a potentially inauthentic agenda. An individual's motive is none of your business, and needing to know before you accept the compliment is an act of negation. Be personally responsible and graciously accept the compliment. Stay clear of another's personal intrigue by refusing to empower it with any of your attention.

- **Authentic self-acknowledgement is a healthy practice:** It is not arrogant to acknowledge yourself. It takes courage, self-respect and honesty. On this journey, there can be much focus on what is potentially distorted or contractive within you, but it is also a necessary part of a balanced healing process to appreciate, honor and compliment what is expansive within you as an act of self-acceptance. How do you expect to create and/or accept the many invitations of love and admiration from the Universe that come through others if you are unwilling to practice an authentic honoring of yourself?

- **Fully receiving a compliment is an act of vulnerability:** To accept a compliment, you must be vulnerable. It can be uncomfortable, but it's necessary for any true growth and expansion. Expansion inspires and creates more expansion. Eventually, you will learn to relinquish your need for protection, surrender your fears and be open to experiencing more. That process begins with being vulnerable.

Here are some tips to consciously recognize, receive and accept a compliment:

Look into the eyes of the individual giving you the compliment: Recognize that a fear of intimacy and issues of self-worth prevents most people from directly looking at the individual who is recognizing them. Allow yourself to be seen. Be present, engaged and conscious in the exchange of energy. It is a gift.

Express "thank you" without any embellishment or commentary: Receive the compliment regardless of what potential agenda may exist. This can be challenging and you will see how tempting it is to diminish this powerful experience for yourself. Instead, fully receive it with self-respect.

Give yourself permission to feel the gesture of admiration: Accept the benefits of this gift by fully feeling the experience of the compliment. Receiving at this depth will release many unconscious beliefs, conditioning and patterns as the process unravels. Allow the compliment to deeply penetrate as you begin to actualize your inherent worth by consciously practicing this small but powerful act of self-love.

The Honoring Adult authentically celebrates accomplishments: In the ever-changing experience of life, if you meet your goals, take the time to celebrate. It offers perspective, builds confidence and creates the possibility of self-reflection to create the foundation for the next series of inevitable challenges. The Honoring Adult offers this sincere acknowledgement as an act of self-recognition.

Self-honoring is not arrogant or boastful: Any form of healthy self-appreciation is a loving act of respect. This creates a deep sense of inner validation. Unlike arrogance or boastfulness, true self-honoring takes courage and vulnerability. It is not a form of insecure posturing. It is a simple and powerful demonstration of honest self-reflection. You are only appreciating what you believe to be true and holding that truth with personal respect.

Examples of Affirmations that Empower the Honoring Adult:

"I honor, respect and appreciate the unique expression of me."
"I always keep my word, honor my agreements and uphold my personal integrity."
"I acknowledge, honor and embrace the infinite abundance of the Universe."

AVAILABLE ADULT

attentive, engaged, beingness, holding space avaialble, present

PROTECTOR

boundaries, guardian, integrity, security, discipline, dicernment

COMPASSIONATE ADULT

tolerance, loving-kindness, sensitivity, caring, empathic, concern

MATURE
INNER ADULT

conscious, mature, responsiveness, awareness, empowered, accountable, expansive

RESPONSIBLE ADULT

capable, responsive, accountable, trustworthy, action-oriented, pragmatic

NURTURER

tenderness, warmth, gentleness, affection, caring, support, cherishing

HONORING ADULT

acknowledgement, appreciation, recognition, grateful, respectful, celebration

THE MATURE INNER ADULT
The Responsible Adult

"It takes courage to grow up and become who you really are."
– E.E. Cummings

Understanding the Dynamics of The Responsible Adult:

The Responsible Adult can be understood as the sensible expression of maturity. It is the ideal practical side of caring. This aspect of the Mature Inner Adult expresses its expression of devotion through taking care of the pragmatic aspects of life. This is the aspect that manages life with focus, attention and capability.

The Qualities of the Empowered Responsible Adult:

- **Has the "ability to respond" to life through empowered action**
- **There is little or no drama or resentment in the execution of practical duties**
- **Experiences life through the lens of an empirical realist**
- **Practical expression of altruistic devotion**
- **Dependable to complete tasks as promised in a timely manner**
- **Expresses caring through a more impersonal or utilitarian manner**
- **Usually grounded in earthly, practical and pragmatic concerns**
- **Expresses a degree of capability, confidence and proficiency**
- **Level-headed commonsense and sensibility**
- **Has been known to effectively multi-task**
- **Being responsible is an active expression of caring**
- **Displays effective decision-making skills**
- **Expresses a service-oriented perspective**
- **Authentic responsibility creates accountability, safety and trust**
- **Result and goal oriented**
- **Expresses a high level of self-motivation, reliability and consistency**
- **The Responsible Adult is a genuine realist**
- **Adept at organizing, scheduling and list making**
- **Cultivates an expansive mindset towards execution and growth**
- **Sincerity of action**
- **Develops, focuses and executes through structure, practical systems and processes**

Responsibility (respond – ability "The ability to respond"): When this behavior is seen from a contractive perspective, responsibility becomes a form of pressured action. In this context, responsibility is associated with being a burden. But if the word was broken down as "the ability to respond" in an expansive framework, it dispels the duty-bound association into an honor-bound expression of appreciation.

When someone is "responding," a certain level of self-awareness, maturity and accountability is always present. It's not an obligation. Just a sense of completing the task-oriented aspects of a productive life. The ability to respond always has an element of conscious choice. One chooses through awareness to be mature, dedicated and responsive.

The Responsible Adult is a realist: This aspect of the Mature Inner Adult is the expression of a realist, an individual inclined to truth and pragmatism. By examining empirical data, they determine their course of action. They accept a situation "as it is," and after scrutiny, act accordingly. This is the level-headed aspect of the Mature Inner Adult that is the most grounded in functional expression of reality.

They tend to be very focused and not easily swayed by opinions, stories, dramas or theories. This does not make them cold, disconnected or distant. On the contrary, this expansive aspect is engaged on a practical level. Being a realist does not mean there is no space for anything else. It just means that a foundation is first built upon realism, and any subsequent action is inspired from that perspective.

There is little or no drama or resentment in the execution of practical duties: This aspect of the Mature Inner Adult is all about action. They are proactive and self-assertive, rather than passive and dependent. They don't feel victimized by life. They do not tend to complain about their role, task or job.

They do not whine or unload problems onto other people; instead, they face their problems or challenges directly and work out solutions rather than depending on others for direction. They will seek assistance, but only in relation to what they sincerely require, as in areas where they lack expertise, not in relation to unresolved emotional needs from the past.

Expresses a degree of capability, confidence and proficiency: Why does the Responsible Adult seem to have an instinctual confidence in its own capacity? A high level of confidence exists not because of some pre-disposition, but rather it is developed through ongoing practice and practical application. Because this aspect of the Mature Inner Adult focuses its attention and efforts on execution and action, there is little indulgence or wasted time in the over-analysis, fear or procrastination. Self-assurance and confidence are cultivated by persevering through many errors, mistakes and failed attempts and learning from them.

The practice of self-discipline: The Responsible Adult has attained and demonstrates a high degree of self-discipline. A well-grounded work ethic is important without sacrificing yourself in the process. A certain amount of awareness needs to be present, so you know how to work and not become distracted from necessary tasks.

Formulating and implementing goals and plans: The Responsible Adult knows the power of goal setting and executing the plan towards the goal. The plan represents the "how to" steps to realize the goal. The plan is the container that you create around the goal. It creates accountability and inspires progress. The container will always evolve and shift as you refine during the process.

Responsible Adults formulate goals and take the appropriate actions to achieve them in a timely manner. They establish their priorities in life, craft a plan and they follow through to the best of their ability. The goal casts an ideal into the unknown and creates a powerful tether to create necessary momentum.

In contrast, people living within a victim-oriented Wounded Inner Child's frame of reference will overreact emotionally to events that are insignificant in the overall scheme of their lives and fail to respond to events that are important or crucial to their well-being. Because the Responsible Adult tends to pursue their goals and priorities earnestly without drama, they exude a certain air of integrity as their outer actions and commitments are more likely to correspond to their words and promises.

Organizing, scheduling, systems and structure: Most people do not take the time to consider the necessity of organization, scheduling, systems and structure in everyday life. We take it for granted when everything is running impeccably. The Responsible Adult is accomplished because of its ability to effectively understand and leverage these organizational principles. Just like a successful business, everyday life needs a good operating procedure to thrive. Because of its down-to-earth and practical approach, the Responsible Adult has a natural talent for the understanding and application of these principles.

Unraveling the expression "Adulting": The pop-culture idea of this expression has become a phenomena and topic of much debate. The concept of "Adulting" loosely refers to the Responsible Adult and the practical "grown-up" duties that fall under its auspices. This includes things like having a job, living independently as well as many mundane aspects of the Responsible Adult such as taking clothes to the dry cleaners, making and keeping appointments, paying your bills, getting your car registered, doing yardwork, and so on.

Depending on different individuals, their perspective and intention, different motivations may be driving the "Adulting" reference. It can be interpreted as a goofy and cute phrase of acknowledging personal responsibility, but if you look at it more closely, you can see that something else is fueling the widespread use of the phrase as well. Adulting commonly has two different meanings:

1. to behave in an adult manner; engage in activities associated with responsible adulthood

2. to make or push someone to behave like an adult; turn someone into an adult

Adulting refers to behaving like an adult, engaging in tasks and duties that "grown-up adults" regularly have to do. And the key word here is "have to," or in other words, somehow being forced to perform these duties as if they are not a fundamental, normal and healthy part of life. When you categorize this aspect of healthy living as "Adulting," you can create a sense of victimhood between you and this foundational aspect of your maturity as if there is something unfavorable or inherently wrong about it.

Those who live consciously as the Responsible Adult can find the term puzzling. Therefore, when the term "Adulting" is spoken from a contractive perspective, it is coming from a fearful place that does not honor the profound power, support and potential from this aspect of maturity. In using the term, you may be unconsciously revealing that the Shadow Inner Adult or the Wounded Inner Child has a greater hold on your consciousness than you realized.

Consider that you are being "invited" to empower this unowned aspect of your maturity and that you may need to explore, reexamine and change your relationship to the idea of responsibility; to see it from a more empowered and expansive mindset.

The Responsible Adult is the practical aspect of the Mature Adult: The Responsible Adult is the practical foundation of maturity that not only provides the structure to support the Radiant Inner Child, it also helps provide the framework for also empowering other aspects of the Mature Inner Adult (Nurturer, Compassionate, Available, Honoring, Protector).

Think of the Responsible Adult as the action-oriented builder, the doer and the sensible organizer who deals with the mundane, conventional and day-to-day issues that keep life humming along smoothly. When those aspects of life are handled, there is more room to explore other aspects of you.

When you are on top of your schedule, then you know when you have free time; when the bills are paid, then you do not need to worry about finances, and so on. When you have an empowered and expansive relationship with the mundane practicalities of life, you will not feel burdened or taxed, but instead more connected, open, confident and free.

The Responsible Adult is effective only because it is aware of its important role in the greater functioning and performance within the being and in life. It does not attempt to be something other than what it is and therefore keeps its attention where it is needed.

Examples of Affirmations that Empower the Responsible Adult:

"I am responsible and accountable for all of my actions."
"I am capable, dedicated and committed to my goals."
"I always create more than enough time to get everything done."
"I have confidence in my ability to achieve my dreams."
"I am present and focused on only what needs to be done."
"I have what it takes to be successful."

AVAILABLE ADULT

attentive, engaged, beingness, holding space avaialble, present

PROTECTOR

boundaries, guardian, integrity, security, discipline, dicernment

COMPASSIONATE ADULT

tolerance, loving-kindness, sensitivity, caring, empathic, concern

MATURE
INNER ADULT

conscious, mature, responsiveness, awareness, empowered, accountable, expansive

RESPONSIBLE ADULT

capable, responsive, accountable, trustworthy, action-oriented, pragmatic

NURTURER

tenderness, warmth, gentleness, affection, caring, support, cherishing

HONORING ADULT

acknowledgement, appreciation, recognition, grateful, respectful, celebration

THE MATURE INNER ADULT
The Protector

*"Boundaries represent awareness, knowing what the limits are
and then respecting those limits."*
– David W. Earle

This aspect of the Mature Inner Adult is regarded as the eternal hero, savior or champion of the being. The Protector is the vigilant sentry and advocate that safeguards all facets of the Inner Child. This archetype is concerned with preservation and security. The Protector is the honorable custodian of boundaries, grounded in virtue, and lives by a strict code of conduct. Empowered by duty, this loyal advocate is watchful, steadfast and confident. And like any responsible guardian or true warrior, it is a peacekeeper first and will only be fierce as a last line of engagement.

Understanding the Dynamics of The Protector:

It is said that the best offence is a good defense. Which better aspect of the Mature Inner Adult to embody this characteristic than the Protector, whose sole duty is to act as a watchful defender of our consciousness. A true Protector is not overtly aggressive. It uses force only when necessary and only as a last resort.

The Protector creates a sense of safety and confidence. This aspect of the Mature Inner Adult is associated with all aspects of creating, maintaining and honoring personal boundaries.

*"Man must evolve for human conflict a method
which rejects revenge, aggression and retaliation.
The foundation of such is a method of love."*
– Martin Luther King Jr.

The concept of the Protector is one of the most distorted aspects of the Mature Inner Adult in our patriarchal society. It is not violent. It exudes the qualities of decisiveness, selfless service, and the courage to do what serves the highest good even when it is a personal challenge to do so. This behavior acts to loyally support established and necessary boundaries with conscious awareness.

The Protector remains calm and centered when confronted with a challenge and is inwardly aligned and integrated. The Protector is in touch with deeper emotions and states of consciousness, is warm and compassionate, appreciative and generous at every opportunity of engagement. This defender fights "the good fight" and draws boundaries to support a position of security and safety. The Protector is only in favor of benefiting the greater good and making life more fulfilling for everyone.

The Qualities of the Empowered Protector:

- **Demonstrates a highly disciplined attitude in many areas of their life**
- **Creates, maintains and safeguards necessary boundaries without rigidity**
- **Cultivates a sense of security, safety and support**
- **Has been known to "fight the good fight" for the highest good**
- **Displays qualities of honor, loyalty and respect for all beings**
- **Highly developed sense of discernment**
- **Displays a keen decisiveness, directness and clarity of thought**
- **Supports selfless service through genuine humility**
- **Displays a high degree of courage to do what is needed even when difficult**
- **Can be known to champion and selflessly support a higher cause**
- **Does not require accolades or compliments and contributes without fanfare**
- **Knows their role in collaborative projects without ambition and competition**
- **Does not oppress through their power, influence, strength or presence**
- **Lives by a sense of purpose or dharma in their actions and behavior**
- **Confrontation, violence or aggression is only utilized as a last resort**
- **Has a high sense of personal integrity in their thought, word and deed**
- **Displays and supports empowered conscious action in all**
- **Exhibits a strength of character, inner alignment, centeredness and self-awareness**

The best and most effective personal boundaries are subtle;
these "quiet" boundaries are so effective they are rarely ever noticed.

Understanding the Importance of Boundaries: Boundaries have a fundamental place in life. Every living creature has its own territory or set of boundaries in which it lives and that it defends against intrusion. Boundaries are the fundamental principles that develop your internal codes of ethics which outwardly create the governing laws, rules and systems used as your code of conduct. Boundaries vary from person to person. Knowing and upholding your personal boundaries creates a necessary sense of safety and security needed for growth.

Healthy boundaries promote healthy development: One may visualize developing boundaries like a series of concentric circles ever-expanding from the center. Consider a developing child who is vulnerable to outside influences. Inherent boundaries and appropriate limits, based on the child's level of development, are created as a protective measure to ensure its security amid its natural development and evolution.

In the beginning, the boundaries can very limited, but this security allows the child to fully explore the confines of its environment. Eventually, as the child develops more competency, skills and courage, it organically extends outward. In a healthy development, this inspires the next concentric extension of safety which extends further than the original buffer for more room to explore, and so on and so forth. Eventually, this process continues as the child develops into a fully aware and competent, mature adult who is now capable of defining and creating their own boundaries based on their personal experience.

Without these initial boundaries that organically expand with natural development, the child would not feel safe from intrusions and outer influences. If the boundaries are too severe, then the child feels stifled and trapped. If the boundaries are lessened too soon, then the child feels threatened and overwhelmed by the possibilities that it has not yet grown to feel confident or capable to handle.

Your understanding of a healthy boundary will be determined by your direct experience of boundaries as you were developing. These dysfunctional boundaries in your development can cause the distorted view of how "healthy" boundaries appear in your adult behavior.

Compromised boundaries create emotional, mental and psychological instability: When boundaries are weak, you may easily become emotional, mentally and psychologically instable and feel overwhelmed by opinions and the needs of others. The line between yourself and others is blurred. You can experience difficulty identifying your own emotions and needs. People with weak boundaries are hypersensitive to what others think and say about them.

Common signs are: overinvolvement in others' lives, perfectionism, people-pleasing, trying to fix and control others with judgments and advice, staying in unhealthy relationships, taking on too much work or too many commitments, and avoiding being alone too much. When your boundaries are too weak, you can feel responsible for everything and everyone.Unconsciously, weak boundaries illustrate a lack of personal awareness as you are somehow disconnected to an aspect of yourself and your own needs.

Rigid boundaries can create disconnection and isolation: For some people, there is a fear of intimacy because of past hurt. They fear being suffocated and the loss of independence. They will attempt to control or avoid connections. This rigidity creates an impenetrable barrier. Loneliness, emptiness, resentment and depression may develop, along with difficulty giving and receiving care and concern. Common signs of rigid boundaries are chronic feelings of loneliness, rejection, hurt, loss and pain. There is a craving for connection while fearing closeness.

Flexible boundaries are the most expansive and create continual growth: Flexible boundaries are the ideal experience. To create appropriately mutable boundaries, awareness and discernment have to be present. These types of boundaries are selective, like a semi-permeable cell wall that consciously decides what to let in or what to keep out. There is an ever-present understanding that change and evolution are the only constant forces of the Universe and that the boundaries need to continue to evolve with the individual.

Common signs of flexible boundaries are a balanced demeanor, confidence, compromise, natural resistance to emotional and psychological manipulation, difficulty to exploit or coerce. They also reveal a lack of attachment to the present boundaries and an awareness for constant refinement and growth.

> *"An intimate relationship is one in which*
> *neither party silences, sacrifices, or betrays the self*
> *and each party expresses strength and vulnerability,*
> *weakness and competence in a balanced way."*
> – Harriet Lerner

Giving permission: The concept of consent plays an important role in creating healthy personal boundaries. If consent is not given, then a level of violation has occurred. It also creates confusion when messages are unclear as to what permission has been given.

Remember that you always have permission to change your mind, renegotiate your position and redefine the boundary as you grow and evolve. Become comfortable saying "no." That is a powerful boundary when it is appropriate for you. And remember that what was permissive in a less aware state of consciousness or in one circumstance is not necessarily appropriate as you become more aware in another situation.

The distinction between you and another: Boundaries can also be described as the differentiating line or the distinction between where you end and another begins. It is your personal recognition of that difference and your ability to respond with self-respect and dignity in maintaining a healthy relationship with that difference intact. Honoring the limits of what feels safe and appropriate for you can only be determined by you.

Personal privacy: Privacy is a kind of personal solitude unique to every individual that refers to something that is inherently special. You always have the right to express yourself in the manner that feels appropriate, authentic and safe to you, and no one has a right to demand otherwise. That inner sanctum of personal privacy is sacred, and the boundaries that protect that inner world must create a sense of security that no one has the right to override.

In a world of social media, unauthorized transparency, instant information access and personal information overload, we can forget the importance of the empowered state of clear boundaries and personal anonymity. You only need to expose what you wish to share, when you wish to do so, and in the manner which you feel safe doing it.

Healthy boundaries are created from expansiveness: Fear does not create healthy boundaries. Fear is a contractive response that is not founded from self-awareness, self-respect or self-worth. But for many, when they begin to create boundaries, it starts there and can be fueled by anger. Even though the initial boundaries may be appropriate, in the beginning they can still be reactive. From this survival protectiveness, the experience of self-respect must emerge to encourage a more expansive foundation based in awareness and the process of self-discovery.

The Different Types of Personal Boundaries:

One may have healthy boundaries around one area of their being and yet they may not be as refined in another. Ultimately, the more deeply you understand these different areas, the more you can develop a powerful, conscious and healthy relationship with them all. This holistic experience of your boundaries will only deepen your sense of personal safety and security.

Spiritual boundaries: These types of boundaries are sometimes difficult to understand because they are non-physical, subjective and unique to every individual. But in general, they can be expressed through the knowing that everyone has the personal right to believe what is authentic to them.

They have the right to explore the divine, God or spirit (or whatever they relate to) in their own unique way as long as it does not infringe on another. No one has the right to impose their beliefs on you and you are not obligated to practice your personal relationship to your inner world in a particular manner that needs to conform to anyone else. Allow your direct experience to always be your guide and your personal barometer.

Some examples of spiritual violation or abuse:

- Discrimination, punishment, shame or abuse for personal spiritual beliefs
- Threatening the imposition of a belief onto you
- The conscious denial of the existence of your direct experience
- Someone utilizing "spiritual justification" to violate you

Emotional boundaries: Weak emotional boundaries are akin to being caught in an emotional storm with nothing to ground you. When you are compromised in this way, you will be greatly affected by others' emotional states. You may feel responsible for others' feelings while compromising your own emotional experience. Emotional boundaries are created when you honor your own emotions in any given circumstance.

Healthy boundaries prevent you from giving unwanted advice, pointing the finger or accepting blame. They protect you from feeling guilty or responsible for someone else's negative feelings or problems and teach you not to take others' comments personally. High reactivity suggests weak emotional boundaries. Healthy emotional boundaries require clear, grounded internal boundaries. They are founded on knowing your feelings and your responsibility (ability to respond with love) to yourself and others.

Some examples of emotional violation or abuse:

- Coercion, pressure or demands that you should feel a specific way that is not authentic to you
- Anything that dominates or overrides your permission to feel a certain way
- Not knowing how to separate your feelings or emotions from another (emotional caretakers)
- Emotional abuse (contractive verbal, emotional attacks)
- Someone imposing an emotional state or mood onto you and making it your responsibility

Mental or intellectual boundaries: Mental or intellectual boundaries revolve around thoughts and how you express those thoughts which reflect your values and your opinions. These types of boundaries are also about choosing to cultivate and maintain an expansive mindset. Like anything, an expansive mindset requires awareness, attention and practice to maintain.

Are you open-minded but still grounded and confident enough in your own understanding to listen with openness without becoming rigid?

Do you easily sway from your core beliefs?

Do you have a strong and discerning mind that can sift through the onslaught of information that is hurled at you?

Can you distinguish what is expansive for you to give consideration?

If you become highly argumentative, defensive or rigid, you may have weak mental boundaries.

How quickly can you get seduced into negative and self-abusive thinking?

Some examples of mental abuse or violation:

- Not taking personal responsibility and accountability for your behavior (blaming another)
- Accepting contractive or abusive dialogue, ideas or judgments about yourself or another
- Sacrificing your plans, dreams and goals to please another
- Being punished or even denied having your personal opinion

Psychological boundaries: Psychology is the study of conscious and unconscious patterns of behavior that form your personal beliefs. This experience also includes emotions and thoughts associated to those behaviors. By examining this internal code of conduct, you can continue to develop more refined boundaries that serve to maintain inherent safety and security but do not limit growth. Psychological boundaries define your experience of personal dignity.

The most common examples of psychological violation or abuse:

- Anything that diminished the self-worth of an individual (humiliation)
- Treating an individual as an instrument or an object (objectification)
- Violations that degrade an individual's value as a human being (degradation)
- Anything that strips a person or group of people of their human characteristics (dehumanization)

211

Physical boundaries: These types of boundaries refer to all the physical or worldly boundaries and how they manifest in your outer world. This includes your physical body, sense of physical space, sexual orientation, and personal privacy. Physical boundaries provide a barrier between you and an intruding or demanding force that desire to violate any of these areas in various ways. You have the right to have physical security and safety.

Some examples of physical violation or abuse:

- Inappropriate touching, sexual advances or sexual violation
- Discrimination based on your appearance or gender
- Physical abuse or violation (holding, grabbing, dominating physical force)
- Viewing and using personal information, files or private information without consent
- How people treat your possessions (borrowing without asking, damaging property)
- Financial infringements (not paying debts, stealing money)
- Disrespecting your sense of personal space (intruding without knocking, unwanted hugs)

Your ever-evolving code of conduct: Poor or unrefined boundaries, rules and/ or a flawed internal code of conduct based on those boundaries are better than no boundaries at all. You must always start somewhere. The more you practice, the more refined and the healthier those boundaries become based on your evolving maturity, experience and consciousness.

You need to test and measure those boundaries through experience and learn what needs to change. That is the process. Perfection is an evolving act of refinement, not a static end goal. There is always more, other and beyond your present experience.

Tips for Setting Healthy Boundaries

- *When you realize you need to set a boundary, be clear, firm and succinct. Use the least words necessary to express your position. Do not over-explain, justify or apologize for the boundary that you are setting. You cannot set a clear boundary if you send mixed messages. Remember that you are informing the individual about the boundary, and it is not up for discussion, and you are not looking for feedback or commentary.*

- *You are only responsible for communicating the boundary in a respectful and clear manner. The boundary is your way of honoring your needs. You are not responsible for what is triggered in another, their reaction or the issues that may arise within them because of your boundary. It is highly likely they will not approve, be put out or disagree with your position, especially if this is a new behavior.*

- *Expect your boundary to be challenged. It is inevitable. This is meant to test your inner resolve and conviction. If you want your boundary to be respected, your behavior must match the boundary you are setting. Do not waver or rescind the boundary. Honor what you need.*

- *Often you will feel selfish, greedy and insecure about the boundary you are setting. This is natural. You will often question yourself and even feel anxiety and fear about taking care of yourself. Setting boundaries takes courage, resolve and inner conviction, and like anything, it takes practice to execute. The reaction in you is an indication that you are pushing out of your comfort zone, and it can feel very strange and unnatural in the beginning.*

- *If you feel resentment or you find yourself angry or put out about a situation, examine if you need to set a boundary. In the beginning, it is difficult to recognize when you are out of alignment with your needs because it may be a familiar pattern. Pay attention, check in, and examine how you feel about the present circumstance. Be honest about what is required, even if it is uncomfortable.*

- *Learning to set healthy boundaries in an ongoing process which you will continue to refine and recreate as you develop more awareness and confidence in trusting yourself. Set boundaries on your own time frame and be willing to shift those boundaries as your needs change. What was appropriate today may not be necessary tomorrow.*

- *Develop a support system of people who respect your right to set boundaries. The support system helps you build confidence and self-empowerment as you learn to trust yourself. Highly toxic and manipulative people do not typically respect boundaries. Be aware of those who dismiss your boundaries.*

Centeredness, self-awareness, inner alignment creates strength of character: The idea of centeredness refers to a deep connection at a core level, a conscious awareness of that connection, and therefore moving in alignment from that centered place. This is a form of inner balance that creates the solid, unflappable baseline from which you may engage. This sense of alignment is necessary to create personal boundaries and to be firm in those boundaries.

There is no need for aggression when there is a sense of centeredness and connection to the source of who you are. From this point, drawing boundaries is effortless, because it becomes an extension of that inner alignment. The conscious self-awareness maintains that connection and is constantly adjusting to flow with the expression of that inner balance.

Your character is the defining quality of your individual nature which is illustrated in your ongoing behavior. Being in alignment can also mean that your actions are congruent with your inner code of conduct, how you feel about yourself, your inner values and your sense of self-respect. If you wish to understand someone's core values, you just have to have the discipline to pay attention to the conscious and unconscious behavior which defines their character.

The Protector will never oppress through their power, influence, strength or presence: There is a difference between "power" and "being empowered." Power is that raw, untapped energetic force that can be utilized expansively or contractively. Sometimes it is fueled by confidence and purpose, but too often it is fueled by the desire to oppress and control.

The one who wields power determines how it will be channeled. When this strength and force is channeled through an honorable expression to serve a higher cause, it can be elevated to a state of empowerment. When you are empowered, you not only draw from your own inner strength, but you can also be supported, fueled and inspired by the energy of an outside source.

The Protector exudes a strength that is apparent. But the Protector always remains vigilant of the unruly ego-activating nature of power and is therefore disciplined to focus that presence and strength into inner and outer expansive behaviors and choices. That conscious focus of power builds boundaries. The powerful influence of strength also creates the foundation for development and growth. But when it is channeled through unconsciousness with a contractive motive of the Shadow Inner Adult or the Wounded Inner Child, it can also be devastating.

Supports selfless service through genuine humility: Humility comes from a sense of knowing that you are playing a part in the greater picture or a larger context – like a single weave in a tapestry following your unique journey while still being aware that your behavior and choices have a ripple effect on the whole.

Authentic humility is not about being inferior, common or lowly, but rather invokes a lack of pretentiousness which demonstrates a genuine courtesy in your actions without pride or arrogance. The Protector knows it possesses a deep strength and internal power but is remarkably unassuming about it and chooses to remain inconspicuous unless it is necessary.

The Protector is always in some form of inner or outer service to something or someone. The Protector may act as an advocate to a wounded aspect of your inner being creating the necessary safeguarding that allows for growth, or the Protector may show up as the honorable defender when called upon to serve and protect. Either way, this aspect is an expression of empowered action and selfless service to a greater good that is always available when needed to "fight for a higher cause."

Lives by a sense of purpose or dharma in their actions and behavior: Without a sense of purpose, life can lack meaning. To experience fulfillment, one must connect deeply to the core of who you are and tap into something beyond the superficial. Living by a sense of purpose is a powerful initiator that exudes a sense of empowered confidence in yourself and your choices. The Protector diligently executes that inner dharma through conscious practice and behavior in your inner and outer worlds. It creates, maintains and defends a secure refuge so you can safely express that purpose.

The conscious Protector aides by the unwritten "Law of non-engagement": A wise and conscious "spiritual" warrior will practice the law of non-engagement. A true Protector never seeks conflict for the sake of conflict, never glorifies conflict, and never defines inner worth based on conflict.

There are no unnecessary pre-emptive or aggressive strikes in order to strike a power position or prove a point. The Protector does not concern itself with matters that have nothing to do with the vital task of security and protection of the Inner Child. It will always mind its own business and does not interfere in irrelevant matters. It does not waste or expend unnecessary energy or attention where it is not needed. The conscious Protector knows fully the implications of a boundary. Engagements between parties create karma or consequences in the outer world that will have to be dealt with at some point.

There is always a ripple effect from every action. Non-engagement also does not mean that the Protector is threatened by the idea of a conflict. It is prepared, ready and willing. But there is an awareness of the power and message of any choice and takes that into consideration when choosing a course of action. In fact, The Protector will pursue engagement only as a last and final resort.

Examples of Affirmations that Empower the Protector:

"I am always safe and secure and create safety wherever I am."
"I lovingly create boundaries for what does not feel in alignment with me."
"I give myself permission to respect myself and my needs."
"I have the strength, discipline and commitment to follow my dreams."
"I am always committed to my own needs."
"I am a living, honorable example of my truth."
"My outer reality is in integrity with my inner reality."
"My actions are in alignment with my beliefs."

Your Personal Mature Inner Adult Dynamics

_____ AVAILABLE ADULT

_____ COMPASSIONATE ADULT

_____ NURTURER

_____ HONORING ADULT

_____ RESPONSIBLE ADULT

_____ PROTECTOR

After reading the chapters about **The Mature Inner Adult,** take some time to consider which of the six archetypes are most empowered and best describe your personal conditioning. Rank them on the above scale of 1-6 (1 being the most consciously empowered and active and 6 being the least).

Remember that the potential for all the Mature Inner Adult archetypes exist within every individual's conditioning, but everyone has a different level of development in each of the different expressions of maturity based on their specific life circumstances and what they have consciously chosen to actively cultivate.

Usually several of the dynamics are more empowered than others in your inner and outer experience. The idea of this process is to isolate the dynamics where you are strong and explore the areas where you are weak so that you can refine and activate as many as possible. When you can create more awareness, you can begin to more consciously work with those archetypes in new and different ways.

Consider the dynamics in your past and present (inner and outer) relationships. If you observe those relationships, you will begin to see the reoccurring patterns playing out and where your strengths and weaknesses lie. Be honest with yourself. It may require some introspection and self-analysis. Remember there is a difference between what you aspire to be and what is authentically empowered within you.

EMPATHIC CHILD

intuitive, emotional,
empathic, feeling,
nuanced, sensitive

GIFTED CHILD

special, remarkable,
unique, self-expression,
self-identity, talented,
extraordinary

PLAYFUL CHILD

celebration, joyful,
freedom, pleasure, light-
hearted, absurdity, playful,
spontaneous

RADIANT
INNER CHILD

expansive, innocence, trust,
vulnerability, awe, passion,
connection, freedom,
spontaneous, childlike

CREATIVE CHILD

artisitc, conscious creator,
innovation, visionary,
originality, imagination

MAGICAL CHILD

fantasy, magical,
wonderment, non-linear,
supernatural, alchemy

SACRED CHILD

spiritual, sacred, ceremony,
ritual, awe, wonder,
devotion

The Radiant Inner Child

The **Radiant Inner Child** is the radiant aspect of the two-fold expression of expansiveness. The term was first referenced in modern psychology by Carl Jung who is considered to be the originator of the concept in the "Divine Child" archetype. Emmet Fox called it the **"Wonder Child"**. Charles Whitfield dubbed it the **"Child Within."** The idea of the Inner Child broke into the mainstream primarily through Hugh Missildine, MD, *"Your Inner Child of the Past"* (1963). But, this powerful and transformational symbolic aspect of consciousness has been explored throughout numerous esoteric, sacred and spiritual systems across the globe throughout recorded history and has become even more poignant for the evolving consciousness of today.

The Radiant Inner Child exudes the qualities from your deeper nature: the subtle, sensitive and more nuanced states that offer meaningfulness. It is expressed through many different archetypes which all illuminate the necessary qualities that create a fulfilling, empowered and sustainable spiritual experience. As you begin to open the doors to accessing more of your own inherent beingness, the illuminating experience of the Radiant Inner Child will begin to emerge.

> *"Let the little children come to Me, and do not hinder them!*
> *For the kingdom of heaven belongs to such as these."* (Matthew 19:14)

The Radiant Inner Child contains the untainted expressions of your divine nature that are longing to be honored, nurtured and expressed. The direct experience can be blissfully intoxicating and deeply fulfilling.

Unfortunately, the most simple and powerful expressions of the **Radiant Inner Child** are dismissed when we become desensitized, jaded and cut off from the true childlike awe of the universe. These qualities – innocence, joy, trust, vulnerability, awe, passion, play, creativity, connection and empathy – are the keys to the gateway of inner realization that can then become integrated into every aspect of life.

In the metaphoric, symbolic and archetypal journey of the Tarot, the first card of the twenty-two major Arcana represents the unrealized ignorance of the Fool. This card represents the asleep and unconscious, almost "childish" nature within us that only has the possibility of awakening through initiations and lessons of the journey.

It is only through the multi-layered process of unraveling, self-inquiry, acceptance, healing and integration on the spiritual journey can true wisdom and realization be attained. This remembered innocence, awe and spiritual vulnerability allows one to deeply connect one to their true nature. This is symbolically represented by the final card in the Tarot deck, depicted as **The Child of the Univers** or the **Universe** card, which symbolically recognizes the eternal journey of remembering fulfilled through the wonderment of the universal child within.

The Archetypal Conditioning of the Radiant Inner Child

It is important to cultivate the different qualities of radiance and understand how an empowered state of radiance can affect the different areas of your being. Once these Radiant Inner Child aspects are embraced and aligned with the Mature Inner Adult, it creates a powerful Expansive Relationship Feedback Loop.

Some people will only focus on one aspect of their Inner Child and ignore the other. They will either "escape" into the radiant nature of the Inner Child or find themselves swimming in the wounded nature of their Inner Child. So, it is important to balance the work in the Wounded Inner Child with empowerment of the Radiant Inner Child to create a truly "healthy" holistic and empowered relationship of balance with totality of the Inner Child.

A large portion of spiritual evolution has to be devoted to
the ego-mind's ongoing return to the natrual state of primordial innocence.

The Empathic Child: This aspect connects each of us to the experience of our emotions, intuition and the empathic connection to those subtle experiences in the inner and outer world. It reveals how we should connect in our relationships and empowers empathy for the world around us. Feeling deeply not only allows us to help heal others, but ourselves. The Empathic Child is the primary access point in the consciousness to the power of direct experience.

The Playful Child: Expansive joy without a goal or agenda explores a powerful aspect of freedom. This aspect of the Radiant Inner Child is the embodiment of celebrating the moment. It relaxes the mind and opens a pathway to the joy of being. Play allows for creativity, magic, ritual and connection while reimagining the world from a humorous and expansive space. It awakens the sense of adventure within, and allows us to laugh at the absurdity of life and to not take ourselves too seriously.

The Magical Child: This aspect of the Radiant Inner Child is deeply attuned to the realm of the imagination where unfathomable visions of fantasy, non-linear magic and make-believe exist as living possibilities. Honoring these dreamy, magical realms allows for the expression and energy of the inner alchemist to create and explore.

The Sacred Child: This aspect is inspired by the feeling of awe and wonder of the universe. The Sacred Child reveals the subtle world of consciousness that lives beyond the mundane. It is the untainted access to the power and presence of ritual, ceremony and sacred rite. It lends a deep sense and experience of the profound and longs for the natural honoring of the spirit realm.

The Creative Child: This aspect celebrates all things creative. It is passionate to explore the beauty and power of the world of artistry through all expressions of life. Beyond the innovative expressions of philosophies, ideas, music, poetry, art, writing, theater, or dance, the Creative Child also awakens the ability to explore the essence of creative manifestation and allows for the realization that we are all inherently creators of our reality.

The Gifted Child: Every individual is uniquely talented and can and will only ever be expressed by and through you. The Gifted Child allows you to channel your unique presence. Attempting to minimize the talents of the Gifted Child condemns this aspect of consciousness into subdued mediocrity. And it diminishes confidence, self-value and the ability to honor and celebrate those unique gifts of consciousness. It is deeply important that the Gifted Child be cherished as beloved and special.

EMPATHIC CHILD

intuitive, emotional, empathic, feeling, nuanced, sensitive

GIFTED CHILD

special, remarkable, unique, self-expression, self-identity, talented, extraordinary

PLAYFUL CHILD

celebration, joyful, freedom, pleasure, light-hearted, absurdity, playful, spontaneous

RADIANT INNER CHILD

expansive, innocence, trust, vulnerability, awe, passion, connection, freedom, spontaneous, Childlike

CREATIVE CHILD

artisitc, conscious creator, innovation, visionary, originality, imagination

MAGICAL CHILD

fantasy, magical, wonderment, non-linear, supernatural, alchemy

SACRED CHILD

spiritual, sacred, ceremony, ritual, awe, wonder, devotion

THE RADIANT INNER CHILD
The Empathic Child

Empathy is a developed inner relationship.
It expresses itself through vulnerability.
This authentic openness offers intimate access
to everything in your inner and outer world
through a direct experience of connectedness.

Understanding the Dynamics of the Empathic Child:

Empathy is a deeply heart-felt quality that creates and fosters connection at an emotional level. It is the ability to have an emotional and intuitive connection to the inner and outer world around us and allows one to gain perspective from that sympathetic nature. This aspect of the Radiant Inner Child empowers the ability to not only understand but also feel another's circumstance, situation and feelings.

As children, we are inherently attentive. This expresses itself in a responsive and warm-hearted nature. This childlike kindness is present because the connection to the emotional and intuitive experience within is untainted, and therefore it allows for that kind of connection to the world around us. It allows one to "walk in another's shoes" "to feel for another" and to be courteous to another's experience. We learn to tune in.

Empathy focuses on the qualities that connects us all. Relating to someone's experience does not mean you agree with what you witness, but rather it is about appreciating and respecting how it may feel. This deeper understanding evokes a desire to help for the "greater good" because one can relate to and recognize the experience.

The Empathetic Child embodies the three-fold expression of direct experience: Emotion, intuition and empathy. The combination of these three elements express the radiance of this archetype.

- **Emotions:** These feelings can be understood as subtle energetic (vibrational), psychological, cognitive and biological states that we experience, express and utilize to communicate the more subtle aspects of consciousness. Emotions are felt as deeply complex, recognizable responses to stimuli in our inner and outer environments.

- **Intuition:** Beyond the gross emotional body, there is a deeper nuanced state of experience that can be felt through and beyond the primary senses which is commonly referred to as intuition. This word originates from the Latin "*intuicioun*" which means looking at or considering insight, direct or immediate cognition beyond the rational or linear understanding. It is often described as spiritual perception.

- **Empathy:** The ability to observe, connect, understand and experience the subtle emotional (inner or outer) landscape of yourself or another and resonate or relate with their position, state or circumstance. This aspect of the Empathic Child can experience this sense of authentic connection and understanding on many levels of consciousness through both emotions and deeper intuition.

The Qualities of the Empowered Empathic Child:

- **Emotionally connected, sensitive and caring**
- **Introspective, thoughtful and sincere by nature**
- **Can relate to another's circumstances or situations**
- **Expresses a deeply intuitive nature**
- **Is connected to their emotional body but not ruled by it**
- **Radiates a sense of warmth, acceptance and safety around them**
- **Demonstrates an unstrained and natural expression of kindness to others**
- **Explores and appreciates all perspectives of an issue**
- **Open-hearted, sincere and authentic**
- **Empowers inclusiveness**
- **The Empathic child is child-like but not childish in their expression**
- **Expresses a deep acceptance of all emotional states**
- **Inspires greater empathy in others through their example**

Understanding the Spectrum of Your Emotional Experience

Your "emotional body" is the part of you that expresses the complex spectrum of human emotions. There is no clear agreement from the scientific community on a definitive definition for emotions. But it is generally defined in psychological terms as:

"a complex state of feeling that results in physical and psychological changes that influence thought and behavior. Emotionality is associated with a range of psychological phenomena, including temperament, personality, mood, and motivation."

"In psychology and philosophy, emotion typically includes a subjective, conscious experience characterized primarily by psychophysiological expressions, biological reactions, and mental states."

There are countless theories, studies and opinions on the mysterious nature of the human emotional experience. But what is true is that while every human being has the same emotional potential, we can have a completely different relationship to varying qualities of that emotional spectrum. Sometimes one individual will consciously or unconsciously favor or disown a particular emotional experience due to our childhood conditioning. But every human being has the same fundamental access and range of human emotions.

Simply put, the emotional body can be described as "E-motion" or "energy in motion" with each emotion reflecting a specific quality and expression of energy and frequency on the spectrum. Each of these different states of emotion can color or affect the other aspects of your being depending on your relationship to each of the different emotional qualities.

The Empathic Child is the aspect of your being that allows for the natural connection and expression of the many different emotional experiences that make up that complete internal spectrum. The understanding of your emotional system profoundly determines your personal ability to empathize and relate to the emotional experience in another. A stunted or repressed internal emotional experience may lead to the limited ability to empathize to an outside situation, while a refined and intimate relationship to your emotional landscape can deepen your degree of empathy.

The Eight Different Emotional Classifications

The emotional body can be broken down into eight different fundamental categories (four expansive and four contractive). Each of these categories contain within them a broad number of variations, descriptions, nuanced expressions and degrees for that particular emotional quality. For instance, in the spectrum of fear one may experience nervousness or anxiousness, which could be classified as a **"lower intensity, more subtle"** expression or one may feel terror or dread, which would exist as a **"higher intensity or degree"** of fear on the spectrum of that particular category.

EXPANSIVE	CONTRACTIVE
Joy	Fear
Sadness	Anger
Gratitude	Guilt
Peace	Shame

It is important to realize that every individual's understanding of their emotional experience is personal, subjective and is determined by their conditioning. Everyone may use different terms to describe the same experience based on their personal awareness, exploration, study and level of practice.

225

The Power and Potential of Your Inner Emotional Weather System: A simple way to think about the active emotional (energy in motion) spectrum is to see it as a constant changing state of weather patterns that shifts and changes throughout the course of the day.

This emotional weather, like normal weather, is always happening. There is always weather outside, even if it is mild and subdued, but if you take the time to notice, there are distinct differences. Sometimes the weather is calm and serene. Other times it is activated like a storm. No specific form of weather is inherently bad or good, exactly like emotions.

We are always being informed by the direct experience of the inner "feeling" weather system, the one that interacts with our thoughts, beliefs, body and outer world. It gives us an experiential perspective on the situation at hand and offers a rich avenue of connections from which to engage. How we engage with our internal emotional weather system of feeling is dictated by our pre-existing conscious and unconscious conditioning.

Some people have a more over-dramatic, expressive manner of engagement and stir up the weather into a storm while others are subdued and less dramatic. Some people barely notice their emotional weather at all. Some people feel deeply but emote very little, and some people avoid their emotional experience because they are threatened by the uncomfortable nature of its inherent power. We can begin to refine and embrace that relationship to our emotions with more awareness.

If that healthy expression of energy (emotion) is repressed, it inevitably begins to infect other areas. This unhealthy suppression of your emotional landscape can lead to powerful conditions, manifestations and even diseases of the mind and body. Try holding back or even redirecting the weather. It is not wise or sustainable. Yet many people have been unconsciously conditioned to do just that in relation to the natural expression of their emotional capacity.

For the most part, our society is not typically encouraged to acknowledge this deeper realm of experience. Most compromise this element of themselves and tend to live predominantly in the superficial aspects of the being. There is very little language or training to inspire this experiential awareness. There is a "gap," and that is why many feel (because they don't feel) empty and cling to the superficial out of fear of the unknown. Some do not even know what is missing.

Without the awakened Empathic Child to connect and channel the emotional body, an individual's capacity for a more profound relationship to themselves, the world and other people is limited and incomplete. Being empathically connected, being informed by your feelings and expressing yourself through your intuitive nature are all fundamental character traits of the human "experience."

*"Emotion is the chief source of all becoming conscious.
There can be no transforming of darkness into light
and apathy into movement without emotion."*
– Carl Jung

The Stages of Emotional Evolution

Emotional Awareness: One must begin their exploration of their emotional body by developing a conscious awareness of their emotional experience. This means distinguishing the differing qualities of emotion and the consequently somatic expressions in the physical body. That awareness builds the foundation for a broader experience in the emotional spectrum.

Emotional Intelligence: Emotional Intelligence refers to an individual's ability to articulate their emotional experience into a language of words. Intellectualizing your emotional state without referencing your direct experience results in superficial expression. Emotional Intelligence requires Emotional Awareness as a foundation or the integrity of your expression is ineffective and lacking depth.

Emotional Alchemy: The combination of a refined Awareness of direct experience + a practiced ability of articulation allows an individual to embrace Emotional Alchemy (the ability to transform something from a lower to a more refined state) as the final stage in the evolution of your emotional experience. In this state you are an active participant in influencing, purifying and refining your emotional body and you are able to use this facet of your being consciously in your expression of empathy and connection to yourself and others.

Other Emotional Dynamics:

- **Your emotional experience is always accessible within you**
- **There are expansive and contractive emotional states of energy**
- **E-motion represents a state of a particular quality of "energy in motion"**
- **To "e-mote" means to express or release that particular state of emotion**
- **Your emotions have a somatic or visceral expression in the physical body**
- **Some of your emotions can have a cognitive component**
- **Your emotions (emotional charge) + mental thoughts create beliefs**
- **Every human being has the same emotional potential**
- **Your emotional depth determines the depth of your empathy**
- **There is no such thing as a bad or wrong emotion**
- **Emotions exist on a broad spectrum**
- **Emotions are highly personal and subjective experiences**
- **Your emotional experience is a direct experience**
- **Emotional awareness empowers, develops and deepens your intuition**

To develop a greater awareness to your emotional world, take some time and consider these questions. It is powerful to explore your answers through journaling. This will create a framework that can begin your journey into your inner and outer emotional relationships and manifest in all of your outer experiences. When possible, use specific examples from your past in your assessment.

- **What was the emotional landscape of your immediate family growing up?**
- **Explore the quality of expression: Was it mostly repressed, suppressed, overdramatic or manic?**
- **What emotions were most embraced, which were not?**
- **What was your parents' relationship to each of the eight emotional categories?**
- **What is your present relationship to each of the emotional categories?**
- **Which emotions do you feel the most comfortable with?**
- **Which emotions do you feel least comfortable with?**
- **Which emotions are most present in your inner and outer experience?**
- **Which emotions do you most notice when you engage in the outer world?**
- **Are you aware of how you feel at any given moment?**
- **Can you identify where the emotion is being somatically expressed in the body?**

Connected to their emotions but not overwhelmed by them: The empowered Empathic Child has an awareness of their emotional nature but is not overwhelmed by the experience. They are not ruled by those emotions nor are they emotionally reactive. Establishing a more conscious relationship to your emotional landscape can be overwhelming and a bit "messy" as you learn and grow to feel and express yourself in a healthy manner. But when you give yourself permission to be connected, much is revealed, especially if there's been a lot of conscious or unconscious suppression.

The ability to accept the full spectrum of the emotional experience shows maturity. It requires one to continue to embrace the contractive as well as the expansive emotions and understand that every expression has its place. The empowered Empathic Child is a living expression of that realization. It does not judge or make any experience of the emotional world "bad." It is vital to continue to explore and embrace your relationships to every aspect of you and discover healthy ways to express even the most contractive feelings. As you become more refined in your emotional world you discover the breadth of the spectrum is rich with experience.

The Empathic Child is "child-like" but not "childish" in their expression: "Childish" refers to a reactive state of expression while "child-like" refers to an empowered state. The most aware and conscious individuals on the planet exhibit a beautiful child-like innocence in their expression.

Radiates a sense of warmth, acceptance and safety around them: Someone who is empowered and accepting of their own sensitive nature will naturally emulate these traits as a living, authentic example of self-respect and self-worth. Others feel a sense of safety around them because they feel that empowered inner acceptance and realize that the individual is compassionate and empathic of their situation, and in most cases will not judge their experience.

Expresses a deeply intuitive nature: People inquire how to deepen intuition. The answer and first step will always have something to do with cultivating a deeper relationship to how you feel. That inner journey through the entry point of the direct experience of emotions eventually leads to a deeper intuitive state. It is inevitable.

This deeper intuitive state is developed through the introspection, practice and refinement of that direct experience. As you realize a deeper relationship with the Empathic Child, you begin to outwardly live integrated to that inherently intuitive nature and it is expressed in your behavior and actions in the outer world.

The Intuitive World of the Empathic Child

Your emotional world is only fully appreciated and understood as a direct experience. That is why emotions are also referred to as "feelings." As you continue to refine your relationship to your emotional landscape, it opens the door to your intuitive faculties and allows you to access a deeper and more subtle energetic world. We often unconsciously refer to this "other" world of experience beyond the mundane through common expressions in our every day language. In any of these examples, there is a recognition of this nuanced energetic and intuitive experience.

- **I got a good sense of what was going on with him.**
- **A got a bad vibe from that guy.**
- **Something was off about that situation.**
- **The atmosphere in the room was very thick.**
- **That girl has such an amazing energy around her. She was radiant.**
- **I got a good "hit" on that idea. It came to me.**
- **Something just feels right about it.**
- **I have a gut feeling about it.**
- **I had a really good feeling about that choice.**

Understanding and connecting to different intuitive faculties: This expansive expression of the Radiant Inner Child known as the Empathic Child is a powerful point of access to emotion and cognition. It also transcends the superficial world of mind beyond rational assessment until it accesses the intuitive faculties of your being.

On the path of self-exploration, many people inquire, "How do I more deeply access my intuitive faculties?" Through the ongoing relationship with the Empathic Child, you can enhance these intuitive experiences by being available to the nuanced experience within you. Through the power of self-observation and direct experience you can unravel your own relationship with your intuition.

Turning the outward senses within: To empower the process, one can access the deeply intuitive nature of the Empathic Child by turning the focus of the physical senses inward and begin to pay attention and be available to the subtlety of the energetic experiences beyond the world of the physical. When these "subtle inner feelings and senses" are combined with intentional self-observation, you will begin to utilize your emotions, feelings and the power of sensation through an empathic connection.

Examples of Affirmations that Empower the Empathic Child:

"I give myself permission to fully feel, embrace and accept all of my emotions."
"I always listen to my inner knowing."
"I am able to easily articulate my emotional experience."
"Even if they are uncomfortable, all my feelings are important and valid,."
"I am open and receptive to honoring the emotions in myself and others."
"I am able to easily track the somatic emotional experience in my physical body."
"I can easily connect with others on an emotional level."

EMPATHIC CHILD

intuitive, emotional,
empathic, feeling,
nuanced, sensitive

GIFTED CHILD

special, remarkable,
unique, self-expression,
self-identity, talented,
extraordinary

PLAYFUL CHILD

celebration, joyful,
freedom, pleasure, light-
hearted, absurdity, playful,
spontaneous

RADIANT INNER CHILD

expansive, innocence, trust,
vulnerability, awe, passion,
connection, freedom,
spontaneous, childlike

CREATIVE CHILD

artisitc, conscious creator,
innovation, visionary,
originality, imagination

MAGICAL CHILD

fantasy, magical,
wonderment, non-linear,
supernatural, alchemy

SACRED CHILD

spiritual, sacred, ceremony,
ritual, awe, wonder,
devotion

THE RADIANT INNER CHILD
The Playful Child

"Like art, play is that quintessential experience
that is almost impossible to define—because it encompasses infinite variability
—but which we all recognize when we see, or experience."
– Hara Estoff Morano

Expansive amusement and celebration of joy for the sake of celebration without a goal or agenda explores a powerful aspect of freedom. This aspect of the Radiant Inner Child is the embodiment of pleasure and merriment of life through celebrating the moment. This relaxes the mind and opens a pathway to the joy of being. Play is the childlike playground that allows for creativity, magic, ritual and connection while reimagining the world from a humorous and expansive space. It opens a place to explore for the love and beauty of pure exploration. It awakens the sense of adventure within us and allows us to laugh at the absurdity of life and not to take ourselves too seriously.

Understanding the Dynamics of The Playful Child:

Play is one of the most expansive aspects of our Radiant Inner child and is one of the highest expressions of human evolution. Play is the ultimate free-form on multiple levels of consciousness. It happens without an agenda and allows for constantly shifting variables and stretches the possibilities of human consciousness.
Through this free-spirited expansive space, the Playful Child is granted permission to intuitively explore evolving behaviors and interactions as it informally explores and celebrates possible options in a safe and uninhibited container. It is an entertaining and adventurous exercise in conscious and unconscious self-definition and personal reflection.

Balanced play empowers an individual to experience a profound state of open creativity that expands and strengthens the neural network of the mind. It promotes creativity, nurtures problem-solving skills and explores the range of human emotional experiences. Play ultimately reveals multiple levels of our choices, desires and dreams without limitation.

Play is an inherent instinctual expression that is observed in all different species. In the context of human expression, play is varied from person to person depending on their individual conditioning, culture and personalities.

The powerful relationship between play and fun: Deeply woven into the experience of play is also the idea of fun. The Playful Child is embodied in expressions like "having fun" or "that was fun" or "time flies when you are having fun." Embracing of the radiant feeling of fun rests at the very heart of the experience of play.

Fun is a manifestation of joy. The effervescence of fun can be experienced in the most difficult or challenging situations, a conscious shift of disposition to view the present situation from the innocent, open and receptive perception of the Radiant Inner Child.

The idea of fun is based on how one chooses to engage with a new experience. When a person is challenged to consciously think expansively to overcome challenges, they push beyond their conventional existence to learn something new.

Fun soothes the utilitarian mind and temporarily releases it from the focus of the routine of daily living, giving it permission to temporarily transcend the mundane and lose itself in the moment. When you are engaged organically in the enjoyment of the moment, the perception of time changes and inevitably "time flies because you are having fun."

The qualities of the empowered Playful Child:

- **Lives with an unburdened and innocent sense of freedom**
- **Does not take themselves or life too seriously**
- **Celebrates in the power of possibility**
- **Lives with a sincere and empowered sense of joy**
- **Embraces experimentation and exploration**
- **Embraces and celebrates the spontaneity of life**
- **Present and in touch with experience of the moment**
- **Not defined by or attached to a fixed agenda**
- **Embraces fluidity – rules are a suggestion, not a mandate**
- **Experiences playful exploration in everything that they do**
- **They are experience driven, not goal oriented**
- **Deep sense of curiosity**
- **They are easily able to pivot or shift from one activity to another**
- **Play is the connection to pure possibility**
- **Uses everything as part of the game – nothing is excluded**
- **On a never-ending quest to embrace inner "joy" through outer "fun"**

Experience driven not goal oriented: As a result of the innocent demeanor and the ongoing quest for play, the Playful Child is not interested in some future goal, but in the joyful experience of the journey. The goal will continue to transform, be disregarded and constantly overlooked for that connection to the joy of the adventure and the process of getting there.

The Playful Child does not base its sense of accomplishment on the attainment of the goal but rather on how much fun it was to get there. The goal serves as a catalyst to keep the game of the adventure alive so that the maximum amount of fun can be extracted and experienced along the way there. The joyful experience of the process will always be the only destination for the Playful Child.

Embraces fluidity because rules are a suggestion, not a mandate: Imagine a free-spirited child completely engaged in a game. As the rules of the game evolve, the child will effortlessly shift to the new paradigm. Confining that sense of fluidity interferes with the sense of fun and diminishes the experience. For the Playful Child, the rules were never a mandate, they were an idea and changeable based on where the energy spontaneously moves. An empowered Playful Child allows an individual to remain flexible with what unfolds and offers the ability to meet that new space with a sense of fluid expansiveness.

The Playful Child can access "everything" as part of the game – nothing is excluded: Everything is included in the process. Everything (person, place, thing) has the potential to become a vehicle to enhance the joy of the game. This sense of inclusiveness is a byproduct of the unifying nature of expansiveness. Through play, we get an illustration of an inclusive relationship that connects everything without judgment.

The power of absurdity is a profound expression of creative playfulness: Where the conventional mind sees absurdity as foolish, childish, useless and ridiculous, the Playful Child sees absurdity as a vehicle to transcend the confines of any conscripted paradigm. The Playful Child embraces it as a radical and boundless opportunity for the infinite possibilities of play. It is not confined by convention and therefore not bound by plausibility.

This thrust into absurdity is not rebellion. It is an innocent and natural expression of how the Playful Child radically celebrates the power of infinite possibility. This ridiculousness is profoundly playful, expansive and can unleash unrestricted, far-fetched irrational and comedic joy that baffles the mind and lifts the heart. For many comedians, artists, musicians, visionaries, scientists and creative thinkers, embracing a sense of absurdity is a solace from the world of conformity where the expected and safe reign supreme. It is no wonder that the Playful Child is a natural empowered expression of this form of creative expansiveness.

"You're only given a little spark of madness – you mustn't lose it."
– Robin Williams

Does not take themselves or life too seriously: The Playful Child always sees the humor and ridiculousness in themselves, their actions, and the world around them. Being able to view the world from that lens prevents you from taking things too seriously. That seriousness creates stress and does not inspire creative solutions or receptivity. An empowered Playful Child is incapable of becoming overwhelmed with its own sense of importance.

This sense of fun is important on many levels. Play shifts our perspective and alters our mood. Research has also shown its expansive impact on our minds, emotions and physiology. It can relax muscles, boost the immune systems, release endorphins, decrease stress hormones, and increases blood flow to the heart.
The Playful Child opens the door to levity in your all relationships. It balances the focused intensity of various aspects of the Mature Inner Adult, the heaviness of life, and prevents the stress of seriousness to dampen expansive connection.

"The struggle of maturity is to recover the seriousness of a child at play."
– Friedrich Nietzsche

The exploration of play through sexuality: Human beings are hard-wired to seek physical intimacy with a partner and enjoy the pleasure that comes from connection. This inherent biological conditioning once utilized pleasure to ensure continued procreation. But today, sexuality is rarely utilized for the sole purpose of reproduction. In fact, it has become one of the most widely accepted, unconscious and misunderstood expressions of adult play.

Sexuality in its purest form is a complex, creative and radiant expression of play. It is one the few forums where adults still give themselves permission to embrace the experience. Consider some of the social rituals of human courtship: giddy attraction, flirtation, banter, posturing, demonstrations of prowess, physical and sexual allure, sensual word play, sexual innuendo, physical foreplay and unbridled creativity around different expressions of exploring pleasure.

Through suppression, society has a developed a dysfunctional relationship to the idea of play and a distorted relationship to sexuality. There are so many layers of indoctrinated belief, conditioned ideas of guilt, shame, condemnation and judgment about every facet of our natural attraction and desire for sexual pleasure. As a result, it has corrupted the naïve and primal desire for the exploration of play through sexuality.

The Mature Adult's reclaimed relationship to the Playful Child has the power to restore the natural beauty in the exploration of sexuality through open-hearted innocence, receptivity and acceptance. With an empowered Playful Child, there can be a wonderous embracing of sexual play that celebrates the joyful freedom of experimentation through the expansive radiance of human communion.

The power of conscious play: The exercise of play is an act of self-definition. Play will reveal yourself to you. It naturally expresses what you are drawn to, what "you want to do," curiosities and deeper aspirations when there are no assigned agendas.

Play connects you to the power of possibility within yourself and reveals something beyond the "have to" consciousness that drives most practical thinking. It unravels the conditioning that muffles your deeper ideas, the ones that manifest a true sense of inherent joy. That joy arises through attunement to this inner experience rather than defaulting to the utilitarian functioning that most have adopted.

People strive to succeed for the sole purpose of creating freedom so, their lives do not have to continue to revolve around "I have to." They long to return to this free-form playful engagement with life where they are not restricted by time, money, status or obligations. They work to attain security so they can finally return to that innocent state.

To learn more, consciously examine your hobbies and your uninhibited moments of free-form play. You may want to journal your answers. A sense of conscious play can uplift your life in every way if you choose to open yourself to and embrace the Playful Child.

Do you allow a lot of "fun" in your life?

Where do you find yourself most playful? In what circumstances? With who?

What type of play do you seem to seek? And more importantly, why?

How can you continue to access that expansive feeling of play?

What avenues can you continue to explore that sense of play to your life right now?

If your Playfiul Child had a voice what would it say to you?

What does this tell you about yourself?

The repressed Playful Child can create over-indulged escapism: A healthy Playful Child offers a powerful platform for development. Through maturation, the play-based world of childhood would naturally develop into a more formal platform of a chosen adult vocation.

A sense of purpose and enjoyment would feed your psychological, emotional, mental and spiritual needs. What if your play became your purpose? The profound suppression of the Playful Child has corrupted this natural evolution. And therefore, most of our work is no longer a natural extension and evolution of our play.

Examples of Affirmations that Empower the Playful Child:

"I give myself permission to be open to all possibilities."
"I allow myself to trust the power of joy."
"I allow myself to explore without an agenda or plan."
"It is safe for me to let go."

EMPATHIC CHILD

intuitive, emotional, empathic, feeling, nuanced, sensitive

GIFTED CHILD

special, remarkable, unique, self-expression, self-identity, talented, extraordinary

PLAYFUL CHILD

celebration, joyful, freedom, pleasure, light-hearted, absurdity, playful, spontaneous

RADIANT INNER CHILD

expansive, innocence, trust, vulnerability, awe, passion, connection, freedom, spontaneous, childlike

CREATIVE CHILD

artisitc, conscious creator, innovation, visionary, originality, imagination

MAGICAL CHILD

fantasy, magical, wonderment, non-linear, supernatural, alchemy

SACRED CHILD

spiritual, sacred, ceremony, ritual, awe, wonder, devotion

THE RADIANT INNER CHILD
The Magical Child

"We can choose to function at a lower level of awareness and simply exist, caring for our possessions, eating, drinking, sleeping and managing in the world as pawns of the elements, or we can soar to new and higher levels of awareness allowing ourselves to transcend our environment and literally create a world of our own – a world of real magic."
– Wayne Dyer

This aspect of the Radiant Inner Child is deeply attuned to the realm of the imagination where unfathomable visions of fantasy, non-linear magic and make-believe exist as living possibilities. Honoring these dreamy, magical realms, characters and the supernatural scenarios allows for the expression and energy of the inner alchemist to conjure, create and explore. In our fact-based linear reality, this aspect is undervalued and shunned in exchange for the pragmatic world without the wonder of magic.

The Origins, History and Definition of Magic
The ancient meaning of the word "magic" has been utilized in cultures all over the world since the dawn of human history. Therefore, it is difficult to pinpoint the exact etymology of the word. It has many meanings:

- **Members of the learned, elite and priestly class**
- **The mysterious art of controlling the actions of supernatural or spiritual**
- **Anything pertaining to, or produced by enchantment**
- **Skilled magicians, astrologers who hold a lineage of ancient wisdom**
- **The uncanny ability to have unexplained influence, power and perception**
- **The manipulation of natural forces to create optical illusions**
- **The fantastic, unreal, fictional realm of make-believe**
- **One who engages in powerful alchemy or transformation**
- **The art of influencing, predicting events or producing marvels using hidden natural forces**

Understanding the ancient symbol of the magician: Though the idea of magic appears throughout history, one of the most common modern interpretations originates from the Tarot deck. The Tarot is a collection of archetypal images which are interpreted to unravel and expose unseen energies, influences and help predict the future. This mysterious set of cards is also shrouded in mystery because many cultures worldwide claim its origins.

The Magician is the first card of the twenty-two Major Arcana in most traditional Tarot decks. It is depicted with the Magician's right hand holding a wand raised towards the heavens, the sky or the element ether, while his left hand is pointing down towards the earth. This iconographic gesture has multiple meanings but is consistent in one who respects the Great Mystery of spiritual immanence and connection.

The powerful association between magic and alchemy: The Magician is recognized as one who is capable of bridging the gap between the heavens and the earth, the known and unknown, or the unmanifested and the manifested. The word "alchemy" is closely associated with the transformational potential of magic. It embodies the idea of altering one substance into another.

Utilizing natural elements (earth, air, fire and water), alchemy is a form of magic for those who are trained and skilled in the ability to change the properties of a physical or metaphysical substance. For example, physically "transforming lead into gold." The ancient practice of alchemy is considered to be the foundation of modern chemistry.

Within the inner realm of the Magical Child, the psychological power and potential also exists to alchemically transform or "raise the unconscious into the conscious." Magic honors the mysterious possibility of change and offers the ability to envision a more expansive reality through the exploration of the fantastic.

Understanding the Dynamics of the Magical Child:

The aspect of the Magical Child empowers the realm within the consciousness where the possibility of the fantastic can exist and flourish beyond the known constructs of accepted and pragmatic reality. This powerful aspect of the Radiant Inner Child can express, through the allegory or representation of this visionary world, its unconscious and repressed psychological needs. It does so with mystical and mythological expressions in a dream-like reality which offers total freedom and safety to explore.

This is the place where the Magical Child is empowered as the architect to explore the archetypes of possibility. This world may draw on ancient mythological symbols, cultural tales and stories as well as outer experiences to offer a personal platform of metaphoric and symbolic expression to unravel and resolve inner conflicts. It allows for an expansive expression of the unknown.

The Magic Child embraces the whimsical, outlandish and the far-etched. But it is important to realize, that not too long ago in recent history what was once considered far-fetched, science-fiction or fantasy has become not only possible but is now manifested in our conventional practical world. Without the ability to recognize and honor the magic of fantasy in the inner world, you cannot create the fantastic in the outer world.

The Qualities of the Empowered Magical Child:

- **Alive with a sense of myste ry**
- **May seem almost magical, dreamy, otherworldly or ethereal**
- **Open and receptive to the possibilities of the unknown**
- **Can practically manifest the impossible**
- **Honors their personal dream and empowers others' dreams**
- **They naturally defy convention**
- **Willing to believe in something beyond the practical and pragmatic realities**
- **Honors and gives appropriate expression to their personal fantasies**
- **May appear as if they "know something" that no one else knows**
- **The power of belief in seeming impossibility**
- **Loves adventure and is passionate about the quest for the unknown**
- **Embraces a sense of awe about the world around them**
- **The childlike ability to dream without limitations**
- **Has the powerful ability to manifest their visions**
- **Holds a powerful relationship with the idea of mystery**

The Magical Child always and only exists outside of the world of convention:
It is important to understand that the Magical Child is not acting out in a rebellious manner. It is not engaging in some underhanded opposition or reaction to the mundane world. In fact, there is no trace of malicious or subversive intent in its immersion, expression and celebration of its far-out, non-linear, fluid, fantastic expression.

It simply does not have any attachment to the idea of conventions or normalcy. It does not understand the notion of "rules." It cannot be anything less than its radiant "magical" expression of possibility and impossibility even if it wanted to be.

The Magical Child always exists, thrives and functions outside of conformity. By its very nature, it does not have the capacity to comprehend or even care about the idea of plausibility. For the Magical Child, everything is always possible. To truly channel this powerful alchemical magic into your practical world, you have to first accept that the Magical Child lives beyond convention in an unadulterated, free-form relationship to the power of unlimited potential.

> *"You cannot do it, unless you can imagine it."*
> *– George Lucas*

The child-like ability to dream without limitations: The paradigm of the conventional world can quietly destroy your inherent ability to dream without rules, limitations or practicality. Without even noticing, you will begin to lose touch and suppress the ever-present Magical Child of your youth. In this world of practicality that you have had to invest in to survive, the seemingly far-fetched dreams of the Magical Child are disregarded as a waste of time and childish as they are relegated to a small corner in your consciousness.

You convince yourself that you are still able to dream, because you have "plans" and create "goals." But if you examine those "pseudo-dreams," you will realize they are minimized to fit within the context of your existing paradigm. Without an empowered Magical Child, very few people will ever envision a reality outside their existing paradigm. Therefore, your radiant, childlike ability to "fantasize" about unlimited possibilities has been systematically quelled at the expense of this powerful Magical Child quality.

People are truly unaware what they sacrifice when they limit their capacity to dream without practicality, convention, or rules. It seems harmless, but this contractive suppression erodes your ability to stretch the elasticity of perception.

The ability to dream without limits is vital if you want to achieve aspirations beyond your existing paradigm. If you cannot imagine yourself outside of the convention of your existing world, how will you ever give yourself permission to reach for more, other and beyond? Without the Magical Child most people settle without ever realizing it a minimized version of their dreams that are only an echo of their true potential.

> *"All the works of man have their origin in creative fantasy.*
> *What right do we have to depreciate imagination?"*
> *– Carl Jung*

Intuitively supports the visions and dreams in everyone: Anyone with an empowered Magical Child has the capacity to "dream big and beyond" and can envision the most outrageous possibility of potential. In this way, the Radiant Inner Child aspect unequivocally and naturally explores their fantastic personal visions. The Magical Child has an inherent and instinctual need to embrace the exploration of the dream world without question. It is in its nature to do so.

In many cases the dream may not come to fruition in the physical world as expected, but the Magical Child intuitively understands the importance of the energy and power of that possibility. That inherent commitment to the dream sparks deeper insight, opportunities and explores multiple facets of consciousness in the process and opens the entire being to a new world of expansiveness.

Because the Magical Child is intuitively devoted to the dream, it will also inspire and actively support the fantastic realms of possibility in another. That is part of the "infectious magic" and influence of this aspect of the Radiant Inner Child. There is nothing more inspiring than to have an authentic expression of the Magical Child in your corner, whose only desire is to empower and share the magical world of fantastic impossibility.

The power of belief through seeming impossibility: The inner belief system of a human being is a sophisticated mechanism that is still not fully understood. What we know, however, is that our beliefs are less tied to physical reality than most of us would admit.

Studies have been done with elite athletes, professional musicians and dancers who have been trained to conceptualize themselves attaining seemingly impossible results or pushing through their limitations. Within an imaginary inner world of fantasy, they see themselves as successful, imagine these results, and practice every detail of their performance until they condition themselves to believe in the impossible. This practice of actively engaging the Magical Child in this way has proven to create extraordinary results in the physical world. Through empowering their fantastic ideas, they have alchemically transformed the impossible into the possible.

Possibility will always remain out of reach and impossible in the outer world
until it is first acknowledged, explored and cultivated in the inner world.
The expression of magic is a sincere and powerful celebration
of the transformation from the impossible into the possible.

The relationship between magic and mystery: The empowered Magical Child is that "sparkle in the eye" of the individual that is alive with a sense of mystery and magic. This type of individual is charming, has magnetism and charm – they are alive with something intangible but spellbinding.

Someone who embraces the idea of magic also embraces the mysterious unknown that have not been fully explored or understood. Magic is the practice and expression of that mystery. An individual that lives embracing the idea of magic is open to mystery and those who embrace the mysterious are open to the possibility of magic. Either way, there is a palpable presence to someone who is invigorated by the empowered Magical Child within them.

Embraces a sense of awe in the world around them: In indigenous philosophies, the infinite power and presence of the Universe is called "The Great Mystery." Embracing the great mystery of life beyond the conventional creates a sense of awe for the sheer magic of the Universe. A receptive and open Magical Child can effortlessly connect, experience and envision the infinite possibilities of creation through the eyes of authentic wonder.

245

The Societal Manifestations of the Alternative World of the Magical Child

One of the most powerful gifts of the Magical Child is its ability to create an alternate reality that can be used to safely explore unresolved issues, conduct healing and investigate one's relationship to different archetypal energies. This is the enchanting power and possibility of fiction.

The Magical Child embodies an imaginary platform with unlimited possibilities to explore metaphor, symbol, healing, resolution, allegory, psychological relationships, and to make commentary on society and the human condition through fantastic personalities, characters, landscapes, scenarios and unreal but relevant narratives.

Human beings are natural storytellers, and the Magical Child not only celebrates but also empowers the journey of those imaginary narratives of fiction in every different form of expression. The magic of movies, plays, art, fictional accounts, and music can all share a creative and fantastic interpretation and alternative view of reality.

Powerful industries tapping into the Magical Child: What was once found in a limited expression in our culture and was only considered appropriate for young children is now exploding into a revolution of one of the fastest growing adult entertainment genres in history. The world of fantasy can now be found in countless online, virtual and in-person, pop-culture platforms of expression: cos-play, digital animation, sci-fi, steam-punk, anime, comic books, toys, collectables, graphic novels, music, books, gaming, fantasy role-playing, theme parks, virtual-reality, costumes, bars, restaurants, clubs, concerts, conventions, fashion, parties, art and more.

Billion-dollar industries have developed based on the creation, dramatization and expression of the otherworldly energy that belongs to the realm of the Magical Child. This long list includes movies, videos games, animated films and series, theme parks, role playing, fantasy games, science fiction, graphic novels, books and associated merchandise which support a powerful Magical Child subculture.

Like never before the narrative of mainstream movies, TV and theme parks are depicting popular supernatural, super-powered beings with extra-ordinary abilities, magical and mystical creatures, mutants, extra-terrestrials and inter-dimensional beings existing in alternate realities, dimensions, worlds and planets, which challenge the notion of what was once considered normal, conventional reality.

The popular fantasy of spectator sports: Another unexpected but accepted forum where many unwittingly play out their different aspects of the Magical Child is through our connection to spectator sports. One's association to a specific sport, team or individual player opens the "fantasy element" of an individual's Magical Child where an individual can virtually and vicariously experience: the thrill of the win; success and achievement through the athletic; technical and practiced skill of the player; experience a sense of belonging to a community; build loyalty and pride for a region, country or specific city while also following the ongoing strategy, statistics and evolution of those game participants and/or teams.

Mascots borrowed from animals, mythology and mystical creatures, songs and chants, team costumes with themed colors, traditions and rituals all creating powerful fantastic worlds and loyal sub-cultures. This live action "reality" theater includes every sport under the sun, all the way to representatives from every country participating in a worldwide Olympics.

The online world of fantasy: Another platform for the Magical Child to express its sense of wild imagination is the online and social media world of fantasy, where people can literally recreate their identity through generated avatars and fictitous personalities and engage as someone or something else. With a healthy relationship to the Magical Child, the discernment of the Protector and the presence of the Responsible Adult in the online world can become a powerful meta-reality for expression and exploration.

This online world of make-believe can mutate into an escapist fantasy if an unconscious and disempowered Magical Child has been hijacked by the Shadow side of the Inauthentic Adult and the Over-Indulgent Child. The Shadow Inner Adult aspect seeks to manipulate this fantastic façade for personal gain, escapism or for an ulterior motive in an alternative and imaginary digital world.

The Unowned Magical Child: Honoring the otherworldly energy of fantasy or magic does not mean that it is always appropriate or necessary to literally "play it out" in the outer world. The powerful energy of the Magical Child must always be explored in a safe and appropriate manner through creative, artistic, symbolic, metaphoric and psychological spaces with conscious attentiveness.

The magic and alchemy of manifestation: The Magician is recognized as the archetype who has the power to bridge the gap between the heavens and the earth, the known and unknown or the unmanifested and the manifested. In a practical sense the magician or the alchemist is responsible for channeling the fantastic otherworldly visions into form by using the physical elements of the earthly plane.

It is one thing to dream, but it is yet another thing to manifest that dream into its closest representation in the practical world. For this skill to be consciously engaged and successful, the Magical Child must be empowered, embraced and channeled into the realm of the practical. This is one of the most powerful alchemical talents and the purpose of a true artist.

At some point, every artist becomes frustrated with the implicit limitations of the physical world. How does one channel those outrageous ideas, larger-than-life inventions, far-fetched, dream-like creations from the fantastic domain of the Magical Child into practical reality? The truth is that there is always something lost in the translation, because the full manifestation of the Magical Child can never be accurately expressed within the limiting rules of the physical world.

But it is the life-long calling and task of the visionary, inventor, prophet, poet or scientist to deepen the ever-evolving relationship with the Magical Child and realm of the fantastic. They are driven to challenge the boundaries of accepted convention, innovate and to continue to practice and refine their abilities to express this Radiant Inner Child archetype through dedication and belief in the impossible.

The most important thing to remember is that even though the full embodiment of the magical world can never fully survive in the land in practicality, the energy and essence of the Magical Child can be powerfully transmitted and deeply imbued and therefore experienced. In that way, the alchemist creates the bridge between the unmanifested and manifested world.

The relationship between magic, science and technology: At first glance, the relationship between these subjects does not seem to make sense. The Magical Child embodies the world of impracticality, fantasy and the unreal possibilities. And the world of science is based in the observable data of the physical and the application of real-world innovation into different forms of technology. How are they related?

Just as the alchemist created the foundation for modern chemistry, the energy of the Magical Child influences the next wave of scientific exploration. It is true that all modern creations have first originated in the realm of creative fantasy. What was once fantastic science-fiction has now become reality.

The inventor Nickolas Telsa describes his process of creation in his writings. He states that by creating alternate realities in his mind he could build, test and examine the functioning of his inventions to prove their effectiveness so he could make refinements and alterations before their actual construction.

"The world is full of magic things, patiently waiting
for our senses to grow sharper."
– W.B. Yeats

When a less sophisticated consciousness is presented with an unexplainable, advanced technology, they first view the phenomenon as powerful magic. The empowered Magical Child can deeply inspire the sense of the magician in the scientist, and at the very least allow science to remain open to the fantastic realm of infinite possibilities.

Examples of Affirmations that Empower the Magical Child:

"I give myself permission to fully feel, embrace my dreams."
"I am open and receptive to the power of possibility."
"I give myself permission to fully embrace my transformation with ease, grace and flow."
"I allow myself to completely believe in myself."
"I empower my ability to manifest my dreams, visions and goals in the world."
"I give myself permission to embrace the "Great Mystery.""
"I give myself permission to recreate myself."

EMPATHIC CHILD

intuitive, emotional, empathic, feeling, nuanced, sensitive

GIFTED CHILD

special, remarkable, unique, self-expression, self-identity, talented, extraordinary

PLAYFUL CHILD

celebration, joyful, freedom, pleasure, light-hearted, absurdity, playful, spontaneous

RADIANT INNER CHILD

expansive, innocence, trust, vulnerability, awe, passion, connection, freedom, spontaneous, Childlike

CREATIVE CHILD

artisitc, conscious creator, innovation, visionary, originality, imagination

MAGICAL CHILD

fantasy, magical, wonderment, non-linear, supernatural, alchemy

SACRED CHILD

spiritual, sacred, ceremony, ritual, awe, wonder, devotion

THE RADIANT INNER CHILD
The Sacred Child

"There is nothing so secular that it cannot be sacred,
and that is one of the deepest messages of the Incarnation."
– Madeleine L'Engle

This aspect of the Radiant Inner Child is deeply connected, attuned and inspired by the direct experience, knowledge and feeling of awe and wonder of the universe. The Sacred Child is the pure, untainted and innocent access to the power and presence of ritual, ceremony and sacred rite.

For the Sacred Child, a deep sense and experience of the profound dwells in the subtle realm of more, other and beyond. It longs for this natural honoring of spirit which creates a physical and symbolic experience that makes space for the essence of everything to thrive.

Understanding the Dynamics of the Sacred Child:

The experience of the Sacred Child dwells in the heart of awareness. Without some level of awareness, the idea of the "Great Mystery" or the "Divine" cannot be felt or expressed. It is a natural and deep acknowledgement of something beyond the world we see. The concept of sacred honors our place in the infinite mechanics of the universe and creates a sense of perspective and humility. This aspect of the Sacred Child allows access to that powerful inner and outer experience. To more deeply understand the dynamics of the Sacred Child, it is important to understand the difference between the mundane and the sacred.

"In the mundane, nothing is sacred,
while in the sacred nothing is mundane."
– Dogen Zenji

Mundane: The word "mundane" is derived from the 15th century word "mundas" which means normal or ordinary. Our perception of something ordinary is usually associated with understanding something from the most basic earthly functionality in its most literal, face-value, earthly or temporal conception. In many ways the concept of mundane has to do with utilitarian functioning capacity of the human experience.

Sacredness: The word "sacred" originates from the 14th century word sacren which means to make holy, anoint, dedicate or confirm. It is based on the notion that something originally seen as mundane can be uplifted, making it special and giving it deeper importance.

The word "sacred" also implies a "personal or internal experience" of something beyond normalcy, something special and profound in nature.

- **To ordain something through conscious intention and attention**
- **To reassure and hold something close to your heart**
- **To bring awareness of the extra-ordinary into the world of the mundane**
- **To make sacred through consecration, worship or veneration**
- **Treating something with great respect and reverence**
- **To recognize the holy or divine**

"The sacred cannot be precisely defined. Each of us perceives it through a lens of personal history. For me, sacredness is an experience of inner radiance of life, the unseen force that transforms and nourishes the physical but is never diminished by it. There is something more to it, a mystery that is never totally grasped."
– Anthony Lawlor

The feeling of sacred is a deeply personal experience: The idea of sacredness and experience is unique to every individual. What is sacred to one is not necessarily sacred to another. Because of this subjective association, it can be difficult for a linear mind to distinguish what is sacred and what is not through rational understanding alone. Sacredness is a deep and personal experience of feeling. Therefore, to truly grasp the idea of sacredness, one must begin to "see, feel and understand through the heart" and embrace the experience.

This aspect of the Radiant Inner Child is also attracted to the esoteric, metaphysical and the nuanced expression of spirit. The Sacred Child will be drawn to the energy of ritual, sacred ceremony and rites of passage. And though the most common forum for this expression is sometimes through the practice of various religions (which are meant to be celebrations of this spiritual nature), the deeper experience of sacred truly transcends these limited man-made paradigms.

Unravelling the connection between sacred and wholeness: The word "sacred" is derived from multiple medieval cultural words which conceptualized the idea "to make holy, bless, consecrate, anoint, sanctify or immortalize."
It is interesting to note that the word "holy" originates from the word "whole" which refers to tthe idea of being intact, untainted, complete or healthy. (This has evolved into our modernized concept and usage of the word "holistic.")

Being holy is not about "being religious" but instead it implies an understanding, practice and relationship of "wholeness" with your inner and outer worlds. This appreciation of wholeness creates a powerful perspective within your internal universe which allows for a much deeper understanding of your inner workings.

This aspect of the Radiant Inner Child is intuitively attuned to the experience and understanding of wholeness. It is inspired by the awe and wonder of recognizing its intimate connection to something beyond itself, as an aspect of the oneness of all things. As a result, the Sacred Child can be deeply affected by its personal investigation through many forms: nature, art, consciousness, the power and presence of ritual, ceremony and sacred rite, prayer, meditation or spirituality.

Understanding the powerful connection between sacred and spiritual: When most people use the term "spiritual," they are referencing that there is a deeper (described as vibrational) aspect to everything. They are describing a relationship to the profound. Someone who is spiritual is engaging in a relationship with the subtle realms of consciousness. And their personal relationship to the sacredness will be completely unique to them.

The Qualities of the Empowered Sacred Child:

- **Embodies a childlike sense of wonder and awe**
- **Expresses a sincere humility of character**
- **Radiates an uncanny sense of depth**
- **Feels drawn to the spiritual, mystical and divine**
- **Has a profound love and respect for all living things**
- **Has a love affair with the natural word**
- **Embraces a holistic perspective of life**
- **Does not polarize easily to extreme views**
- **Gravitates to stillness, quietude and sincerity**
- **Loves sacred practices, ceremony and ritual**
- **Lives beyond the superficial world of the mundane**
- **Has the capacity to be deeply devotional**
- **Lives intentionally inspired by a deeper purpose**

The Relationship between devotion and sacredness: One of the most prevalent characteristics of the Sacred Child is its relationship to devotion. The root word "devote" originates from the Latin *devotus* which indicates the inward act, state or feeling or to zealously dedicate oneself by vow or promise. It refers to a behavior affecting the use of something that has been consecrated, something that is held sacred. Devotion arises from a feeling that is difficult to articulate.

For instance, if one feels a deep sense of devotion to their family, they may say that their family "is dear to their heart," which is another way of saying that they hold that relationship sacred. They may have deep feelings of gratitude and love for their family, and as a result there is a sense of loyalty and commitment. The expression of devotion will be personal and completely unique to that individual.

This expression of raw devotion from the Sacred Child is a vulnerable expression that can be quite naïve. Without the presence of the Mature Inner Adult, this feeling of sacredness can be inappropriately projected onto another person or group and easily manipulated. It is important to understand that the experience of devotion is never anything less than radiant because it is a pure expression. It is the lack of maturity, guidance and discernment that makes devotion problematic.

For this reason, however, we can become afraid to openly express devotion. The vulnerability is real. Like anything, an appropriate expression of devotion is learned by example and through accumulating wisdom through direct experience. And since there are only a few safe forums for the Sacred Child to be expressive, it is suppressed and limited to socially accepted and appropriate forums.

Sacredness and religion: Even though sacredness and devotion are associated with religious practices, organized religion is not necessary for either experience. The creation and structure of religions originated from a feeling of sacredness and were personified as a means to honor and celebrate that experience.

The deepest feelings of sacredness are evoked from the sense of knowing there is more beyond our present perception. The feeling of awe, humility and respect that is ultimately born from the sense of connection to a greater wholeness. Organized religion can function as a forum to explore this sacredness and provide a forum for devotion, but it is not necessary.

For instance, sitting down every morning and relaxing with a cup of coffee or tea, talking a walk at the end of the day of work to unwind, visiting your favorite café every week, walking home the same way from school every day, the familiarity of maintaining a weekly workout schedule, lighting candles and creating the atmosphere for inner contemplation when you take a bath, or regularly playing specific, soothing music on the car ride home from work to let go of the workday can all be sacred.

By simply being more aware of the powerful potential in these personal rituals, you can not only deepen your inner experience, you may also consciously enhance their effectiveness through your attention and intention. This is the power of the Sacred Child.

Whatever you place your consciousness and intention on
more deeply reveals itself to you in your inner and outer world.

The world of the Sacred Child is not linear, practical or rational, but you can use these mature tools of observation to explore the non-linear reality beyond the mundane. This translates as imagery, color, metaphor, symbolism, vision, sensory and empathic feelings, emotions, intuition, transmission, synchronicity and inner knowing. Those are the vehicles to awaken the subtle realms in your existing life:

> *"A symbol, like everything else, shows a double aspect.*
> *We must distinguish, therefore, between the 'sense' and the 'meaning' of the symbol.*
> *It seems to me perfectly clear that all the great and little*
> *symbolical systems of the past functioned simultaneously on three levels:*
> *the corporeal of waking consciousness, the spiritual of dream,*
> *and the ineffable of the absolutely unknowable…"*
> *– Joseph Campbell (The Symbol Without Meaning)*

Displays an uncanny sense of inner depth and presence: When one embraces the Sacred Child within, they will effortlessly express an intangible sense of imbued presence. The feeling of inner sacredness, respect, devotion and humility creates a sense of depth that radiates through the countenance of that individual. When one has connected to those inner feelings, explored the realms of direct experience and accepted the Sacred Child within, the depth of that relationship permeates through their personality and behavior. It is palpable.

Gravitates to stillness, quietude and sincerity: When one quiets themselves and turns their conscious awareness inward, they will eventually access the powerful stillness that is expressed through the Sacred Child. As a result, the Sacred Child is drawn to meditative environments which allows this stillness to flourish. This allows for a deeper connection in every relationship.

Does not polarize easily to extreme views: As a result of the increased receptivity and being open to the deeper mysteries of the universe, an empowered Sacred Child does not easily polarize extreme views or superficial moral debates. It is less interested in the rigid conceptual positions of right and wrong and far more aligned with the feeling of the "sacred flow" of the universe.

Expresses a sincere humility of character: Most people are an expression of an unconscious, beaten-down world that lives with a repressed and disconnected relationship to the Sacred Child. Because of this, they are not capable or willing to give themselves permission to experience being deeply "affected" by anything. Without this ability to connect beyond the superficial, it is impossible to be humbled by the sacredness of life. It can be uncomfortable to journey into the deeper realms of the world of the Sacred Child and yet there is a deep, human longing to be embraced by the depths of this inner connection to Source.

One of the most profound expansive qualities of the Sacred Child is its humility. The innocent, open receptivity and devotion to sacredness evokes a permeating sense of humility. The Sacred child is a vehicle to that sense of connection and sincere humility.

There is a profound and deep respect for the sacred that is woven through every aspect of life. The example and practice of ritual, prayer and ceremony and the deep respect for the planet and its treasures hold the key for the continued expression of the Sacred Child.

The sacredness of the Earth: For the Sacred Child, one of the most tangible experiences of sacredness can be explored through the relationship to the Earth. In many ancient spiritual practices, the Earth is considered the physical manifestation of the Divine. The Sacred Child is empowered by revering the natural world and the sense of homeostasis that maintains the delicate balance of life.

"Nature is your nature."
– Samjhi

This passion is expressed through a love of animals, a connection with the outdoors, a love of nature, a fascination for growing, the desire to protect the environment, an appreciation for the interconnectedness of all things, a deep love for the earth as well as an unquenchable desire to understand the inner mechanics of our natural world. For many, their first connection to the sense of wonder of the Sacred Child was inspired through the direct experience of the natural world.

Sacredness of aboriginal societies: The aboriginal and (once considered) primitive cultures are far more sophisticated and connected in their relationship to sacredness than the rest of the world. They embrace the Sacred Child and have imbued many of its empowered qualities as an integrated way of living in harmony with the Earth. The living example of practice of ritual, prayer, ceremony and the honoring of the planet and its treasures holds the key for empowering the Sacred Child. These cultures are endowed with an inclusive and holistic practice of balance and respect for every expression of life. Their alignment to the natural world is an undeniable remedy to lost sacredness.

A disempowered and disconnected experience from the sacred: The feeling and empowered experience idea of something sacred is so unacknowledged that people do not realize it until it is taken away. In a society that actively turns its back or belittles the idea of the sacred experience and glorifies the secular, where is the Sacred Child to be expressed? And what becomes of an individual that has lost their respect, connection and sense of wonder to the idea of the profound and their devotion to the Earth?

Meaninglessness, cynicism, and a jaded lack of connection to something beyond the superficial world leads to an isolated and mundane existence. Without that internal connection to the inherent Great Mystery of life, self-abusive narcissistic attitudes and behaviors will continue to destroy ourselves and the planet. The divine aspect is a requirement for a society to retain its values and someday restore balance.

Examples of Affirmations that Empower the Sacred Child:

"I give myself permission to be affected by the mysteries of life."
"I am open and receptive to the wonder, beauty and power of the natural world."
"I give myself permission to embrace the Great Mystery with ease, grace and flow."
"I allow myself to be humbled by the awe of the universe."
"I invite more, other and beyond into my daily experience."
"I open my heart to the mysteries of the Universe."
"I give thanks and gratitude to Mother Earth who sustains us all."

EMPATHIC CHILD

intuitive, emotional, empathic, feeling, nuanced, sensitive

GIFTED CHILD

special, remarkable, unique, self-expression, self-identity, talented, extraordinary

PLAYFUL CHILD

celebration, joyful, freedom, pleasure, light-hearted, absurdity, playful, spontaneous

RADIANT INNER CHILD

expansive, innocence, trust, vulnerability, awe, passion, connection, freedom, spontaneous, Childlike

CREATIVE CHILD

artisitc, conscious creator, innovation, visionary, originality, imagination

MAGICAL CHILD

fantasy, magical, wonderment, non-linear, supernatural, alchemy

SACRED CHILD

spiritual, sacred, ceremony, ritual, awe, wonder, devotion

THE RADIANT INNER CHILD
The Creative Child

"But unless we are creators, we are not fully alive. What do I mean by creators?
Not only artists, whose acts of creation are the obvious ones of working with paint or
clay or words. Creativity is a way of living life, no matter our vocation
or how we earn our living. Creativity is not limited to the arts
or having some kind of important career."
– Madeleine L'Engle

The Creative Child connects, honors and celebrates all things creative. It is passionate to explore the beauty and power of the original worlds of artistry through all expressions of life. Within the innovative expressions of philosophies, ideas, music, poetry, art, writing, theater, or dance, the Creative Child allows for the realization that we are all inherently creators of our reality.

Understanding the Dynamics of the Creative Child:

The Creative Child connects to all things original, alternative and inspired specifically by its unique consciousness. Creativity allows us to conceive, conceptualize and uniquely express ideas in the outer world. In this way, everyone is, on some level, an individual artist. Consciously owning and expressing your personal creativity enables access to your inner divine potential and the process required to empower a conceptual idea into a tangible form.

Being an empowered conscious creator: We are creative beings by nature. The ability to express that creativity connects you to your divine nature. The fact of our existence means a perpetual state of creating on some level of consciousness. Your present state of being, energy, emotion, word, thought or deed are all powerful creative forces which reveal themselves in the inner and outer worlds.

So many people choose to limit the forum from which they allow themselves to be creative. They only allow themselves to focus their creativity into a specific project or narrow platform. But how expansive could your experience become if you allowed your Creative Child to flourish?

"You can't use up creativity.
The more you use, the more you have."
– Maya Angelou

The Qualities of the Empowered Creative Child:

- **Expresses a passionate curiosity and a love for self-discovery**
- **Skilled at innovative problem solving**
- **Does not get trapped in the conventional or mundane**
- **Experiences life as a creative experiment**
- **Embraces taking a risk**
- **Forges innovative, new and sometimes radical approaches**
- **Expresses confidence in new situations**
- **Avoids stereotyping—prefers individuality, uniqueness and differences**
- **More easily accepts and embraces change and new alternatives**
- **Accesses the feminine and masculine through creative partnership**
- **Powerful capacity for creating associations, combination and arrangement**

Expresses a passionate and curious love of self-discovery: The Creative Child exemplifies a curious passion for self-discovery. This innate expression of curiosity is exhibited as a self-inspired appetite for knowledge, and the associated feeling of expansion that accompanies the thrill of that discovery and the act of creation. It supports an experience of optimistic exploration and continued quest for more information. In other words, the Creative Child wants more raw material to draw from, more diversity and more "data points" of experience to use in the creative process. When you embrace the Creative Child, you embrace the beauty of self-discovery. Engaging in the conscious act of creation creates direct access to a fundamental aspect of your divinity and the inherent potential that you unknowingly possess.

Because the Creative Child utilizes every aspect of your consciousness as source material, it naturally supports and inspires the process of self-investigation. It empowers the path of self-discovery, transformation and healing as you become your own creative experiment.

The relationship between creativity and artistry: There is confusion about the difference between creativity and artistry. They are related, but they are not the same. In any discussion about creativity you will hear someone announce that they are not an "artist" or that they have no artistic talent and therefore they do not view themselves as being creative. Most people typically refer to the word "artist" as someone who has developed a level of proficiency in the area of the arts (painting, sculpture, dance, acting, pottery, culinary cuisine, performing arts, music, photography, graphics arts... etc).

And the idea of artistry usually refers to someone who has cultivated a certain level of craftsmanship or skill in a particular field of study. There is a powerful relationship between creativity and artistry because artisans "create" works of art and employ the qualities of the empowered Creative Child in their work.

They imbue that inner expansive relationship to the process of how they approach their craftsmanship and this affects how and what they create. This could involve creative problem-solving, innovation, unconventional associations, complex ideas merged with the skill of executing those ideas in a creative manner.

Not everyone who has embraced the Creative Child will naturally become a proficient artist. But with the empowered inner relationship, they will be able to consciously apply the expansive qualities of creativity in any aspect of their life through their inner and outer relationships, endeavors, projects or tasks. All the so-called mundane aspects of life can be enhanced through a conscious relationship of creativity, artist or not.

The relationship between creativity and originality – It has been said there is no true "original" ideas. But creativity isn't about pure originality, it's the re-configuration of known elements into a new expression. It may have been done before, but it was never channeled through the unique expression that is you.

> *"There are not more than five musical notes, yet the combinations*
> *of these five give rise to more melodies than can ever be heard.*
> *There are not more than five primary colors,*
> *yet in combination they produce more hues than can ever be seen.*
> *There are not more than five cardinal tastes,*
> *yet combinations of them yield more flavors than can ever be tasted."*
> *– Sun Tzu (The Art of War)*

The Creative Child embraces risk taking: With every act of creation there is a level of risk involved. Creativity requires you to move beyond your comfort zone. True expansion can only happen at the far end of your known world. And to access this creative spark, you must be willing to be vulnerable enough to take a chance.

One of the radiant qualities of the Creative Child is its uncanny ability to lean into risk and see it from the expansive perspective as an undiscovered landscape for creative potential. Not every creative endeavor is successful. Some creative ventures fall short of the initial vision. But taking that creative risk offers you invaluable experience that you would not have necessarily taken if you played it safe.

Taking a risk can open new potential, another path, alterative approach and vital learning that can only be gleaned from being available to the experience that you gave yourself permission to have. Taking "a leap of faith" is about having faith and confidence in your ability as well as trusting your own capacity to respond to the unknown situation with an expansive perspective. In the beginning, it will be scary. But the more you take a chance, the more creatively resourceful you can become. No risk means no challenge, and no challenge means you won't access the depths of your creative potential unless you take a chance.

More easily accepts and embraces change and new alternatives: The creative process is never static. The completion of one endeavor will inspire the next one. The creative process is always in an expansive state of transformation. Because of the innocent and childlike receptivity, the Creative Child is flexible and can more easily embrace new alternatives. Change is inevitable and you cannot be too attached to what was if you want to continue to explore what can be. This sense of exploration is driven by the expansive joy of creative expression and the beauty that can be discovered in the process.

Avoids stereotyping—prefers individuality, uniqueness and differences: This dynamic approach to creative investigation usually leads the Creative Child away from the focus of "stereotyping." This aspect of the Radiant Inner Child usually sees more creative potential in exploring uniqueness, individuality and differences. Stereotyping is an over-generalized belief, based on contractive assumptions and not rooted in fact. For the Creative Child, differences are something to be embraced. Individuality and personal creative expression is deeply connected to you, as you are always exploring your unique creative viewpoint in the process.

The Creative Child experiences life as a grand and ever-changing creative experiment: The great canvas of life is the ultimate creative experiment. It is filled with infinite possibilities, unique opportunities and wonderous options just waiting to be explored. This expansive and playful approach to the experience of life also offers countless opportunities for joy through open, nonjudgmental experimentation. It is the pioneering spirit of the creative process that ignites the beauty in this grand experiment. And everyone has the power and opportunity to create their unique adventure.

Examples of Affirmations that Empower the Creative Child:

"I honor, respect and appreciate my unique creative expression."
" I am willing to step into the unknown with confidence."
"I listen and act on my inspiration."
"I give myself permission to be a conscious creator of my dreams."

EMPATHIC CHILD

intuitive, emotional, empathic, feeling, nuanced, sensitive

GIFTED CHILD

special, remarkable, unique, self-expression, self-identity, talented, extraordinary

PLAYFUL CHILD

celebration, joyful, freedom, pleasure, light-hearted, absurdity, playful, spontaneous

RADIANT INNER CHILD

expansive, innocence, trust, vulnerability, awe, passion, connection, freedom, spontaneous, Childlike

CREATIVE CHILD

artisitc, conscious creator, innovation, visionary, originality, imagination

MAGICAL CHILD

fantasy, magical, wonderment, non-linear, supernatural, alchemy

SACRED CHILD

spiritual, sacred, ceremony, ritual, awe, wonder, devotion

THE RADIANT INNER CHILD
The Gifted Child

"You are a unique flower, a beautiful and exquisite
One-Time-Happening in the universe.
It is a time in which the universe has condensed into your form
with such unique intensity that is trying to realize itself
in a One-Time-Happening for all time.
This is the sacred event of a human birth."
– David Spero

This aspect of the Radiant Inner Child embodies the specific talents of every individual that can and will only ever be expressed by and through you. Empowering the individual qualities of the Gifted Child is the act of channeling your unique presence. Attempting to minimize the talents of the Gifted Child pushes this aspect of consciousness into subdued mediocracy. It diminishes confidence and the ability to celebrate those unique gifts. It is deeply important that the Gifted Child be cherished.

Understanding the Dynamics of The Gifted Child

One of the key purposes of this aspect is the ability to value one's own remarkableness. In a society that encourages conformity, the idea of being "gifted" seems to be reserved for a rare few who have had some extraordinary virtue bestowed upon them. These people are revered for their apparent talent by those who experience themselves as plain or ordinary.

However, the idea of being gifted is a conditioned mindset, a belief that empowers one to discover inherent talents and pursue them, which leads to proficiency and outstanding displays of eventual mastery. The honoring of those unique and sometimes extraordinary aspects of the Gifted Child opens that possibility for transcending the restriction of "normalness."

The more one observes how rare each individual being is, like a single leaf of a tree, the more the possibility that inherent uniqueness has a place to thrive. This ultimately creates an environment of intriguing diversity as well as the confidence and foundation for exploring a growing depth of self-love.

The Qualities of the Empowered Gifted Child:

- **Fluid perception, lateral and unique thinking**
- **A sense of internal confidence in their own abilities or uniqueness**
- **Adept at exploring and adapting to new information without fear**
- **Radiates a sense of natural appreciation for the talents of everyone**
- **Displays persistence for their own unique or personal perspective**
- **Views the idea of normal as "What feels right for them"**
- **Inspires others through the example of their own expression**
- **Displays exceptional abilities in a specific area = talent**
- **Sees all forms of talent as something to embrace, encourage and celebrate**
- **Has the desire to hone and refine their skills**
- **Embraces unknown and new challenges**

The Journey of discovering your unique giftedness: The exploration of uniqueness is one of the most important aspects of embracing the Gifted Child. It begins with a desire to seek connection to your unique self. As you consciously embrace the expansiveness of that inner communion, you naturally translate that experience through your personal expression in the outer world. This is the first phase of igniting the power and potential of the Gifted Child.

Once that investigation has created that inner connection, you begin to discover the different forums for that inner expression. In the next phase of the process, you begin to explore your inherent talents. It can be anything: writing, music, speaking, sports, humor, etc. The more you connect and explore the experience of that natural giftedness, the more you will want to hone that expertise. Honoring your inner uniqueness allows you to discover your talent. Your expansive experience of that talent can then inspire you to explore mastery of your skills.

Views the idea of normal as "What feels right for you": The general understanding of "normal" can minimize the unique expression of the Gifted Child. But someone with an empowered Gifted Child chooses to view the idea of being normal from a different perspective. They base the concept of normalcy on harmony, on what "feels right." That experience is not obligated to follow a prescribed, typical or expected path. This radical understanding of normal is always formed from referencing and embracing that inner alignment.

Following and exploring your talent is an expansive act of self-expression: In many cases, people have unconsciously bought into the belief that it is not prudent to explore, embrace and practice your inherent talent unless that "gift" can be translated into something practical. They will first seek to cultivate practical skills (even if they are not passionate about them) to survive in a utilitarian society at the expense of their secret passion or personal dream. They sacrifice the investigation of their talent and self-expression in exchange for developing a practical skill that can help them survive in the world.

Often, those talents are relegated to the world of hobbies out of necessity and will only get explored, if at all, after one is able to make a living. In many cases, those radiant talents are completely abandoned because of lack of support, fear or doubt. If you want to uncover the unfulfilled dreams and passions of any individual, examine what they do in their "spare time" in their hobbies and pastimes. Within those activities you can usually see the unfulfilled longings of the Gifted Child.

The idea of being special is not sustainable by outer recognition alone: In the trendy, pop-culture world, the idea of being special is based in public recognition. In many cases, you are gifted or talented if you successfully achieve something that the general society deems as valuable or important. What is seen as important is what is considered the most relevant for the particular culture to maintain a specific idea of itself. If you fit the profile, people look up to you and you may gain significant recognition. In this case, the idea of being special has been determined by outer criteria that is only supported by temporary circumstances and potentially shifting opinions when trends eventually change.

In this outward model of recognition, your deeper value is never based on your own sense of inner worth. Instead, it is based on how you serve to satisfy the outer paradigm. And just because you are publicly acknowledged does not necessarily mean that you are talented or that you demonstrate a level of mastery in a specific area.

As a result, many have made their "special talent" the ability to get recognized within their culture, because they know how to embody what is publicly desirable. It is important to not to deny recognition from the outer world. It is not wrong or insignificant. It can be healthy to enjoy this recognition as long as you do not allow that to become your only source of validation to determine your inner value. So many people confuse this public adoration for feeling special and having value, but in comparison with being aligned to the direct experience of feeling your own value, this form of outer glorification will always be superficial and unsustainable.

Standardization and status quo can numb personal expression: If you attempt to subdue your own individual perspective for the need to be accepted by the status quo, you are suppressing your inherent spark of uniqueness. You can never be the truly remarkable being you want to be if you default to status quo.

The irony of the situation is that the very people who take radical paths and challenge standardization are the ones being celebrated by the very status quo that sought to ignore them for standing apart from the crowd.

After they have reached a specific level of success, these bold mavericks become idealized and coveted because they had the courage to stand apart. The empowered Gifted Child absolutely refuses to be numbed or minimized by standardization or status quo even if they must stand alone.

Inspires others through the example of their own expression: This kind of inner conviction inspires others to follow their own path and discover this kind of connection in themselves. An empowered Gifted Child radiates natural appreciation for not only their own talents, but also the talents in others. A person who is authentically secure with their empowered Gifted Child is not threatened by another's talent or giftedness. They do not scorn, judge or diminish another's personal expression, but instead, they embrace and revel in the expression of that giftedness.

The Gifted Child exemplifies fluid perception, lateral and unique thinking: Embracing the inner uniqueness of your Gifted Child enhances lateral thinking, the ability to solve problems through a creative approach, typically through viewing the problem in a new light. This kind of thinking requires you to embrace your own sense of uniqueness.

> *"You cannot solve a problem*
> *from the same consciousness that created it.*
> *You must learn to see the world anew."*
> *– Albert Einstein*

Embracing the unique, odd, strange, unusual and different is the foundation of creating a fluid perception. Empowering this perception allows you to experience life "outside of the box." This creates a sense of freedom to investigate the relationship to all things in a new manner. Uniqueness is and will always be a radiant gift that offers a different perspective to enhance your perception.

Diversity creates inner and outer strength and empowerment: There is nothing bad about the strange or unusual; it is just different. Appreciating these oddities is another way of embracing the beauty of diversity. The empowered Gifted Child has a natural affinity for differences and intuitively understands the power that resides within them.

Diversity serves an important role in evolution by allowing an adaptation to new circumstances and different environments. Diversity contributes to the health and robustness of any system. But when the levels of differences in any given environment are diminished, the system becomes infinitely more weakened and is less able to adapt to a changing environment.

Your inherent uniqueness contributes to the radiant expression of human diversity. The expression of differences allows variation to be present to support healthy interaction, growth and adaptability. Anyone who embraces and empowers the uniqueness of the Gifted Child enhances the health and wholeness of not only themselves but also the larger human population.

Examples of Affirmations that Empower the Gifted Child:

"I honor, respect and appreciate my uniqueness."

" I am special and the expression of my individuality matters."

"I give myself permission to be different."

"I am in alignment with my personal experience and expression of normal."

"Normal is what feels in alignment within."

"I allow myself to effortlessly discover, embrace and express my unique talents."

Your Personal Radiant Inner Child Dynamics

_____ **EMPATHETIC CHILD**

_____ **PLAYFUL CHILD**

_____ **MAGICAL CHILD**

_____ **SACRED CHILD**

_____ **CREATIVE CHILD**

_____ **GIFTED CHILD**

After reading the chapters about **The Radiant Inner Child,** take some time to consider which of the six archetypes are most empowered and best describe your personal conditioning. Rank them on the above scale of 1-6 (1 being the most consciously empowered and active and 6 being the least).

Remember that the potential for all the Radiant Inner Child archetypes exist within every individual's conditioning, but everyone has a different level of development in each of the different expressions of maturity based on their specific life circumstances and what they have consciously chosen to actively cultivate. Usually several of the dynamics are more empowered than others. The purpose of this process is to isolate the dynamics where you are strong and explore the areas where you are weak so that you can refine and activate as many as possible. When you can create more awareness, you can begin to more consciously work with those archetypes in new and different ways.

Consider the dynamics in your past and present (inner and outer) relationships. If you observe those relationships, you will begin to see the reoccurring patterns playing out and where your strengths and weaknesses lie. Be honest with yourself. It will require introspection and self-analysis. Remember there is a difference between what we aspire to be and what is authentically empowered within you. It helps to explore specific examples in your life through journaling. Use the information in the chapters regarding the six **Radiant Inner Child** as a guide to help you in your process.

The Expansive Inner Relationship Feedback loop

An empowered relationship between **MATURITY** and **RADIANCE** embodies the most powerful expansive feedback loop that is available in your inner and outer relationships. This supportive alignment deepens and enhances one another. It creates a powerful self-sustaining synergy that is filled with unlimited possibilities for continued expansion. Without the empowered qualities of maturity, the **Radiant Inner Child** cannot be fully nurtured to reach its full potential, and without the infusion of the radiance, the **Mature Inner Adult** can never reach its full zenith.

To experience a more sustained experience, the full potential of this expansive feedback loop must be consciously developed. This process requires you to refine your inner relationship to each of the six expansive aspects that make up the Radiant Inner Child and the six expansive aspects that make up the Mature Inner Adult.

It is important to first understand your existing relationship to the elements in both quadrants of expansiveness. Which archetypes do you have an empowered relationship with? Which elements have never been explored? Which archetypes do you need to develop and refine? This ongoing investigation also invites you to not only understand and empower each of the six archetypes in each quadrant, but to then also explore how each of the mature and radiant aspects in both quadrants align and support each other.

This process of inner investigation is vital because this will be the expansive foundation of how you will interface with all your outer relationships. In an outer relationship, you are attracted to theses empowered radiant and mature qualities in another. You are also attracted to those aspects of the Radiant Inner Child and the Mature Inner Adult that are not fully developed on yourself. With awareness, an outer relationship offers a powerful invitation to experience those unowned qualities within. But in the unconscious process of relating to these qualities in another, many feel a powerful sense of "completion" by their partner. As a result, many develop co-dependent relationships that seek to satisfy those unfulfilled archetypes within through the outer experiences of those qualities in another.

The more deeply you empower these missing elements, the less likely you will attempt to satisfy them in your outer relationships. Your Expansive Inner Relationship Feedback Loop offers you an unparalleled experience for expansive connection in every outer relationship. With this powerful Inner relationship engaged, there is an unfathomable potential to develop those radiant and mature archetypes through each other.

Your Expansive Inner Relationship Feedback Loop

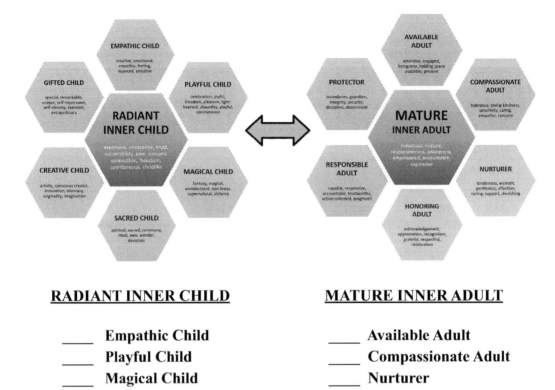

RADIANT INNER CHILD

_____ Empathic Child
_____ Playful Child
_____ Magical Child
_____ Sacred Child
_____ Creative Child
_____ Gifted Child

MATURE INNER ADULT

_____ Available Adult
_____ Compassionate Adult
_____ Nurturer
_____ Honoring Adult
_____ Responsible Adult
_____ Protector

The expansive aspects of your **Radiant Inner Child** and **Mature Inner Adult** influence every inner and outer relationship in your life. Transfer your observations and ranking for both quadrants from the previous sections and examine the relationship between the different archetypes in the radiant and mature expression of expansiveness. Explore the unique configuration of your expansive Inner Relationship Feedback loop.

Tips to Exploring Your Expansive Outer Relationship Dynamics

It can be uncomfortable to examine your existing unconscious relationships to radiance and maturity. But remember that each of these unexplored aspects offers profound opportunities as they are further developed. Have patience with yourself as you begin to investigate the unconscious dynamics of the Radiant Inner Child and the Mature Inner Adult.

1. If you cannot easily determine your internal dynamics, then begin by investigating your past and present relationship dynamics. What reoccurring behaviors or patterns do you notice? Pay attention to your existing and past roles. What do you see? The recurring behaviors that show up in your different relationships are clues and invitations from the outer world to help you see the unowned and unexplored behaviors inside of you.

2. It may help to make a list of your past and present relationships and journal your initial observations. It may also assist you, as part of your process, to ask a close and trusted friend, existing partner, spouse or family member for their observations about your patterns.

You will ALWAYS project the unconscious elements of the Adult/Child dynamics into every relationship at some level as long you are not aware of the inner dynamics.

Use the below worksheet to explore how you play out these relationship dynamics in the world. Explore different forms of relationships to get a better idea of how these patterns express themselves.

For example, you may use your boss, co-workers, neighbor, siblings, past romantic partners, past or existing friends, extended family members and parents. Explore the inner conditioning and which of the different expressions of the *Expansive Relationship Feedback Loop* that you are attracted to and how you respond to them.

Here is an example of how to complete the worksheet.

In my relationship with *my good friend Stephen*
I am most attracted to the Radiant Inner Child dynamic of *The Creative Child*
I am most attracted to the Mature Inner Adult dynamic of *The Available Adult*
WHY: *Creativity is always a powerful way for me to engage with another.*

Also examine how you respond with expansiveness. When someone expresses a radiant or mature dynamic, you may respond in two different ways:

1. **You may mirror the same radiant or mature dynamic**
2. **You may respond with a different mature or radiant dynamic**

RADIANT EXAMPLE:

Here is an example of a mirrored RADIANT response:

In my relationship with *my good friend Stephen*
When he/she expresses the Radiant Inner Child dynamic of *Playful Child*
I usually respond with the dynamic of *Playful Child*
WHY? *Because it is easier to be playful with someone who is already playful – we are in sync.*

Here is an example of a different RADIANT response:

In my relationship with *my nephew Jacob*
When he/she expresses the Radiant Inner Child dynamic of *Playful Child*
I usually respond with the dynamic of *Creative Child*
WHY? *Fun and playfulness always inspires my experimentation and creativity.*

Here is an example of a MATURE response:

In my relationship with *my daughter Skye*
When he/she expresses the Radiant Inner Child dynamic of *Playful Child*
I usually respond with the dynamic of *Honoring Adult*
WHY? *I love to celebrate and honor playfulness because no one did that for me growing up.*

MATURE EXAMPLE

Here is an example of a mirrored MATURE response:

In my relationship with *my girlfriend Tanya*
When he/she expresses the Mature Inner Adult dynamic of *Available Adult*
I usually respond with the dynamic of *Available Adult*
WHY? *Because it is easier to be available with someone who is available*

Here is an example of a different MATURE response:

In my relationship with *my colleague Christie*
When he/she expresses the Mature Inner Adult dynamic of *Available Adult*
I usually respond with the dynamic of *Responsible Adult*
WHY? *When she holds space, I feel more inspired to get things done.*

Here is an example of a RADIANT response:

In my relationship with *my aunt Era*
When he/she expresses the Mature Inner Adult dynamic of *Available Adult*
I usually respond with the dynamic of *Gifted Child*
WHY? *When I feel seen and supported, I am more able to express my uniqueness.*

Your Expansive Outer Relationship Feedback Loop Worksheet

1. In my relationship with:_____

I am most attracted to the **Radiant Inner Child** dynamic of:_____

I am most attracted to the **Mature Inner Adult** dynamic of: _____

WHY?_____

When he/she expresses the **Radiant Inner Child** dynamic of: _____

I am most likely to **respond** with the dynamic of: _____

WHY? _____

When he/she expresses the **Mature Inner Adult** dynamic of _____

I am most likely to **respond** with the dynamic of: _____

WHY?_____

2. In my relationship with:_____

I am most attracted to the **Radiant Inner Child** dynamic of:_____

I am most attracted to the **Mature Inner Adult** dynamic of: _____

WHY?_____

When he/she expresses the **Radiant Inner Child** dynamic of: _____

I am most likely to **respond** with the dynamic of: _____

WHY? _____

When he/she expresses the **Mature Inner Adult** dynamic of _____

I am most likely to **respond** with the dynamic of: _____

WHY?_____

3. In my relationship with:_____

I am most attracted to the **Radiant Inner Child** dynamic of:_____

I am most attracted to the **Mature Inner Adult** dynamic of: _____

WHY?_____

When he/she expresses the **Radiant Inner Child** dynamic of: _____

I am most likely to **respond** with the dynamic of: _____

WHY? _____

When he/she expresses the **Mature Inner Adult** dynamic of _____

I am most likely to **respond** with the dynamic of: _____

WHY?_____

4. In my relationship with:_____

I am most attracted to the **Radiant Inner Child** dynamic of:_____

I am most attracted to the **Mature Inner Adult** dynamic of: _____

WHY?_____

When he/she expresses the **Radiant Inner Child** dynamic of: _____

I am most likely to **respond** with the dynamic of: _____

WHY? _____

When he/she expresses the **Mature Inner Adult** dynamic of _____

I am most likely to **respond** with the dynamic of: _____

WHY?_____

5. In my relationship with:_____

I am most attracted to the **Radiant Inner Child** dynamic of:_____

I am most attracted to the **Mature Inner Adult** dynamic of: _____

WHY?_____

When he/she expresses the **Radiant Inner Child** dynamic of: _____

I am most likely to **respond** with the dynamic of: _____

WHY? _____

When he/she expresses the **Mature Inner Adult** dynamic of _____

I am most likely to **respond** with the dynamic of: _____

WHY?_____

6. In my relationship with:_____

I am most attracted to the **Radiant Inner Child** dynamic of:_____

I am most attracted to the **Mature Inner Adult** dynamic of: _____

WHY?_____

When he/she expresses the **Radiant Inner Child** dynamic of: _____

I am most likely to **respond** with the dynamic of: _____

WHY? _____

When he/she expresses the **Mature Inner Adult** dynamic of _____

I am most likely to **respond** with the dynamic of: _____

WHY?_____

PART VI
EXPANSIVE MEDICINE

Healthy Relationship Dynamics:
The Expansive Feedback Loop Between Maturity and Radiance

*The most balanced human beings are able to sustain
the intricate relationship between being an aware adult
while supporting the child-like qualities of their inner and outer self.
Both sides of expansion are empowered and both are celebrated
because each aspect accepts its unique role in expansiveness.*

The Mature Inner Adult offers different remedies of healthy and empowered maturity which support, uplift and enhance the different archetypes of the Radiant Inner Child. In turn, the Radiant Inner Child revitalizes the radiance back into the Mature Inner Adult archetypes. The mature archetypes can now operate at a deeper and more enhanced level. This is the beauty and synergy of the expansive relationship between maturity and radiance. As you begin to understand the subtleties of your inner dynamics and conditioning, it is important to utilize the transformational medicine from the different archetypes of radiance and maturity to ongoingly support the Expansive Feedback Loop.

The Mature Medicine of The Available Adult

The Available Adult is also vital to support all aspects of the Radiant Inner Child. It is this aspect of maturity that is necessary to develop a healthy inner relationship with the Radiant Inner Child. Without the Mature Inner Adult engaged, actively "holding space" and creating safety for the Radiant Inner Child, none of the radiant traits can emerge. In the healing process, it is far more common to hold space for a wounded aspect than to consciously support a radiant aspect. But there can be no development or refinement to any the different radiant archetypes of the Radiant Inner Child if you cannot be sincerely available for them.

The Available Adult and the Empathic (intuitive) Child: The Available Adult is the mature aspect of your being that allows the understated, but complex and deeper movements of the Empathetic Child to be seen, acknowledged and respected. Without a safe inner platform of self-recognition, this vital aspect will remain unrealized. The non-judgmental support of the Available Adult is necessary for the Empathetic Child to emerge.

The Available Adult and the Gifted Child: The Available Adult is the aspect of the Mature Adult that gives you permission to acknowledge the individual greatness of the Gifted Child as a unique expression that can only be offered through and by you. When you become available to your own uniqueness, you can then allow yourself to affirm this unexpressed potential. The Available Adult holds space for you to embrace and support the exploration of your gifts and talents. Without it, you will not have the confidence for you to allow those talents to emerge.

The Available Adult and the Creative Child: We are always in a perpetual state of creation through every thought, feeling, word or deed. The Creative Child is the radiant expression of creativity in all of your relationships. The Available Adult is the powerful medicine of unimpeded recognition and loving support. Without it, you can never fully access your creative potential and channel it into your daily life. And you cannot consciously manifest your dreams into reality if you are unwilling to first acknowledge your creative nature more deeply. Once the Creative Child is seen and acknowledged by the Available Adult, it becomes empowered.

The Available Adult and the Sacred Child: Without the Available Adult, the Sacred Child will be disowned and ignored. The Available Adult respectfully embraces the idea of the possible unknown aspects of the Great Mystery around us without judgment or condemnation. This sense of "things beyond" provides a profound opportunity for exploration, development and expansion. The acknowledgment and recognition of sacredness in your daily life creates connection and inclusion as part of the process of growth.

The Mature Medicine of The Compassionate Adult

The Compassionate Adult supports, gently empowers and lovingly inspires all the different aspects of the Radiant Inner Child. The radiant aspects of the being need this form of supportive nourishment to fully open, explore and safely express their inherent potential.

The Compassionate Adult and Empathic Child: Compassion and empathy are deeply connected. The Compassionate Adult is very attuned to the healthy expression of the Empathic Child. The Compassionate Adult can be understood as the active, mature and discerning influence that helps navigate the complex relationship with the "suffering component" of empathy.

Because the nature of the Empathic Child is so innocent, the medicine of the Compassionate Adult offers a more mature understanding and grounded support in responding to human suffering. Without this mature element, the Empathic Child can be easily overwhelmed by the intensity of suffering, react or become repressed because of fear.

The Mature Medicine of The Nurturer

It is not enough to simply acknowledge the expansive archetypes within you. Those expansive elements all require a certain level of consistent nurturing to be fully empowered. The powerful supportive medicine of the Nurturer manifests as a loving sense of support and is the necessary expansive fuel that inspires each archetype to reach its full potential.

Though all expansive aspects require nurturing, some archetypes will require different levels and forms of attention and support at different points of the process of evolution due to your individual conditioning.

The Nurturer and the Playful Child: Nurturing the freeform expression of playfulness in the Playful Child can take on many forms. But one of the most important expressions of medicine from the Nurturer is the ability to consciously let go and simply allow the spontaneous expression of joy to bubble up from within. Releasing agendas and preconceived notions about fun, accepting its fluidity and actively celebrating the expression of that joy is powerful medicine for nurturing the inherent radiance of the Playful Child. The spontaneous expression of freedom cannot be controlled or manipulated in a specific way; it must consciously be allowed to flow.

The Nurturer and the Empathic Child: The medicine of the Nurturer supports the evolution of your emotinal, intutitive and empathetic nature through sensitivity and loving attention. That support allows the Empathic Child to connect, acknowledge and most importantly explore a direct experience of "feeling" of the different qualities of emotional energy. Without this, you will never create a fully integrated relationship with your feeling nature or empathically connect from an empowered and sustainable position. Nourishing the process allows your inner awareness to evolve and shift with your deepening relationship to the Empathic Child.

The Nurturer and the Sacred Child: The Nurturer allows you to be moved by a sense of awe, gratitude and humility which endears itself to a deeper experience of sacredness. For the Sacred Child to flourish, you have to consciously be willing to recognize it, accept the experience, then allow yourself to be affected by it. It is a choice to develop the ongoing sensitivity to broaden the bandwidth of your perception through nurturing this receptivity.

The Nurturer and the Creative Child: Nurturing the art of creativity is only empowered through a conscious shift of mindset beyond the conventional; embracing bold and occasionally radical approaches. Without active development, the Creative Child can easily be absorbed by overwhelming temptation of the status quo. But, the medicine of the Nurturer supports life as a creative experiment and embraces individual curiosity. It supports the development of unconventional self-expression, artistry and originality.

The Nurturer and the Magical Child: The medicine of the Nurturer supports the Magical Child through empowering the belief in possibility. The Nurturer helps develop the Magical Child's relationship to fantasy and lovingly embraces the exhilaration of mystery, wonder and imagination. It nourishes the Magical Child's wonderment by allowing this seemingly improbable world to become probable through actively nourishing those "unrealistic" visions. The Nurturer lovingly transcends the contraction, restriction and judgment that limit the possibility of dreams.

The Nurturer and the Gifted Child: Nurturing raw talent accelerates competency, ability and mastery. But without loving attention and expansive support, the gift of raw talent may never become realized. The Nurturer provides that ever-evolving loving support that is required to shift your unique potential into actuality.

The Nurturer and The Honoring Adult: These two aspects are similar, and work best in harmony. For example, the Honoring Adult may uplift the different aspects of the being through self-esteem building, while the Nurturer may take a broader approach as it actively supports the ongoing evolution through many different expressions of loving attention. Honoring Adult medicine offers respect and worthiness through celebration and different forms of acknowledgement. The Nurturer promotes the ongoing development of the being through its nourishing and caring.

The Mature Medicine of The Honoring Adult

It is necessary to recognize, appreciate and honor the various aspects of the Inner Child. Valuing the expansive and radiant nature of all the different archetypes of the Radiant Inner Child not only supports the continued evolution of this aspect of your being, it also sustains it.

Therefore, it is vital to the healthy development of the Radiant Inner Child that you appreciate the different gifts that these archetypes of expansion offer. The uplifting energy of the Honoring Adult empowers each of these aspects to continue to expand and develop. Supporting and uplifting expansion only creates more expansion.

The Honoring Adult and the Empathic Child: The medicine of the Honoring Adult offers the deep respect, and appreciation for this expression of the Radiant Inner Child. Because the expression of the Empathic Child is energetic and nuanced by nature, it requires care, conscious attention and consideration.

It is important to understand that the unacknowledged, disrespected and ignored sensitivity of the Empathic Child will eventually "go underground" into the unconscious and feed the emotional reactivity in various expressions of the Wounded Inner Child. The Honoring Adult offers that necessary mature support and acknowledgement for the Empathic Child. Without this mature element the Empathic Child can easily remain ignored and become repressed.

The Honoring Adult and the Gifted Child: The Honoring Adult understands that it is deeply important that the Gifted Child be cherished and promoted. This aspect of the Mature Inner Adult supports, praises and exalts the uniqueness of the Gifted Child. When it is honored in this way, the self-recognition of that unique "specialness" creates the inner confidence. (Think about the coach who believes in the unexpressed talent in a player or the teacher you who supports the undeveloped potential in a student.) With this loving appreciation those unique gifts finally have the space to emerge. The medicine of the Honoring Adult celebrates the evolution of personal potential.

> *"You can only become special through Self-Recognition."*
> *– David Spero*

The Honoring Adult and the Magical Child: The Magical Child embodies the "power of possibility through the realms of impossibility." The Magical Child lives in an "otherworld" that celebrates the make-believe, whimsical, fantastic, non-linear, surrealistic and mystical.
The Honoring Adult offers acceptance as it acknowledges and celebrates the Magical Child and its realm of dreams. This aspect of the Mature Inner Adult recognizes that the Magical Child thrives in the realm of the imagination where unfathomable visions of fantasy, fiction, non-linear magic and make-believe exist as living possibilities.

Honoring these realms, characters, creations and the supernatural scenarios that are expressed in this dreamtime reality allows for the expression and energy of the inner alchemist to conjure, create and explore. It also allows the psyche to explore powerful healing narratives, process pain, explore archetypal energies, investigate alternate realities, and offers a true sanctuary for everything that does not fit into the idea of "normal."

The Honoring Adult and the Sacred Child: The Sacred Child is attuned to the experience and understanding of wholeness. It is inspired by the awe and wonder of recognizing its intimate connection to something beyond itself, as an aspect of the oneness of all things. The Honoring Adult celebrates this investigation of human consciousness. It respectfully honors that journey through the various forms of archetypal, metaphoric and symbolic experience. Without this recognition, the Sacred Child would be unempowered to explore its sacred connection to the whole.

The Mature Medicine of The Responsible Adult

The more you own and empower the presence of any aspect of your Mature Inner Adult, the more the aspects of the Radiant Inner Child feel safe to express themselves in new and wonderous ways. Subtle levels of the Radiant aspects flourish with the empowered support from the different flavors of the Responsible Adult.

The Responsible Adult and The Playful Child: The medicine that the Responsible Adult offers to support a healthy Playful Child is simple yet vital for its expression and ongoing development. This Mature Inner Adult aspect offers its dedication and dependable commitment to being responsible so that the Radiant Inner Child can be free to discover and celebrate all the many facets of play. The Responsible Adult maintains the balance of the pragmatic world so the Radiant Inner Child is not restricted in any way, and also provides the necessary care for all the worldly necessities so the Playful Child never has to be burdened by the reality of a mature adult world.

Consider some young children immersed in glorious play outside in the backyard of a family home. They have no care or concern for anything but exploring the next adventure. And the Responsible Adult is inside the house preparing dinner, watching the time, keeping an eye on the activities through the window and fetching the playing children when it is time to have a meal.

They are ushered inside to wash up and have some food. The children who are not ever aware of their own hunger simply follow the instructions because they trust the Responsible Adult. They bolt inside, sit down at the table to eat exclaiming stories and the joy of their escapades. The child has no idea about all the planning, coordination and careful consideration required to effortlessly execute the entire process... and it never should.

The Responsible Adult and The Creative Child: The Creative Child is only interested in the pragmatic mechanics of life only as it applies to the facilitation of its creative expression of consciousness. It longs for a sense of freedom, safety and permission to allow the conscious relationship of creativity to thrive and flourish in every aspect of your life.

Because the Responsible Adult is devoted to facilitating the practical mechanics of life, it provides space for conscious creativity to explore itself. There is always a responsible element that is required to fully to support the creative process. The Responsible Adult handles the utilitarian side of the creative process. For example, it creates the necessary funds required to obtain the raw materials that the Creative Child needs. It facilitates the time in the schedule that allows the space to create, handles the cleanup, storage and maintenance of the tools of the trade and everything else for the radiant process to find its way into expression.

When the medicine of the Responsible Adult is dedicated and devoted to the functioning of the pragmatic world it provides the inner and outer platform for the Creative Child to be devoted to what it does best—create.

The Mature Medicine of The Protector

For the different qualities of the Radiant Inner Child to flourish in a healthy manner, boundaries and safeguards need to be present. Inner and outer security – feeling secure enough to explore and celebrate radiance – is one of the many ways that the Protector shelters these expansive traits as they grow. The Radiant Inner Child, just like the Wounded Inner Child, also needs an advocate to safely support the inner and outer relationship of exploration with self and others.

The Protector and the Empathic Child: The Empathetic Child has issues with understanding and distinguishing clear and healthy boundaries between themselves and others. There can be a tendency for the Empathic Child to become over-empathic with another which can lead to an inner imbalance. To fully accept and feel the spectrum of your emotional state and practice a healthy expression of that inner connection requires safety, understanding and boundaries. The grounded and centered influence from the Protector is vital to regulate and buffer this intensity. A healthy relationship with the emotional body always requires a level of inner discipline.

The Protector also creates the supportive container to ensure that the Empathic Child has the security to explore all the aspects of this nuanced world without fear or judgment. In this way, the Protector functions as the watchful and stabilizing mechanism for all emotional, intuitive and empathic relationships.

The Protector and the Gifted Child: The Gifted Child always needs an advocate to protect the unique dream or vision and the "extra" ordinary expression within. The Protector supports your quest to discover yourself and offers the strength and conviction to stick with your unique path and see it though. Without that strength, support and conviction, most of those unique dreams fade before they are ever allowed to be fully expressed.   This aspect of the Mature Adult will protect and shelter your gifts, talents, and dreams.

The Radiant Medicine of the Empathic Child

The Empathic child infuses all archetypes of the Mature Inner Adult with a better connection to the emotional body. It also invites the different aspects of the Mature Inner Adult into a deeper relationship with your innate sense of intuition.
 The Empathetic Child and the Nurturer: Having a consciously developed relationship with the Empathic Child allows the Nurturer to connect with more sensitivity. This allows the kind attentiveness of the Nurturer to be more "tuned in" and available to the emotional experience while it is fostering a nurturing environment.

The more developed sense of intuition profoundly aids the Nurturer as it functions as the loving provider. The deeper the connection the Nurturer can make, the more it is able to offer its expansive contribution of nourishment. That enhanced emotional sensitivity and intuitive sense of empathy affect your capacity to offer nurturing and support in all of your inner and outer relationships.

The Empathetic Child and the Compassionate Adult: Compassion and empathy are profoundly connected. The innocent radiance of the Empathetic Child that is emotionality and intuitively connected, coupled with the innate human instinct of the Compassionate Adult creates a profound space for healing the wounds of suffering. When the Compassionate Adult can draw on these powerful aspects of the Empathic Child, it is better able to empathically recognize and relate to the struggle. It is sourced by those subtle but radiant energies of the Empathic Child which allows for deeper connection. That connection offers an emotionally and intuitively supported form of compassion that transcends intellectual understanding.

Since compassion is also expressed as an active sense of empathy, the deeper your inner realization of self-empathy, the more effective you will be with another who desperately needs that loving support.

The Empathetic Child and the Available Adult: Consciously connecting to the empowered Empathic Child allows the Available Adult to draw on this deeper sensitivity to be empathically connected. When you can intuitively access an emotional landscape, you can be present without interference.

The more deeply one can access that relationship with the subtle energetic realms beyond the world of mind within themselves the more present they can be for another in that manner. Being emotionally and intuitively connected to the process, allows the space holder to be more responsive to the direct experience of the environment. The deeper the inner connection to these inner states, the more likely one will be less affected by the potential emotional charge and shifting energies of the outer circumstances for which they are holding space.

The Empathetic Child and the Honoring Adult: When the Honoring Adult fosters an empowered bond with the Empathic Child, its capacity for recognizing the world of the subtle is amplified. The Honoring Adult is now able to more deeply appreciate and value the (inner and outer) nuanced states of consciousness. This opens the potential for more cherished attention and support at deeper levels. The combination of emotionally connected empathy along with intuitive connection always creates a more expansive experience of validation.

The Empathic Child and Other Archetypes of the Radiant Inner Child: In many ways, the Empathic Child is the emotional and intuitive heart of the Radiant Inner Child. It offers each of the different aspects the opportunity to connect, experience and understand a sense of feeling and intuition though every archetype more deeply. Conscious attunement to the experience of your emotions and innate intuition is the foundational support that uplifts and empowers every aspect of the Radiant Child.

The Radiant Medicine of the Playful Child

The Playful Child and the Responsible Adult: The Responsible Adult has a reputation of being non-nonsense. It can take its position of the practical "get it done" archetype very seriously. The light-hearted and playful radiance of the Playful Child can help soften that intensity. It joyfully opens the Responsible Adult to a more relaxed way of approaching pragmatic aspects of life. With the influence of playfulness, this aspect of the Mature Inner Adult can learn to respond with more ease, grace and flow and appreciate the joy of the task while still honoring the need to accomplish the goal.

The Playful Child and the Magical Child: The combined influence of these two radiant aspects creates an unprecedented synergy. With the jubilant and spontaneous energy of play, the Magical Child is given permission to delve even more deeply into its more whimsical creations and worlds of the fantastic. This alignment creates a "Playful Magic" that is deceivingly transformational.

The Playful Child and the Creative Child: Fun and creativity always go hand-in-hand. Curious and spontaneous investigation is always a necessary ingredient in the creative process. Playful trial-and-error allows the freedom for those wild ideas to be explored and come to fruition. In this way, these two radiant aspects create an incredible synergistic alliance of "playful creativity" that amplifies the possibility of expansiveness.

The Playful Child and the Gifted Child: With the light-hearted approach of the Playful Child, the Gifted Child is given the freedom to explore its unique potential with less self-consciousness. Since play has no agenda except maximizing joy, the Gifted Child feels safe to come out and explore itself. There is nothing more joyful than embracing your inherent talents and discovering yourself. In this powerful alignment, play is utilized as a transformational invitation for self-discovery.

The Radiant Medicine of the Magical Child

The Magical Child can have a direct influence on the Mature Inner Adult as well as other aspects of the Radiant Inner Child. Infusing the qualities of magic, infinite possibility and the ability to dream are powerful radiant expressions that allow the possibility of powerful alchemy when channeled through the different expansive archetypes.

The Magical Child and the Honoring Adult: The medicine of the Magical Child is whimsical, surreal, fantastic and otherworldly. When this sense of magic from the Radiant Inner Child is injected into the celebratory atmosphere of the Honoring Adult, it can manifest a fantastic space for celebration.

Just consider if the Magical Child medicine was infused into a young child's birthday party. The atmosphere could include magical creatures, superheroes, jumping castles, costumes, circus performers, amusement rides and magicians. The Magical Child brings the enchanted dream-world as a form of celebration while the event honors and celebrates an individual, a special occasion, or change of season.

The Magical Child and the Nurturer: The Magical Child is a powerful ally for the Nurturer. The Magical Child can offer another dimension of possibility for nurturing. This magic is another tool in the expansive toolbox that can be utilized to help the support and sense of nourishment that the Nurturer strives to create.

The Nurturer will leave the magic to the magic-maker and draw on that energy to assist it in its process. Sometimes an individual, especially a young child, needs faith to envision an allegory, and create a make-believe world to explore the possibility of feeling loved and adored. "If you could create anything in your special space, anything at all, what would it look like, who or what would be there and what magical abilities would they possess?" This powerful alliance offers that opportunity.

The Magical Child and the Responsible Adult: The Magical Child is about drawing the unknowable aspects of consciousness from the universe and infusing it into the world. It offers the powerful medicine of alchemy to the pragmatic Responsible Adult. This combination creates the energy of an "inspired scientist" who is able to take the magical world and leverage those unrealistic ideas into practical systems and pragmatic containers. It also helps the sensible realist understand that anything is possible, and that all problems have a solution, even if some of those solutions may be unconventional and fantastic. Together this seemingly odd duo can create a transformational power of alchemy through the real-life application of magic.

The Magical Child and the Creative Child: Blending the whimsical, fluid, non-conventional energy of the Magical Child with the Creative Child's unique lateral thinking and ability to creatively express itself is exceptionally powerful.

The interdependent alliance between these two Radiant Inner Child aspects creates an unparalleled force for creative manifestation and alchemy. Empowered by The Magical Child, the Creative Child expands it canvas to go to magical, unprecedented inner space to access the mystical sense of fantasy. This partnership is an expression of alchemy, transforming an already powerfully radiant space to something much greater.

The Magical Child and the Sacred Child: Because the Sacred Child already revels in sacredness, it is deeply receptive to receive the radiant medicine from the Magical Child. It opens all the spaces of the fantastic, the esoteric and the impossible with a feeling of reverence.

Magic and Sacredness both dwell in deep communion with the mysterious and the unknown aspects of the consciousness. Therefore, there is already a profound common bond between these two aspects of the Radiant Child. They source in each through their relationship to the Great Mystery. The "Sacred Magic" they create is a deeply penetrating energy with great spiritual power for alchemical transformation.

The Magical Child and the Playful Child: The Playful Child lives for the joy and amusement of the moment. It explores life with an unconstrained sense of freedom, without a goal or agenda in flow with the movement of the Universe.

There is an added sense of unconventional fantasy and magic that is offered by the medicine of the Magical Child that expands this play to another level. "Playful Magic" is infectious as it lightens the heart and relaxes the mind and allows a deep sense of surrender to the moment. This creates a profound transformation through the joyful expression of the fantastic and a sense of adventurous curiosity for the unknown.

The Radiant Medicine of the Sacred Child

There is an intimate and powerful relationship in an empowered Sacred Child with varying aspects of the Mature Inner Adult. It imbues a sense of inner connection, purpose and intentionality. Supported by deep meaningfulness and humility, each archetype can operate from a much-enhanced perspective.

 The Sacrèd Child and the Available Adult: When the Available Adult forms an alliance with the profound world of the empowered Sacred Child, its sense of receptivity is amplified and spiritualized. As a result, the Available Adult radiates an even deeper experience of availability. And though it may not be understood, it can be experienced through its ability to hold space for another. This imbued reverence and sense of devotion allows the Available Adult to create a profoundly "sacred space."

The Sacred Child and the Honoring Adult: The Honoring Adult and the Sacred Child have a powerful interdependent partnership. The Mature Inner Adult aspect of the Honoring Adult sincerely acknowledges the (inner or outer) world with genuine respect and appreciation. The Sacred Child fosters deeper access to the more subtle aspects of consciousness providing a deeper opportunity for recognition. Sacredness opens the potential for more cherished attention and support. Combining that already uplifting support with a sense of childlike wonder, awe and humility creates a deeply expansive experience of "sacred honoring." This expansive relationship provides one of the most revered states of devotion that empowers and amplifies each of the archetypes.

The Sacred Child and the Protector: What the Sacred Child offers to The Protector is an empowered and sacred sense of devotion. When the already honorable Protector is imbued with a sense of "sacred devotion," it inspires an enhanced relationship with a deeper sense of something greater.

The alliance of these two expansive archetypes creates a "sacred protection" of safety, along with necessary discernment and code of conduct for the appropriate expression of the innocent, childlike devotion. This Protector becomes an even more powerful and purpose-driven "Spiritual Warrior," who now also has complete access to the radiance of the empowered Sacred Child.

The Sacred Child and Other Archetypes of The Radiant Inner Child: Sacredness empowers every aspect of the Radiant Inner Child in a profound manner. Empowered sacredness and devotion manifests as a direct experience and profound attunement to a deeper world of intrinsic meaning. Sacredness can now be uniquely expressed, celebrated and revered through each aspect of the Radiant Inner Child.

The Radiant Medicine of The Creative Child

Creativity opens the world of possibilities for every archetype. It reimagines any conventional behavior of the Mature Inner Adult and the Radiant Inner Child into something even more dynamic. The Creative Child may also "connect the dots" offering different insight as it reconfigures each expansive archetype into something beyond its present potential. This ongoing creative innovation is the key to evolution.

The Creative Child and the Nurturer: The Creative Child can be of great assistance to the Nurturer through the combined energy of "creative nurturing." Through this powerful alliance, the Nurturer is ignited to discover creative and innovative ways to offer support. That spark of creative ingenuity allows the Nurturer to use unconventional methodologies and lateral thinking to help create a supportive environment of growth and development.

The Creative Child and the Responsible Adult: When the Creative Child is empowered and supporting the Responsible Adult, the results are astounding. This powerful amplification of creative energy allows the Responsible Adult to "stretch" its thinking far beyond the bounds of its conventional approach and pragmatic sensibility. The Creative Child amplifies its already keen sense of responsiveness to any situation through the addition of creative radiance. This powerful expansive feedback loop can now support and sustain a transformational force inspired by radiance, focused into maturity and channeled into practicality.

The Creative Child and the Available Adult: The Creative Child strengthens the creative perceptiveness of the Available Adult. When creativity is infused into its presence, it unleashes an impassioned and energized space that quietly supports self-discovery.

The Creative Child and the Protector: The Protector is the vigilant, discerning sentry and advocate that safeguards all facets of the Inner Child. The Creative Child gives it an awakened sense of creativity that inspire its actions, strategy and approach to any situation. This allows the Protector to be creative and conceptual in its thinking, planning and execution. Like an artist with a muse, this sense of nonconventional, innovative creative energy is infused in every aspect of the hero's discipline, integrity, discernment and engagement.

The Radiant Medicine of the Gifted Child

The medicine of the empowered Gifted Child allows you to recognize, accept and explore your unique expression. Your inherent talent can be channeled through the various expressions of the Radiant Inner Child and the Mature Inner Adult. This allows you to find more ways to explore and express your perception and viewpoint with the world in an expansive manner.

The Gifted Child and the Creative Child: With the activated energy of the Gifted Child, the Creative Child becomes even more empowered. The process of creation now includes a deeper imprint of your unique expression. For example, this can be seen when an artist does a personal rendition of another's song. They may use the structure of the song but will "interpret" the song in a different manner. This artistic interpretation is an illustration of the uniqueness of personalized creativity in action.

The Gifted Child and the Magical Child: The radiant medicine of the Gifted Child infused into the fantastic realm of the Magical Child creates an extraordinary synergy. When your inherent talent is channeled through the alchemical possibilities of the Magical Child, it offers an opportunity to express the mysterious and intangible essence of your uniqueness into the world. The Magical Child's empowered belief of possibility offers the fantastic a limitless forum to explore your specialness, individuality and uniqueness.

The Gifted Child and the Sacred Child: There is a transformational synergy in the relationship between the Gifted Child and the Sacred Child. When the awareness of your own uniqueness becomes sincerely honored, it can empower a richer expression of your inherent nature. When you experience your uniqueness through the lens of sacredness, it generates a deeply transcended experience that can access unprecedented heights of radiance and humility.

The Gifted Child and the Responsible Adult: When the Gifted Child is infused into the pragmatic responsiveness of the Responsible Adult, it creates a powerful space for the practical application of inherent talent. The Responsible Adult channels the essence of you through pragmatic systems and forums to make it useful in the world. And because the Responsible Adult is responsive to your uniqueness, it never sacrifices your talent for the efficiency of the system or process through which it operates. Through the grounded lens of the Responsible Adult, you will find a way to responsively "get it done," while always doing it in your own unique manner.

Reacting to the Expansive (Radiant and Mature) Archetypes:

Not everyone immediately accepts expansiveness with radiance or maturity. If there are deeply ingrained patterns of unconscious conditioning, it can be uncomfortable and sometimes difficult to fully trust and appreciate the expansive dynamics of the Radiant Inner Child and the Mature Inner Adult. This is especially true if you did not have a lot of expansive examples or experiences.

It can take time to work through and process your reactions. But remember, all of these unconscious dynamics offer profound opportunities for self-awareness and growth. Have patience with yourself as you begin to investigate the unconscious reactions to the Radiant Inner Child and the Mature Inner Adult. Once you better understand these patterns, you will be more likely to choose something different.

- If you cannot easily determine your internal dynamics, then begin by investigating your past and present relationship dynamics. What reoccurring behaviors or patterns do you notice? Pay attention to your existing and past roles. What do you see? The recurring behaviors that show up in your different relationships are clues and invitations from the outer world to help you see the unowned and unexplored behaviors inside of you.

- It may help to make a list of your past and present relationships and journal your initial observations. It may also assist you, as part of your process, to ask a close and trusted friend, existing partner, spouse or family member for their observations about your patterns.

Use the below worksheet to explore how you play out these relationship dynamics in the world. Explore different forms of relationships to get a better idea of how these patterns express themselves. For example, you may use your boss, co-workers, neighbor, siblings, past romantic partners, past or existing friends, extended family members and parents. Explore the inner conditioning and which of the different expressions of the **Expansive Relationship Feedback Loop** that you are attracted to and how you respond to them.

When you encounter dynamics of expansiveness, you may react with either:

1. **The Shadow Inner Adult**
2. **The Wounded Inner Child.**

Here are some examples.

In my relationship with *my younger brother Mathew*
I most often unconsciously react with the Wounded Inner Child dynamic of the *Frozen Child*
I most often unconsciously react with the Shadow Inner Adult dynamic of the *Enabler*

When he expresses the Radiant Inner Child dynamic of *Playful Child*
I am most likely to unconsciously react with the: *Internal Critical Parent*
WHY? *Because it is irresponsible, and I NEVER got the chance to let go and just have fun.*

When he expresses the Mature Inner Adult dynamic of *Protector*
I am most likely to unconsciously react with the: *Frozen Child*
WHY? *No one honored my boundaries and I am waiting for them to be disrespected.*

In my relationship with *my co-worker Cyndy*
I most often unconsciously react with the Wounded Inner Child dynamic of the *Needy Child*
I most often unconsciously react with the Shadow Inner Adult dynamic of the *Controlling Inner Adult*

When she expresses the Radiant Inner Child dynamic of *Gifted Child*
I am most likely to unconsciously react with the: *Over-Dramatic Child*
WHY? *I feel insecure and jealous with her ease in expressing herself and I often overreact.*

When she expresses the Mature Inner Adult dynamic of *Responsible Adult*
I am most likely to unconsciously react with the: *Inauthentic Handler*
WHY? *I want to look as good as she does, so I will do what I have to keep my image up.*

Your Reactive Outer Relationship Worksheet

1. In my relationship with:_____
I most often unconsciously react with the Wounded Inner Child dynmaic of:_____
I most often unconsciously raect with the Shadow Inner Adult dynamic of:_____
WHY? _____

When he/she expresses the **Radiant Inner Child** dynamic of:_____
I am most likely to unconsciously react with (**Wounded or Shadow**):_____
WHY? _____

When he/she expresses the **Mature Inner Adult** dynamic of _____
I am most likely to unconsciously react with (**Wounded or Shadow**):_____
WHY? _____

2. In my relationship with:_____
I most often unconsciously react with the Wounded Inner Child dynmaic of:_____
I most often unconsciously raect with the Shadow Inner Adult dynamic of:_____
WHY? _____

When he/she expresses the **Radiant Inner Child** dynamic of:_____
I am most likely to unconsciously react with (**Wounded or Shadow**):_____
WHY? _____

When he/she expresses the **Mature Inner Adult** dynamic of _____
I am most likely to unconsciously react with (**Wounded or Shadow**):_____
WHY? _____

3. In my relationship with:_____
I most often unconsciously react with the Wounded Inner Child dynmaic of:_____
I most often unconsciously raect with the Shadow Inner Adult dynamic of:_____
WHY? _____

When he/she expresses the **Radiant Inner Child** dynamic of:_____
I am most likely to unconsciously react with (**Wounded or Shadow**):_____
WHY? _____

When he/she expresses the **Mature Inner Adult** dynamic of _____
I am most likely to unconsciously react with (**Wounded or Shadow**):_____
WHY? _____

4. In my relationship with:_____
I most often unconsciously react with the Wounded Inner Child dynmaic of:_____
I most often unconsciously raect with the Shadow Inner Adult dynamic of:_____
WHY? _____

When he/she expresses the **Radiant Inner Child** dynamic of:_____
I am most likely to unconsciously react with (**Wounded or Shadow**):_____
WHY? _____

When he/she expresses the **Mature Inner Adult** dynamic of _____
I am most likely to unconsciously react with (**Wounded or Shadow**):_____
WHY? _____

5. In my relationship with:_____
I most often unconsciously react with the Wounded Inner Child dynmaic of:_____
I most often unconsciously raect with the Shadow Inner Adult dynamic of:_____
WHY? _____

When he/she expresses the **Radiant Inner Child** dynamic of:_____
I am most likely to unconsciously react with (**Wounded or Shadow**):_____
WHY? _____

When he/she expresses the **Mature Inner Adult** dynamic of _____
I am most likely to unconsciously react with (**Wounded or Shadow**):_____
WHY? _____

1. Which Mature Inner Adult archetypes do you react to the most? Why? Which Mature Inner Adult archetypes do you react to the least? Why

2. Which Radiant Inner Child archetypes do you react to the most? Why? Which Radiant Inner Child do you react to the least? Why?

3. Are you more likely to react to the Radiant or the Mature expansive archetypes? Explain.

4. Which Wounded Inner Child dynamics do you react with the most? Why?

5. Which Shadow Inner Adult dynamics are you least responsive to? Why?

6. What other observations do you have about your reactions? Explain.

PART VII
MATURE MEDICINE

The Mature Medicine of the Mature Inner Adult

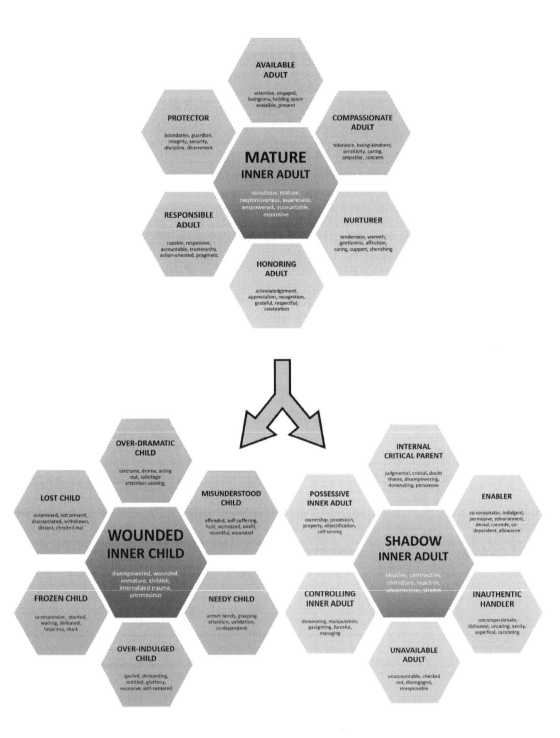

The Mature and Radiant Medicine
For the Shadow Inner Adult and the Wounded Inner Child

The Radiant Inner Child and the Mature Inner Adult can provide powerful remedies for the unhealthy patterns of the Wounded Inner Child and the Shadow Inner Adult. Treating the contractive issues and transforming the inner relationship with the expansive medicine of radiance and maturity will help restore balance. As you begin to more deeply explore and understand the subtleties of your inner dynamics and conditioning, it is important to practice utilizing the transformational medicine. There is often confusion when a contractive archetype presents itself as expansive. Understanding the differences between the archetypes assists you in choosing the most effective medicine for your underlying issues.

The Mature Medicine of The Available Adult

Being sincerely available is always the first step to shifting your relationship to any aspect of yourself. Without the ability to hold space without judgment, there can be no safe space for growth or transformation. This can be difficult to master because being objective requires conscious awareness and intentionality.

Holding a neutral space without the need to actively change or fix anything allows for true observation. This gives you the ability to investigate your existing relationship to the contractive aspects of your consciousness.

The Available Adult vs the Unavailable Adult: The detached behavior of the Unavailable Adult prevents any sense of personal and moral responsibility. The behavior is highly untrustworthy, unreliable, insensitive, unstable and aloof. The conscious and empowered choice to be sincerely available is the most potent medicine for the reckless escapism of the Unavailable Adult. Healing this Shadow aspect is based on deepening its ownership with honesty. The non-invasive and non-judgmental sensitivity of the Available Adult infiltrates the willful ignorance of its Shadow side. By holding space, the Unavailable Adult becomes aware of the depth of its own unavailability, and slowly awareness and responsibility begin to emerge. Once that awareness is established, the new expansive behavior will slowly begin to stabilize.

The Available Adult vs the Enabler: Because the Available Adult appears "not to be doing anything" through its neutrality, it can be mistaken for the Enabler. But "being present" is not the same as willfully doing nothing.
The difference lies in the accountable choice to be present to what is going on instead of turning a blind eye to a situation for self-serving purposes. When the Enabler begins to become present and available to its contractive behavior through the medicine of the Available Adult, the journey of transformation can begin.

The Available Adult and the Over-Dramatic Child: The respectful presence of The Available Adult invites mature, conscious and devoted availability to an unseen wound or pattern that just wants to be acknowledged. Once you become available to see, the drama will guide you to the source of the issue, and the intensity of the drama is no longer needed to get your attention. The Available Adult begins by holding a safe and neutral space for the next phase of healing to occur.

The Available Adult and the Lost Child: The Lost Child's frustration lives in the fact that it does not know, and it does not know why it does not know. The root of this isolation is intense trauma. The price for protection is isolation. The tradeoff is connection.

The Available Adult brings back a connection and the light of awareness into the dark secret that has been protected through the survival mechanism and begins the process of loving recognition through its availability. The neutrality and acceptance lighten the heavy shame that originated from the initial trauma as well as the internal judgment for the behavior of repression.

The Available Adult holds a safe space for the possibility for a sensitive and respectful introspection. The spark of presence is enough to bring awareness to this lost and isolated wound and allow the fragmentation to eventually be lovingly accepted and acknowledged.

The Mature Medicine of The Compassionate Adult

Compassion for all the Shadow aspects of your being is the key to be able to accept and shift your relationship to them. It is easy to condemn and judge yourself for the presence of the shadow, immaturity and its reactive elements. The road to true acceptance always begins with self-compassion.

Compassion for all aspects of the shadow and disempowered aspects of your being is a vital part of the healing process. It assists the Wounded Inner Child to feel empathically nourished and allows the Shadow to be seen and understood without defensiveness. You need an expansive expression of compassionate support to create any new path.

You cannot create self-love through the same fear or abuse that created the shadow, and you cannot heal woundedness through more toxicity. The Wounded Inner Child and the Shadow Inner Adult crave this healthy loving-kindness and sensitivity to feel safe enough to feel accepted and embrace a path of transformation and healing.

Compassionate Adult vs Enabler: Compassion is empathic to suffering, but unlike the Enabler, it always includes awareness and never feeds co-dependency or disempowerment. It is kind, connected and considerate. It also requires a level of discernment on the part of the giver. You must always consider the context of the situation when giving because not all giving in all circumstances is expansive or helpful.

302

The compassionate Adult is always sensitive to the greater (sometimes long-term) good, rather than superficially soothing immediate desires or acting from a place of pity or self-gratification. It realizes that assistance may not always feel more comfortable, especially if what is needed does not enable immediate desires.

Compassionate Adult vs the Inner Critical Parent: The Inner Critical Parent is the most recognizable form of abuse because it is expressed through your contractive-ego as the "inner voice" of criticism, judgment and condemnation. This is what makes the Compassionate Adult so necessary. Until the inner voice of abuse is replaced with its counterpart of loving kindness and compassion, every aspect of the healing process will be crippled by the conscious and unconscious barrage of negative self-commentary.

This is one of the major keys to significantly shifting your inner and outer relationships. Compassion for others always begins with compassion for yourself. As you change the relationship on the inside, you also invite a different experience on the outside. You become open to receiving more expansion, especially in the form of kindness and compassion from the outer world.

The Compassionate Adult and the Misunderstood Child: The Misunderstood Child is desperately attached to its self-suffering. This creates a feeling of lack of compassion for self and a profound feeling of isolation that also leads to self-misunderstanding and self-repulsion. The Compassionate Adult provides loving acknowledgement and empathic understanding. It soothes the intensity of struggle and creates a sense of solace. It is the (inner and outer) recognition that the Misunderstood Child needs to finally allow itself to break the self-imposed exile and feel the warmth of empathy and inner kindness.

The Compassionate Adult and the Over- Dramatic Child: The Over-Dramatic Child is harshly judged because it is so loud, dramatic and over expressive. The loving-kindness of the Compassionate Adult shifts the intense judgment and disgust to patience, compassion and acceptance. It helps relax the overdramatic behavior and offers the desperate need to be seen. Once there is compassion and acceptance for this conditioning, it builds the bridge for a new, expansive relationship. Eventually that contractive attention-seeking energy can be channeled into positive, expressive and "expansive drama."

The Compassionate Adult and the Lost Child: The Lost Child has tremendous difficulties with its dissociative tendencies. The Compassionate Adult offers a loving invitation of reconnection for this traumatized aspect of the Wounded Inner Child. This gentle medicine demonstrates that it can be safe to stay present. This assists the Lost Child in realizing that escape is not the only option.

The Mature Medicine of The Nurturer

Everything requires some form of nurturing and support for healthy development and evolution. This is especially true for the Shadow Inner Adult and The Wounded Inner Child. In order to shift the dynamics into something expansive, the Nurturer offers uplifting nourishment and a renewed invitation into wholeness.

The Nurturer vs the Enabler: Unlike The Enabler, the awareness-driven Nurturer is always considering what long-term needs can be nourished to create a secure, sustaining environment for ongoing growth and expansion, even if it means temporary discomfort. On the contrary, patterns of enabling seek to only satisfy short-term desires and appetites without much thought for the future consequences of those contractive choices.

For example, the Enabler is not considering the long-term effects of enabling an addict to continue abusing a substance, the repercussions of excessive unhealthy food choices for a child, or the consequences for supporting destructive tendencies. Sincere medicine of nurturing always provides the consistent, sustainable support that eventually unravels the illusion of support that the Enabler seems to offer.

The Nurturer vs the Inauthentic Adult: The Inauthentic Adult will never be a sincere nurturer even though it can spend much of its time posing as one. It builds a convincing argument to itself and others that it is exhibiting genuinely caring behavior. The image and outer story can be so compelling that the Inauthentic Adult begins to believe its own act (This is referred to as delusional narcissism).

This is contrary to the Nurturer, who is devoted to its task without an audience or validation. It can selflessly support anonymously. The nurturing is an organic expression of the connection and empathy for another expressed through devotion and loving-kindness.

The Nurturer vs The Possessive Parent: The Possessive Parent will appear to be intensely interested and invested in nurturing and supporting. But the real inspiration for their compulsive smothering or excessive devotion is fueled by self-serving intentions.

The Nurturer is so empathically connected, they could never use another as a selfish vehicle to satisfy their desires or fulfill some unmet aspect of themselves. It is invested in "mothering without smothering." Unlike the Possessive Parent, it inspires expansiveness, connection and growth through a genuine offering without a selfish agenda. And the one being nurtured feels deeply cherished, seen, and validated.

The Nurturer vs The Internal Critical Parent: The voice of the Internal Critical Parent has become so normalized because of conditioning that we fail to recognize it as contractive. The complimentary perspective of the Nurturer provides an expansive alternative and medicine to this constrictive self-narrative. This consistent reassurance will eventually unravel the shadow offering of the Internal Critical Parent.

"Nurturing is not complex. It's simply being 'tuned in' to the thing or person before you and offering small gestures toward what it needs at that time."
- Mary Anne Radmacher

The Nurturer and The Misunderstood Child: The Nurturer offers gentle understanding and support to this aspect of the Wounded Inner Child. It can melt the perpetual mistrust and misunderstanding into feelings of being empathically acknowledged. Through the sincere act of caring and devotion, the perpetually victimized wound of the Misunderstood Child cannot be maintained. The genuine, empathic connection is a remedy for the self-imposed exile. It simply cannot continue to justify anger for not being loved when the caring is so genuinely apparent and abundant.
If this aspect of the Mature Inner Adult can patiently sustain the uplifting attitude and validation, the Misunderstood Child will come out of its self-imposed hiding, step out of the wound and eventually receive the love it so desperately desires but cannot give itself.

The Nurturer and The Needy Child: The Needy Child aspect of the Wounded Inner Child has experienced the deep loss of unfulfilled and unmet needs. Caring from the Nurturer can forever shatter the illusion and unhealthy belief in the notion of scarcity and the fear of self-sustaining those needs. This devotion and loving-kindness support the new sense of inner self-worth that the Needy Child can and does deserve to be cherished and have all its needs met. When the Needy Child finally feels valued, the fear-based grasping outside of itself finally ends.

The Nurturer and The Frozen Child: Debilitating, unprocessed trauma is the root cause that defines this aspect of the Wounded Inner Child. A sense of guilt and shame further complicates the frozen state making it feel utterly hopeless. The Nurturer lovingly challenges the notion that it is unsafe to move. The patience and encouragement of the Nurturer melts the frozen state through, and delicately allows for, small movements to be possible. The gentle validation is the kind-hearted support that the Frozen Child needs to begin to release and heal the fear of the past trauma and begin to move on.

The Mature Medicine of the Honoring Adult

Once of the most powerful functions of the Honoring Adult is the power of recognition without judgment. The Honoring Adult brings awareness and eventual illumination by honoring each of the contractive aspects that are now outdated but were once necessary survival mechanisms. When the contractive patterns are recognized and acknowledged, it is only a matter of time, commitment and practice until your relationship to them is transformed.

Without authentic self-love through the Honoring Adult, the various aspects of the contractive patterns can never be fully seen and acknowledged. The conscious recognition honors the wounds so they can be explored, validated and purified. Therefore, the Honoring Adult plays a vital role in the healing process with healthy, sincere, sensitive recognition. Learning to give this to yourself or another is a transformational catalyst in developing self-love.

The Honoring Adult vs the Enabler: The Enabler unconsciously indulges desires. It will justify "celebration" to fuel escapist behavior. This form of self-indulging behavior of the Enabler taints the true act of validation.

Unlike the Enabler, the medicine of the Honoring Adult is intentional and steeped in awareness and purpose. It uplifts celebration to a sacred act of recognition and honoring beyond self-indulged pampering. This conscious attention is also reflected in discernment and composure, which elevates the appreciation. This palpable feeling of depth and sense of presence will always cut through the indulging behavior of the Enabler and transform the superficial into something meaningful.

The Honoring Adult vs The Inner Critical Parent: The Inner Critical Parent will create doubt about internal honoring and dismiss it as arrogance. Expressions like "who do you think you are?", "Why do you think you deserve to be treated liked that?" or "What makes you so special?" are some common examples from this inner critic.

The entire purpose of the Honoring Adult is true expansive self-validation. That process requires awareness to observe the depth of criticism in your existing inner dialogue, conscious effort to change the inner perspective and a consistent inner practice of self-acknowledgement.

Honoring Adult vs The Possessive Parent: The Possessive Parent never truly honors, respects or even acknowledges the authentic needs of the (inner or outer) Wounded Inner Child. For this reason, the Honoring Adult is an essential medicine in cracking through the self-absorbed, disassociated and sociopathic behavior of possessiveness. The behavior pattern of the Possessive Parent is always dishonorable. When you begin to listen with awareness, recognize and sincerely acknowledge the true needs of the inner child and respect those needs through authentic honoring, the weak illusion of the Possessive Parent is dismantled. The Honorable act of true validation begins healing the wounds and allows the child to be freed from oppression and possession.

The Honoring Adult and The Misunderstood Child: The Misunderstood Child is attached to its perpetual self-imposed suffering. The Honoring Adult offers recognition of the isolation and the pain that drives it. And it does so without getting lost in the seductive nature of that pain.

Without that acknowledgement, the Misunderstood Child will never be elevated out of living in the wound. The Honoring Adult offers ongoing validation and builds the bridge to self-understanding and self-recognition. This provides the opportunity to let go of the self-imposed suffering and build an expansive relationship for true transformation.

The Honoring Adult and the Needy Child: The Honoring Adult acknowledges and respects the unmet needs and wounds of the Needy Child and brings inner awareness to them. Without conscious attention, those needs will never be explored enough to ever be fulfilled, and the Needy Child will continue its constant outer grasping to feel loved. The healing begins with this self-acknowledgement. This creates the necessary safety to seek fulfillment of those needs in outer-world relationships. This act of self-love turns loving attention inward and helps the Needy Child transcend the fear that it will not be recognized and cherished.

The Honoring Adult and The Lost Child: One of the biggest challenges for this Wounded Inner Child aspect is the ability to recognize its own withdrawn state. This aspect of the Mature Inner Adult offers the recognition needed to honor the struggle and isolation that comes with the conditioning. It also provides the opportunity for acknowledgement of the deep trauma that continually instigates the dissociative patterns.

Sincerely honoring the ongoing challenges are difficult when you may not even recognize the source of the contractive behavior. But with the continued practices of self-respect and self-appreciation, one begins to value the process of investigation. And this respect opens the door to finally acknowledge the unknown trauma, face it and discover peace through deepening acceptance. The Honoring Adult's support and recognition allows the Lost Child to feel safe enough to be present and opens the door to the healing journey of self-discovery.

The Mature Medicine of the Responsible Adult

Practical responsiveness is always supported by awareness. The sincere responsiveness, earnestness and devotion that radiates from the Responsible Adult will expose the reactive behaviors that lack conviction and sincerity. The key to the relationship of the Responsible Adult and the different contractive elements is its dedication, attention and grounded consistency. This commitment creates safety.

The Responsible Adult vs the Controlling Inner Adult: The Responsible Adult takes responsive action. Unlike the Controlling Inner Adult, it is conscious, mature and expansive with a high level of accountability. The relationship to action is not impulsive, nor is it an attempt to manage through control. Even if the behavior may seem similar with these two aspects, the inspiration originates from completely different places.

The Responsible Adult vs the Inauthentic Handler: The non-personal objectivity of the Responsible Adult and its intense, systemic approach can sometimes appear uncaring. Unlike the Inauthentic Handler, however, the devotion is channeled into mature and empowered action. The unyielding attentiveness of the Responsible Adult will quickly unravel the illusionary projection of smoke and mirrors of the Inauthentic Handler and expose its lack of commitment and conviction.

The Responsible Adult vs the Unavailable Adult: The Unavailable Adult lives in a state of complete inaccessibility and neglects responsibility. The Responsible Adult can re-engage this unavailable aspect through connection and being present with life instead of avoiding it. It is unaffected by the excuses and justification of inaction and is immune to the avoidance tactics of the Unavailable Adult. If the tenacity of the Responsible Adult can be maintained and executed through a program of concerted action, the Unavailable Adult will eventually have to deal with its repressed fears and its own self-neglect.

The Responsible Adult and The Needy Child: Scarcity rules the unconscious behavior of the Needy Child. The Responsible Adult provides healing by demonstrating what it is like to be cared for in the physical world. It attends to all pragmatic, practical and physical needs. This develops security for the Needy Child and assists the understanding and experience of abundance. Steadfast accountability and reliability build trust. This ability to respond with maturity and consciousness channeled through action assists the Needy Child in realizing its needs in the physical world will always be met. This allows the Needy Child to believe that this can happen in all the other areas of life.

The Responsible Adult and The Frozen Child: One of the most difficult things for the Frozen Child is not knowing how to make the leap into action. The Responsible Adult is the archetype of pragmatic action. It inspires action like no other aspect of the Mature Inner Adult because of the purity in its relationship to execution. It is unaffected by the drama of the waiting game. It does not accept excuses and demonstrates that mistakes can made.

That sometimes you do not have to know how, you can just act and figure it out in the process. The unshakable confidence that has been acquired through its experience soothes the Wounded Inner Child, builds its confidence and demonstrates that it is safe to move.

The Mature Medicine of The Protector

Your character is not determined by what you say you are going to do, but rather by how your behavior reflects your intention. Being consistent in your thoughts, words and actions creates an unshakable integrity. A conscious Protector always responds from this space of self-awareness as a living example of honorable character.

Every Wounded Inner Child needs an inner champion to advocate on its behalf. Once you have saved yourself, you will not rely on a "knight in shining armor" from the outside world to save you. Instead, you learn to draw your own boundaries and create inner support. This sense of security and stability builds a healthy foundation for the development of self-respect and self-love. It also creates the inner trust that allows yourself to love and be loved.

The Protector vs the Controlling Inner Adult: These two aspects can be confused, and the contractive ego-mind can use this murky similarity to justify behavior that is nothing more than reaction or subversive control. *"They deserved it! No one has the right to treat me that way! They got what they deserved."*

The Controlling Inner Adult is directly fueled, consciously or unconsciously, by unprocessed fear. The Protector is not. It does not react or lash out without discernment. It is always motivated by expansiveness. It attends to the needs of different archetypes by creating thoughtful boundaries. As a conscious custodian, the boundary is always drawn out of self-respect, self-care, security, necessity and a deep sense of devotion. Therefore, the Protector is never drawing a boundary "against" someone, in order to dominate through control. It only draws a boundary "for" an aspect within you.

If you are drawing a boundary for yourself, always be clear what aspect of yourself you are drawing it for, how you are going to consciously execute that boundary and why it is necessary. In other words, be conscious, clear and decisive and do what needs to be done from a place of self-awareness.

The Protector vs the Inauthentic Handler: One of the characteristics of this aspect of the Shadow Inner Adult is its willingness to break its word and shift its moral position when it becomes more favorable for its inner or outer image. The Protector counteracts this mercurial behavior. Its steadfast behavior and commitment to a strict moral code of conduct makes the Protector a truly authentic and dependable advocate for the deeper needs of the Wounded Inner Child. The Protector is completely immune to vanity, outer image or social status. It challenges the Inauthentic Handler to be accountable for its lack of conviction and exposes deceitful behavior. Unlike the Inauthentic Handler, the Protector is fulfilled by its dutiful and devoted service to the Inner Child.

The Protector vs the Enabler: Like the Inauthentic Handler, the Enabler will also justify its erratic change in position as its behavior shifts between the polarities of denial and indulging. The grounded and consistent nature of the Protector can offer powerful medicine to the Enabler. It demonstrates the discipline of inner commitments and the conviction of meeting goals without being distracted by fleeting desires.

The Protector also offers the necessary boundaries and the active discernment to make responsible choices that are in the best interest for security and safety. Discipline offers a path of conscious preservation in place of the unconscious devastation of addiction. One of the most powerful tools for any addict to stay on the path of recovery is always building self-respect, security and inner confidence through consistency and steadfastness. With these boundaries in place along with upholding personal integrity, there will be little space for the flip-flop behavior of indulging or denying. The Protector will also enforce the necessary accountability to stay on the honorable path.

The Protector and the Lost Child: Because this Wounded Inner Child aspect never had an advocate during the initial trauma, it does not understand the feeling of safety that comes from the assurance of the ever-vigilant Protector. Since the Lost Child will lose track of time, forget events and details and feels disconnected, which keeps the fragmentation active, it desperately needs the Protector to help build the bridge to bring itself back. The stability of the Protector allows it to feel safe enough to stay present. This is necessary for the Lost Child to confront its healing process and inspires the necessary courage to face and process the fears.

The Protector and the Over-Indulged Child: In order to break the indulgent behavior of the Over-Indulged Child, the boundaries, discipline and temperance of the Protector are required. A commitment to create boundaries combined with the discipline to maintain them creates an appropriate container to regulate the insatiable appetite of the Over-Indulged Child. The Protector's influence of humility helps dissolve the heightened sense of entitlement.

One of the other powerful gifts offered by the Protector is the dedication to selfless service. Since the Over-Indulged Child rarely considers anything or anyone else, shifting the focus to caring for another can mitigate the extreme level of selfishness. Through the watchful supervision, the Protector offers the essential boundaries that can regulate and protect the Over-Indulged Child from its own destructive conditioning.

PART VIII
RADIANT MEDICINE

The Radiant Medicine of the Radiant Inner Child

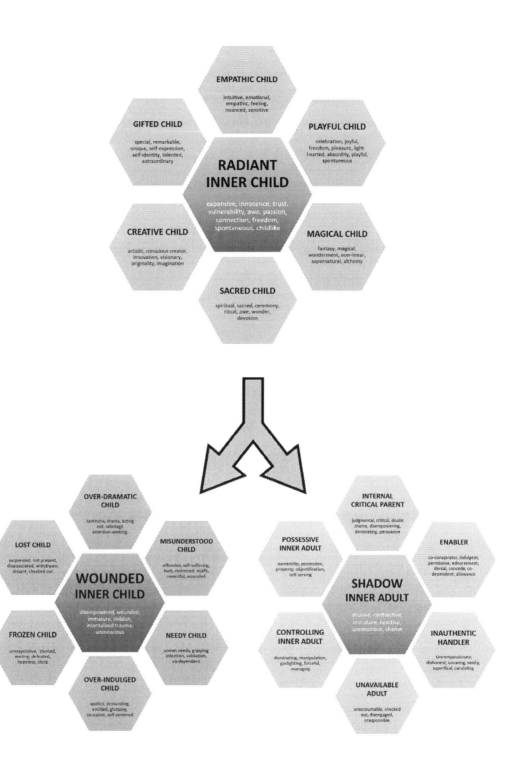

The Radiant Medicine of the Empathic Child

The more you give yourself permission to feel, the more deeply you access the subtle nuances of your consciousness and allow yourself to heal. Empathic connection offers a transformational pathway of healing for any contractive aspect. The Empathetic Child is the essential foundation of creating awareness, and sincere change and empathy is the key to connection.

The Empathic Child and the Unavailable Adult: The Empathic Child offers this contractive archetype an invitation to re-establish connection. The passive-aggressive behavior of the Unavailable Adult is steeped in unconscious fear and anger. Once that inner connection is accessed, it can experience the root of its pain. It can empathize with the emotional consequences of its passivity and understand the devastation of self-abandonment. Honestly embracing those suppressed emotions re-activates the detachment and transforms it into deeper availability. This eventually brings the Unavailable Adult out of hiding.

The Empathetic Child and the Inauthentic Handler: The Inauthentic Handler functions exclusively in the superficial world and has little connection to deeper emotions. It is adept at posturing in the outer world that fuels the façade at the expense of feeling. The Empathic Child makes it extremely difficult to deny, suppress and ignore the inner reality. It forces the Inauthentic Handler to confront the emotional consequences of its inauthenticity. When powerful, authentic feelings are accessed and felt, there is a deeper connection, and the fragile masquerade eventually collapses.

The Empathetic Child and the Over-Dramatic Child: The acting out of the Over-Dramatic Child is an avoidance tactic to prevent connecting to deeper feelings of scarcity, fear and anger. When the source of these wounds is accessed through the Empathetic Child, the drama is no longer ignited by the unconscious. This offers the opportunity to resolve the wounds instead of managing them through childish drama.

The Empathetic Child and the Misunderstood Child: The over-sensitive nature of the Misunderstood Child has a powerful connection to the emotional body but cannot effectively process emotional pain. The victimization perpetuates an emotional story but does not authentically connect or deal with the deeper feelings. The Empathic Child opens the door to the full spectrum of the emotional body, and the pain-focused story of struggle dissolves in the presence of radiance. The Misunderstood Child must finally process the source of the emotional pain that led to its victim mentality.

The Empathetic Child and the Lost Child: The Lost Child unconsciously escapes the deep, traumatic emotional pain of its past. The Empathetic Child invites the Lost Child to be present with those painful emotions. The only way to heal that pain is to face it. But more importantly, one must feel through the trauma to find resolution. The more the Lost Child can allow itself to feel, the more deeply it can heal. The Empathic child offers the gift of feeling, which eventually releases the Lost Child from its cycle of escapism.

The Radiant Medicine of the Playful Child

The medicine of the Playful Child can have a powerfully radiant influence on the deep sense of pain and hurt of the various archetypes of the Wounded Inner Child. Because of its uplifting nature, it can offer an alternative to the unconscious suffering and lighten the relationship to the specific forms of woundedness.

The Playful Child and The Over-Dramatic Child: The medicine of the Playful Child offers permission to the Over-Dramatic Child to act out without the contractive ripple effect. Play is an expansive solution that uses drama as an outlet. It does not sabotage or negatively impact the inner or outer world. One could say that conscious play can create "positive drama" scenarios that are helpful and enriching instead of hurtful and damaging without the shame-based kickback that inevitably comes from being "overdramatic.
"

The Playful Child and The Misunderstood Child: The Playful Child lightens the heavy burden of the Misunderstood Child. The light-hearted approach to life gives the Misunderstood Child permission to let go and enjoy itself. It does not have to continue to perpetuate suffering as a way of being and offers an opportunity to experience, if even for a brief moment, the simple joy of play. This opens the door to possibilities that the Misunderstood Child has ignored or believed it did not deserve. Every moment of expansive play uplifts and lightens the attachment to self-victimization.

The Playful Child and the Over-Indulged Child: Being spoiled or indulging in "excessive fun" is the flipside of "conscious play." Expansive play becomes contractive when it unconsciously begins to draw from woundedness and pain. The Playful Child is always inspired by joy. This creates a sense of freedom and abundance of possibilities. Childlike playfulness is filled with wonder and awe and enjoys the experience of play without an agenda. This can help cure the Overindulged Child of its self-absorbed nature and allow it to have fun without the selfishness and immaturity.

The Playful Child and the Frozen Child: The presence of joyful play safely stimulates action and lightens the fear of spontaneity. Play offers the invitation to get unstuck through investigation, humor and fun. Engaging in that sense of fun allows the Frozen Child to let go of its self-imposed fears and its fearful "what if" scenario. When the Frozen Child can move forward in play it inadvertently is giving itself permission to also act in other circumstances.

The Radiant Medicine of the Magical Child

The Magical Child offers powerful alchemy to all the contractive aspects. This unprocessed "lead" (contraction) has the potential to be transformed into "gold" (expansion) through the fantastic world of imagination.

The Magical Child and the Lost Child: The Magical Child is deeply connected as an active participant in its personal realm of fantasy. This inspires a disengaged Lost Child to practice connection through magic. It allows the Lost Child to expansively engage in a safe place where it can have complete power over the narrative, the characters and the situations – something that it did not experience in the original trauma. In this magical world, it can finally have the courage to face those fearful demons of the past and conquer them.

The Magical Child and the Frozen Child: The Magical Child opens the door to infinite possibilities and assists this aspect of the Wounded Inner Child to trust its decisions. The land of "make-believe" inspires the power to believe. The Magical Child offers the "alchemy of action," and by playing out possible scenarios in a fantasy world, this gives the Frozen Child a place to develop confidence to move forward.

The Magical Child and the Misunderstood Child: The behavior of the Misunderstood Child can be described as a "negative fantasy." The Magical Child offers limitless opportunities in the world of fantasy to explore different expansive possibilities. The radiant energy of hope, belief and possibility slowly unravels the contractive feedback loop of the Misunderstood Child and creates a safe place to explore and resolve its relationship to suffering.

The Magical Child and the Needy Child: The Magical Child offers a world for the Needy Child to transform its feelings of scarcity. Through the alchemy of the fantastic world, all the unmet needs of the Needy Child can be experienced where trust and belief can be re-established. The Needy Child can recognize and explore its needs and begin to heal its wounds.

The Magical Child and the Overdramatic Child: When the Magical Child is infused into unconscious drama, it transforms childish attention-seeking to childlike fantasy. It allows for the celebration of a world of "radiant drama." The Overdramatic Child learns to experience a place of acceptance where everything is not only explored but also encouraged. There are no limitations to how overdramatic one can be in the world of fantasy. The Over-Dramatic Child can be the main character of its own magical universe. It can focus its energy, which was once consumed with attention-seeking, towards exploring the limits of this world, which minimizes its need of constant outward affirmation.

The Radiant Medicine of the Sacred Child

The Sacred Child reveres every aspect of life through the transformational experience of sacredness. All the unconscious, immature and shadow aspects of the being are held with great respect. The Sacred Child recognizes that even the contractive states play a role in the mysterious unfolding of life and are necessary for growth and evolution. Everything is sacred as part of the whole.

The Sacred Child and the Unavailable Adult: This aspect of the Shadow Inner Adult does not value its presence, responsibilities or behavior with any sense of sacredness. Because it is so disengaged from itself, it cannot directly experience any level of self-respect. The Sacred Child elevates the contractive behavior through a conscious invitation into a deeper relationship with meaningfulness. This opens a direct experience that can break down the apathy which unconsciously fuels the unavailability.

The Sacred Child and the Possessive Parent: The Possessive Parent dominates for selfish gratification without concern about consequences. The Sacred Child challenges the notion that the so-called "object" of possession has no meaning besides what it can do or offer for the Possessive Parent. Sacred appreciation and reverence are the remedies for this sociopathic conduct. It inspires humility which can eventually unravel the arrogance and unworthiness attached to possessiveness.

The Sacred Child and the Needy Child: The Needy Child was conditioned to believe that its needs were never important and feel undeserving of attention. It feels shame for secretly wanting these needs to be met. The Sacred Child offers the medicine which respects and values all the needs of this aspect of the Wounded Inner Child. This sense of respect inspires the Needy Child to appreciate that just because its needs were unmet does not mean that it does not have value. Sacredness inspires importance, value and self-love, the very things the Needy Child seeks

.

The Radiant Medicine of the Creative Child

The Creative Child expresses a passionate love for discovery that inspires powerful, active and radiant energy. Where the contractive archetypes react and project fear into the unknown, the Creative Child embraces curious exploration through imagination and conscious creativity.

The Creative Child and the Frozen Child: The Creative Child offers the Frozen Child the opportunity to embrace risks. When the fear of the unknown begins to thaw, the Frozen Child will feel less "stuck." The Creative Child meets the unknown as an opportunity and creative adventure. This expansive approach is helpful to combat the contractive rigidity and procrastination of the Frozen Child. It can meet any situation knowing it has a creative perspective to discover the resolution.

The Creative Child and the Overdramatic Child: The Creative Child can offer a "radiant innovation" to solve the problem of getting attention by exploring other creative solutions that are not destructive. The key is in consciously creating a relationship to new and expansive tools so the dependency on outer drama can be replaced with something healthy and self-sustaining. When the Overdramatic Child begins to realize that it has the power to create something else much more fulfilling through its own creation, it no longer needs to focus on unhealthy drama that it craves from others.

The Radiant Medicine of the Gifted Child

The Gifted Child invites the contractive elements of the being to remember, embrace and explore the freedom of empowered personal expression. This conscious self-acknowledgement is transformational for feelings of unworthiness and allows you to expansively explore your uniqueness without judgment or fear.

The Gifted Child and the Misunderstood Child: Being misunderstood begins with undervaluing your own uniqueness. The Gifted Child shatters the disempowered illusion of victim consciousness. When the Misunderstood Child begins to appreciate its individuality and its sense of personal expression, it will be transformed. This radiant appreciation stops feeding the "sob story" of the lone, misunderstood outcast.

The Gifted Child and the Frozen Child: The Gifted Child allows the Frozen Child to believe in its unique unfolding journey instead of doubting its value. When you can trust in the value of your uniqueness, you embrace the talent that comes from that individuality. It also gives you permission to take the leap and explore yourself through action. The Gifted Child knows that the more you consciously explore your uniqueness, the more you will appreciate and refine the expansive expression of your personal talents.

The Gifted Child and the Possessive Parent: The Gifted Child embraces the uniqueness of your inherent beingness. When you honor yourself, you cannot be dominated, manipulated or taken advantage of by the Possessive Parent. You will not accept the demeaning role imposed onto you.

Responding to the Contractive (Wounded and Shadow) Archetypes:

It is important to recognize the empowered aspects of your Radiant Inner Child and Mature Inner Adult. This allows you to know your strengths and where you may need to put more attention to develop more conscious inner and outer relationships of expansiveness. Because we are a collection of interacting personality fragments, you may be highly developed in some of the expansive archetypes and disempowered in others, and be very responsive in certain circumstances and not developed at all in others. Everyone has their personal blind spots and empowered facets of their being.

For example, you may know how to effortlessly respond to the Wounded Inner Child with compassion and nurturing, but you may not be able to draw boundaries. You may have developed a healthy relationship with your creativity and be highly playful, but it is difficult to connect to your feelings. You may be very comfortable with certain shadow aspects in others but have a lot of difficulty consciously responding to disempowered behaviors. In some cases, you may even show up with those radiant and mature behaviors for another, but you have never been comfortable doing that for yourself.

This exercise offers another opportunity to explore your relationship to those expansive archetypes. The only way you are going to empower these unowned, radiant and mature aspects of your being is through awareness, self-investigation and practice. All these unconscious and unrecognized dynamics offer profound opportunities for self-awareness and growth. Have patience with yourself as you begin to investigate your relationship to the Radiant Inner Child and the Mature Inner Adult.

1. If you cannot easily determine your internal dynamics, then begin by investigating your past and present relationship dynamics. What recurring behaviors or patterns do you notice? Pay attention to your existing and past roles. What do you see? The recurring behaviors that show up in your different relationships are clues and invitations from the outer world to help you see the unowned and unexplored behaviors inside of you.

2. It may help to make a list of your past and present relationships and journal your initial observations. It may also assist you, as part of your process, to ask a close and trusted friend, existing partner, spouse or family member for their observations about your patterns.

Use the below worksheet to explore how you play out these relationship dynamics in your inner and outer world. In the worksheet, we will investigate both relationships to see how you utilize the radiant and mature medicine.

Examine different forms of relationships to get a better idea of how these patterns express themselves. For example, you may use your boss, co-workers, neighbor, siblings, past romantic partners, past or existing friends, extended family members and parents. Explore the inner conditioning and which of the different radiant or mature responses you are most likely to gravitate to when encountering specific contractive archetypes.

When you encounter dynamics of contraction in yourself or others, you may consciously respond with either the Radiant Inner Child or the Mature Adult. Here are some examples.

In my relationship with my *son Max*

When he expresses the Wounded Inner Child dynamic of: *Needy Child*
I am most likely to consciously respond with the expansive dynamic of: *Available Adult*
WHY: *I have a lot patience for his neediness, and I know I he just needs to feel my availability.*

When he expresses the Shadow Inner Adult dynamic of *Controlling Adult*
I am most likely to consciously respond with the expansive dynamic of *the Playful Child*
WHY: *I lighten the control with playfulness so he can learn to relax.*

In my relationship with my *friend Wendy*

When she expresses the Wounded Inner Child dynamic of: *Needy Child*
I am most likely to consciously respond with the expansive dynamic of: *Compassionate Adult*
WHY: *I really see the pain of her unmet needs and I feel compassion.*

When she expresses the Shadow Inner Adult dynamic of: *Inauthentic Handler*
I am most likely to consciously respond with the expansive dynamic of: *Protector*
WHY: *I will not indulge the inauthentic behavior and I draw very strong boundaries.*

In my relationship with my **mother**

When she expresses the Wounded Inner Child dynamic of: *Over-Dramatic Child*
I am most likely to consciously respond with the expansive dynamic of: *Protector and Available Adult*
WHY: *I want to be neutral but I also need to draw boundaries with the drama.*

When she expresses the Shadow Inner Adult dynamic of the *Unavailable Adult*
I am most likely to consciously respond with the expansive dynamic of *Responsible Adult*
WHY: *When she checks out, I have naturally become more responsible to get things done.*

In my relationship with my *friend Dan*

When he expresses the Wounded Inner Child dynamic of: *Frozen Child*
I am most likely to consciously respond with the expansive dynamic of: *Magical Child*
WHY: *I know that he responds very well to fantasy so we talk about sci-fi movies.*

When he expresses the Shadow Inner Adult dynamic of: *internal Critical Adult*
I am most likely to consciously respond with the expansive dynamic of: *Honoring Adult and Sacred Child*
WHY: *When he is judgment of himself, I choose to share something inherently beautiful about him.*

Responding to the Contractive Archetypes Worksheet

1. In my relationship with:_____
When he/she expresses the **Wounded Inner Child** dynamic of: _____
I am most likely to consciously respond with the **expansive dynamic** of: _____
WHY: _____

When he/she expresses the **Shadow Inner Adult** dynamic of:_____
I am most likely to consciously respond with the **expansive dynamic** of:_____
WHY: _____

2. In my relationship with:_____
When he/she expresses the **Wounded Inner Child** dynamic of: _____
I am most likely to consciously respond with the **expansive dynamic** of: _____
WHY: _____

When he/she expresses the **Shadow Inner Adult** dynamic of:_____
I am most likely to consciously respond with the **expansive dynamic** of:_____
WHY: _____

3. In my relationship with:_____
When he/she expresses the **Wounded Inner Child** dynamic of: _____
I am most likely to consciously respond with the **expansive dynamic** of: _____
WHY: _____

When he/she expresses the **Shadow Inner Adult** dynamic of:_____
I am most likely to consciously respond with the **expansive dynamic** of:_____
WHY: _____

4. In my relationship with:_____
When he/she expresses the **Wounded Inner Child** dynamic of: _____
I am most likely to consciously respond with the **expansive dynamic** of: _____
WHY: _____

When he/she expresses the **Shadow Inner Adult** dynamic of:_____
I am most likely to consciously respond with the **expansive dynamic** of:_____
WHY: _____

5. In my relationship with:_____
When he/she expresses the **Wounded Inner Child** dynamic of: _____
I am most likely to consciously respond with the **expansive dynamic** of: _____
WHY: _____

When he/she expresses the **Shadow Inner Adult** dynamic of:_____
I am most likely to consciously respond with the **expansive dynamic** of:_____
WHY: _____

6. In my relationship with:_____
When he/she expresses the **Wounded Inner Child** dynamic of: _____
I am most likely to consciously respond with the **expansive dynamic** of: _____
WHY: _____

When he/she expresses the **Shadow Inner Adult** dynamic of:_____
I am most likely to consciously respond with the **expansive dynamic** of:_____
WHY: _____

7. In my relationship with:_____
When he/she expresses the **Wounded Inner Child** dynamic of: _____
I am most likely to consciously respond with the **expansive dynamic** of: _____
WHY: _____

When he/she expresses the **Shadow Inner Adult** dynamic of:_____
I am most likely to consciously respond with the **expansive dynamic** of:_____
WHY: _____

8. In my relationship with:_____
When he/she expresses the **Wounded Inner Child** dynamic of: _____
I am most likely to consciously respond with the **expansive dynamic** of: _____
WHY: _____

When he/she expresses the **Shadow Inner Adult** dynamic of:_____
I am most likely to consciously respond with the **expansive dynamic** of:_____
WHY: _____

Follow up journaling questions:

1. Which Mature Inner Adult archetypes are most empowered in you? Why?
   Which Mature Inner Adult archetypes are least empoweredin you? Why?

2. Which Radiant Inner Child archetypes are most empowered in you?
   Which Radiant Inner Child archetypes are least empowered in you? Why?

3. Are you more empowered in the Radiant or the Mature expansive archetypes?
   Explain.

4. Which Wounded Inner Child dynamics are you most responsive to? Why?
   Which Wounded Inner Child dynamics are you least responsive to?   Why?

5. Which Shadow Inner Adult dynamics are you most responsive to? Why?
   Which Shadow Inner Adult dynamics are you least responsive to? Why?

Investigate your inner responsiveness to your own contractive patterns of woundedness and Shadow.

6. Which Wounded Inner Child dynamics within you are you the most responsive to? Why?

Which are you the least responsive to? Why?

7. Which Shadow Inner Adult dynamics within you are you the most responsive to? Why?

Which are you the least responsive to? Why?

AFTERWORD

Now that you have completed reading the book, review your completed survey, evaluations, journaling questions and different sets of worksheets from the various chapters. It may take some time to evaluate all that you have discovered about yourself. This new awareness can have a tremendous ripple effect in your relative personality structure and in your behavior because you have taken such a deep dive into the unconscious.

Remember that it took many years of exposure to experiences to fortify these patterns within you until they have become your habitual behavior. Therefore, it will also take some time, continued practice and commitment to unravel the unconscious conditioning, notice the dynamics, and eventually re-program a more conscious relationship with the different expansive and contractive archetypes. Get to know your personal expression of these inner archetypes and make it part of your personal process to self-reflect on what you have learned.

Review your IRAM dynamics from the previous pages and use this map as your ongoing reference.

RADIANT INNER CHILD

____ Empathic Child
____ Playful Child
____ Magical Child
____ Sacred Child
____ Creative Child
____ Gifted Child

MATURE INNER ADULT

____ Available Adult
____ Compassionate Adult
____ Nurturer
____ Honoring Adult
____ Responsible Adult
____ Protector

WOUNDED INNER CHILD

____ OverDramatic Child
____ Misunderstood Child
____ Needy Child
____ Over Indulged Child
____ Frozen Child
____ Lost Child

SHADOW INNER ADULT

____ Internal Critical Parent
____ Enabler
____ Inauthentic Handler
____ Unavailable Adult
____ Controlling Inner Adult
____ Possessive Inner Adult

Have patience with yourself and use the information in this book as an ongoing resource. Continue to become more familiar with the subtleties of how your inner and outer relationship dynamics manifest. Daily journaling and self-introspection to review your dynamics and behavior is a powerful way to continue to observe and understand your patterns. It will also teach you to see your behavior in terms of the underlying dynamics beyond the "story" or the worldly circumstances.

As you continue to discover that every behavior is a product of inner dynamics, you will become more intimate with your own conditioning. As a result, you will notice how the different archetypes continue to unconsciously manifest in every interaction of your life. As you integrate this material, you will be astounded at how your inner and outer relationships begin to shift. This is transformational inner work. If you pay attention, apply the material, utilize the tools and use the map to navigate your behavior, the change you seek is inevitable. It is only a matter of time and practice.

As part of your process, you may also want to share this information with your partner, spouse, family members or friends who are also interested in self-introspection and cultivating more conscious inner and outer relationships. Under the right conditions, this material can foster a powerful space for an intimate, ongoing dialogue and offer a common language to support each other in developing deeper awareness. Safe, respectful and loving inquiry with others about the nature of your patterns can provide objective insight and support on your journey of self-discovery.

Remember that the basis of your inner conditioning was profoundly influenced from the conscious and unconscious experiences of your family of origin. When you are unconscious, by default you become nothing more than a product of that conditioning. If you are a parent who is empowering the journey of self-investigation, the IRAM can be an instrumental resource to offer your children these powerful tools of awareness as they engage in the world of inner and outer relationships.

The more you refine your relationship to this inner map of dynamics and familiarize yourself with your own conditioning, the more you will become adept at recognizing the archetypal patterns in those around you. This system of understanding and navigating relationship dynamics has boundless applications in every facet of life. The possibilities are endless.

As a counselor, teacher, therapist or coach, this powerful tool can assist you to better empathize and understand your clients and students and assist them in their own journey of self-exploration. This process can empower them to discover their own personal relationship dynamics and develop awareness to navigate how their unconscious experience of the different archetypes may influence their choices and decisions. The ability to better understand yourself and others is an invaluable skill in the world of relationships.

With the IRAM, you are empowered to navigate your inner and outer dynamics and make the necessary changes to create conscious relationships in every facet of your life. You now have the tools to consciously create the expansive relationships of your dreams.

The insight, intimacy and understanding to enhance every relationship in your life is possible. Those experiences are all within your reach. Now that this powerful relationship map is in your hands, how far you go with it and what you decide to do with it is entirely up to you. Enjoy the journey of self-discovery as you consciously engage your inner and outer world.

"People say that what we're all seeking is a meaning for life.
I think that what we're really seeking is an experience of being alive,
so that our life experiences on the purely physical plane
will have resonance within our innermost being and reality,
so that we can actually feel the rapture of being alive."
– Joseph Campbell

ACKNOWLEDGEMENTS:

I do not think anyone is ever prepared for the years of searching, false starts, life challenges, disillusionment, exploration, self-examination, healing, journaling, research, notes, discussions, case studies, countless hours of painstaking editing, revisions and rewrites that are necessary to complete this kind of book. I had no idea what I was getting myself into to see this labor of love to completion.

And without a doubt, it would never have been completed if it were not for the unshakable devotion, love and support of my beloved wife Samhji, who not only prompted me to delve into this process but never gave up on me, even when I was ready to give up on myself. She is my inspiration, my muse and my heart.

I want to express my deepest gratitude to my children, Max and Skye, for the privilege of being your parent. I am deeply humbled by the extraordinary beings that you are, and I am continually in awe of both of you as you continue to evolve. You inspire me to be a better human. And to my parents and all my family members who played their part in this journey, thank you.

Without the guidance of every person who in some way assisted me on this path: teachers, psychologists, metaphysicians, mentors, guides, shamans, masters, gurus, healers, spiritual teachers, friends, family, colleagues, clients, students and, of course, my masterful editor and friend Stephen R. Burns, you would not be holding this book in your hands.

I extend my deepest gratitude to the following:

David Spero, who is one of the most remarkable Teachers I have every had the privilege of meeting. His transmission of radiance, consciousness and wisdomcontiues to inspire profound self-reflection and awaken inner realization. His honesty, integrity and articulation of Truth is unlike anything I have ever encountered in this life. And his commitment to love has restored my hope in the Universe and myself. Thank you.

My first mentor, Carolyn Doull, who opened her heart to a wild, young man on the verge of psychological collapse and took him under her wing to nurture and support when no one else would. You gave me purpose and focus. Thank you from the bottom of my heart. You never got the true acknowledgement that you deserved. I also want to recognize my late teacher and metaphysician, Doris "Let it go" Kula who officially introduced me to the esoteric world of metaphysics through her intelligent, quirky, straightforward and no-nonsense devotion to spirituality.

I want to acknowledge my clients and students who continue to challenge me to become a better coach, mentor, counselor and teacher. You literally teach me how to teach. Thank you for trusting me with your pain, your process and your sacred journeys of self-discovery. You inspire me. I am deeply grateful.

Thank you to all those brave and inspired writers, poets, artists and gifted teachers who speak Truth with conviction and eloquence even when it is unpopular, unconventional and misunderstood. There are those of us who are listening. You continue to inspire me to discover and refine my own voice.

Markus William Kasunich has developed a thriving international coaching practice. He is a prolific speaker, author, teacher, artist , father, husband and seeker. He facilitates transformational in-person and online retreats, workshops and events.

Markus utilizes a Holistic (Mind, Body, Spirit) approach to explore the Universe of You. Combining practical and esoteric understanding and techniques, he assists his clients to develop and sustain the necessary awareness to completely transform their lives.

Markus weaves his diverse background, life experiences, perspective, training and education into the process. And he utilizes comprehensive systems and practical tools in the world of business, relationships and all aspects of daily life. He supports his clients to empower their lives, discover their purpose and truly realize their unlimited potential.

For more information Contact:

Website: **https://markuskasunich.com/**
Universe of You Website: **https://members.markuskasunich.com/**
Email: **info@markuskasunich.com**
Instagram: **@markus_kasunich_coach**
Facebook: **https://www.facebook.com/markuswkasunich/**
Twitter: **@markuskasunich**

Made in the USA
Las Vegas, NV
18 April 2022

47675025R00190